D1490375

Do-It-Yourself Gun Repair

Gunsmithing at Home

February, 2010

STILLWATER

PUBLIC LIBRARY

Stillwater, Minnesota 55082

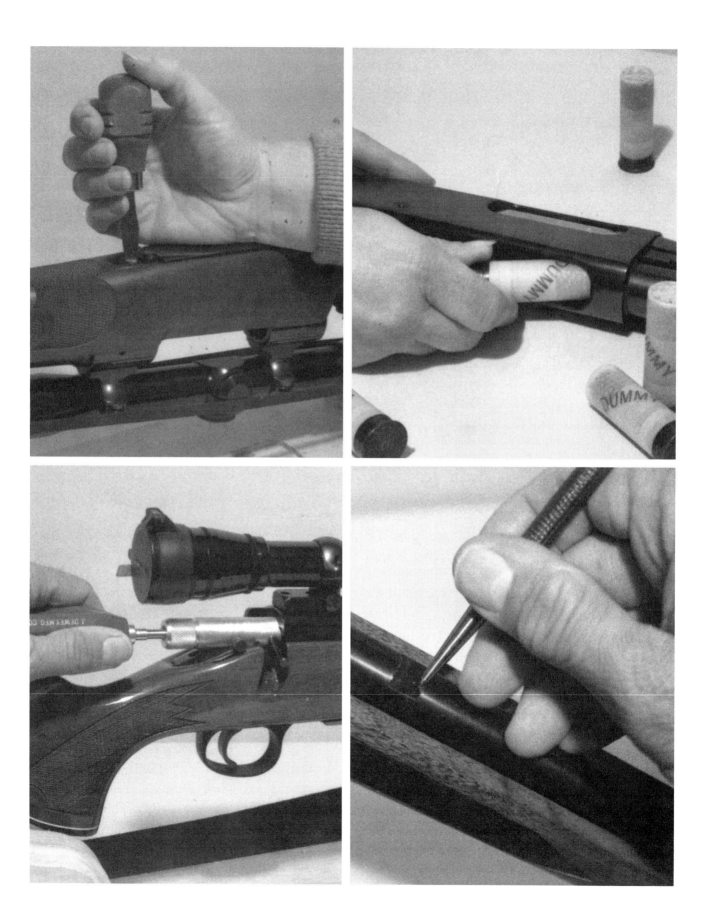

OUTDOORSMAN'S EDGE®
GUIDES

Do-It-Yourself Gun Repair

Gunsmithing at Home

Edward A. Matunas

CREATIVE
OUTDOORS™

Trade paperback edition frist published in 2004 by

CRE▲TIVE
OUTDOORS™

An imprint of Creative Homeowner®, Upper Saddle River, N.J.
Creative Homeowner® is a registered trademark of Federal Marketing Corporation.

Copyright © 2003 Woods N' Water, Inc. and Bookspan
All Rights Reserved

Brief quotations may be used in article reviews. For any other reproduction
of the book including electronic, mechanical, photographic, recording, CD-ROM,
videotaping, laser or computer disc, or other means, written permission must
first be obtained from the copyright holder and the publisher.

Front Cover Photo: ToshBrown.com/Dan Thornberg
Back Cover Photo: Brownells Inc.
All other photos and illustrations by the author unless otherwise noted.

Please be advised that the author and publisher assume that the mechanical
and safety essentials of all the firearms mentioned or covered in this book
are in "factory original condition," with all the specs and measurements
for all parts as originally made by the manufacturer of each firearm.
Making any alterations to a firearm part can be unsafe. Therefore, the author and
publisher strongly suggest that the reader should have all firearms carefully
inspected by an experienced gunsmith. The author and publisher disclaim any
and all responsibility for possible accidents related to the advice in this book.

Printed in the United States of America
Current printing (last digit) 10 9 8 7 6 5
Library of Congress card number: 2004103774
ISBN: 1-58011-203-X

CREATIVE HOMEOWNER®
24 Park Way
Upper Saddle River, NJ 07458

TABLE OF CONTENTS

PART 4
ADVANCED TECHNIQUES

PART 5
THE FINAL STEPS

Cars are tuned by master crafsmen, but they are also tuned by average owners. Part of the enjoyment of a car can be knowing that you, the owner, made it run its very best, having improved acceleration, smoothness, even fuel economy. And so it is with gunsmithing.

You can have your favorite rifle repaired or tuned by the very finest artisan. Indeed, as with auto repairs, there are gunsmithing jobs that should never be attempted by the average owner. But, there are also many repair and maintenance jobs that can be completed in a limited home workshop. Doing these can provide a great deal of pleasure.

It's a source of pride to know that it was your work that transformed your rifle's accuracy from mediocre to near minute-of-angle accuracy. And you can save considerable money when you add some custom feature or make some needed repair with your own labor. These savings can be converted into more ammunition, firearms, or accessories, which are always worthwhile goals.

Not everyone should attempt even minor gunsmithing, but if you have patience, a steady hand, good eyesight, and a bit of mechanical ability, you can accomplish a great deal of home gunsmithing. It is hoped that this volume will help you accomplish those tasks while avoiding the disappointments or damage that could accompany many well-meaning, but uninformed attempts at gunsmithing.

Gun maintenance or repair always requires top-grade precision tools as well as the needed parts. Since these are not always readily available, an Appendix lists the sources of many tools and parts discussed in the text. If you need an item not available, contact the sources shown. Patience in this area will help insure that the job goes smoothly and without disappointment.

By the very nature of the topic, no gunsmithing book can be truly complete. The best gunsmiths, even after fifty or more years at their trade, will admit they are still learning. However, it is hoped that this effort will enhance each reader's knowledge and make a number of specific jobs go easily.

ACKNOWLEDGEMENTS

A book of this kind demands a great deal of assistance from a large number of people and companies—far too many to mention. The author and publisher acknowledges such help and thanks all for their valuable assistance, especially those at Brownells.

Very special thanks for extensive assistance go to John Realmuto for his guidance in my earliest attempts at gun repair and to those countless persons who brought me their cherished firearms for repair, alteration, or customizing during my twelve years of commercial gunsmithing. It was that experience which laid the foundation for this work.

– Ed Matunas

PART 1

AN APPROACH
TO GUNSMITHING IN
THE HOME WORKSHOP

1
DOES THAT FIREARM NEED WORK?

Before a firearm is subjected to any home repair attempts it should be absolutely in need of the planned repair. Too many firearms are reduced in value, by too many well-meaning gun owners, because the owners were unable to determine that their firearm really did not need the extensive work undertaken.

For example, Joe Huntzmuch takes a bad spill and his favorite .30-30 carbine finds rest among some less than smooth forest floor debris. Upon recovering his rifle, he finds a few minor scratches on blued surfaces, several similar marks on the buttstock, along with one rather serious dent. Instead of deciding upon the judicious application of a touch-up bluing pencil for the metal scratches and the application of a steam pad to the stock dent, followed by an overall application of a stock polish, Joe decides upon major surgery. He disassembles the rifle and sands down the metal and wood. Heavy doses of cold blue and stock finish leave the rifle looking less like one that has seen a bit of use and more like one that had been so battered as to require complete refinishing. Now, knowledgeable persons will view the value of Joe's carbine at about half of its worth before all of his attention.

There is an old saw's expression which states—if it works don't fix it. When applied to firearms this is indeed sage advice. There is little reason to redo a perfectly satisfactory

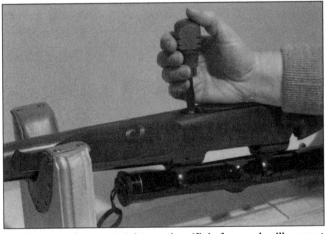

Keeping guard screws tight on the rifle's fore-end will correct many so-called accuracy problems.

blue job or stock finish when the presence of some minor dings justifies appropriate touchup, but no more. Even some ghastly stock dings can be corrected with the topical application of a steam pad and some touch up finish.

Another example of too much effort is Eddie Goodshot's discovery that his rifle was not smartly ejecting fired cases. Despite the fact that the "problem" was typical of a bolt being worked rather too slowly, such as Eddie had done at the range when he discovered his "trouble," he embarked on an extensive program of grinding, filing, and polishing of extractor and ejector. Finally, he had altered these parts so much that they truly refused to work and had to be replaced. Eddie needed firearms manipulation instruction, not repair effort.

Tommy Slideit considered his pump shotgun to be troublesome. It simply failed to kick out fired cases effectively. The trouble was that Tommy failed to realize that pump guns are meant to be operated vigorously rather than timidly, which was how Tommy most often manipulated his action. Tommy was also convinced that his semiautomatic .30-06 needed work as it sometimes failed to feed smoothly when the bolt was eased forward on the first round from the magazine. Again, he

These torn cartridge rims resulted when the ammo was used in a semiauto rifle. The problem was traced to the ammo, not the firearm.

simply did not realize that, to function properly, a semiauto needs to have its bolt snapped shut on the first round, as it would in a normal firing cycling. Others have replaced sights, reamed chambers and performed other unneeded work simply due to lack of understanding the basics of manipulation, usage, or care of their firearms.

There have been countless times when shooters have brought me their favorite rifles for rebedding or new barrels, when absolutely nothing was wrong with the current bedding or barrel. Yet, these shooters strongly complained of poor accuracy from a rifle that was once very accurate. A brief glance into the muzzle often revealed the problem—an extensive buildup of copper fouling from bullet jackets. Sure these shooters clean their guns, but their cleaning is often ineffective either due to the use of solvents not up to the task or a lack of knowledge as to what constitutes proper cleaning procedure.

Sometimes the mere tightening of action screws has corrected an accuracy problem. Or, the tightening of sight mounting fasteners has all too often been the only gunsmithing necessary to correct inaccuracy.

Obviously, the firearm owner needs to know when repair, replacement, or maintenance is in order. Oversimplified, it could be stated that when a condition other than normal is present, some remedial effort is in order. But as shown in the examples, the steps taken need to be in keeping with the degree of abnormality incurred. It is important, therefore, to know what is normal and what is abnormal.

With respect to firearm manipulation, this means that proper operation should be fully understood. To avoid any malfunctions due to mismanipulation, simply operate all firearms as you might under field conditions. This is to say, work a rifle's bolt as though you had just missed a shot at a big buck and were hurrying for a follow-up shot. Ditto for the proper handling of a pump or lever action rifle. Apply the same principle of vigorous manipulation to rimfire rifles and shotguns.

Remember that all semiautomatics require the full compression of the bolt return spring (recoil spring) and the rapid release of that compression to achieve full forward bolt velocity and energy. Thus, when chambering the first round from the magazine be sure the bolt is fully drawn to the rear before releasing it smartly for its forward travel. Avoid any tendency to ease the bolt forward.

In addition, ammunition must be properly loaded into the firearm. For most tubular magazines, this means being certain that the cartridge is fully pressed into the magazine, allowing any retainers or cartridge stops to snap into place behind the cartridge head.

With clips or box magazines, the cartridges must be positioned with their heads fully to the rear and snapped into place so that they correctly seat below any retaining ears or receiver protrusions. Thumb pressure should always be applied to push the cartridge rearward and downward, after each cartridge is in the magazine.

A great many assumed feeding problems are caused by the use of incorrect ammunition. Not every repeating rifle chambered for the .22 LR will feed properly if loaded with .22 Short or .22 Long ammunition. Moreover, some .22 semiautomatics were designed to function only with either standard velocity or high velocity Long Rifle ammo, but not both types. Nor will every rifle chambered for the .357 Magnum properly feed .38 Special ammo. Ditto for rifles chambered for the .44 Magnum and their functioning with .44 Special ammo. In short, you need to be sure the correct ammunition is being used.

Sometimes the correct ammunition selection becomes subtle. As an example, almost all semiautomatic rifles, chambered for non-handgun cartridges, should be used only with ammunition that has the case mouth crimped into a bullet cannelure. Many handloaders forget this important aspect. As another example, many semiautomatic pistols require the use of round nose ammunition, simply not being designed to function with sharp or flat nose bullets.

In addition, light powder charges, as sometimes employed in target ammunition, will often fail to function semiautomatics. This varies to great degrees with firearm design. For instance, the Marlin semiautomatic Camp Carbine, when chambered for the .45 Auto cartridges, will completely cycle its bolt, ejecting the case and feeding a live round, even if the fired cartridge contains no powder. The pressure created by the primer alone is sufficient to drive the bolt fully rearward while forcing the bullet into the barrel throat.

Interpreting the need for maintenance or repairs is not difficult, but it requires mature thinking and a commonsense approach to avoid any tendency to overkill. Recognizing the signals of trouble, or impending trouble, is the beginning of the necessary approach to knowing if a firearm needs attention.

For example, if the problem is poor accuracy, the first item to be suspect should be the condition of the bore. If a rifle is accurate at the beginning of a shooting session but shoots poorer and poorer with succeeding shots, it may well be that the problem is no more than bore fouling. Most centerfire cartridges produce enough barrel fouling so that maximum accuracy will be lost after the firing of fifteen or twenty rounds. In addition, by the time sixty rounds have been fired, only so-so accuracy can be obtained.

Of course, all this is relative and applies to rifles with which shooters can obtain 1½-inch or smaller groups at one hundred yards for five shots. Rifles that will do no better than 2½-inches or 3-inches under the same circumstances can often be fired one hundred or more times before any falling off in

accuracy, due to barrel fouling, can be detected.

Rifles chambered for cartridges with velocities of 2800 feet per second or more can be expected to perform best for no more than fifteen or twenty rounds before cleaning. Those chambered for cartridges that produce lower velocities can be fired more often before a quantity of accuracy-destroying fouling accumulates.

Bore fouling is also related to the smoothness of the barrel. Rough bores accumulate fouling more quickly than smooth ones.

To determine if fouling is accumulating, simply look into the muzzle end of the barrel (fouling is heaviest where the velocity is highest—all else equal). If the lands and grooves near the muzzle have taken on a heavy copper color, then the barrel's accuracy would benefit from a thorough cleaning.

If accuracy deteriorates with firing, but not due to bore fouling, one can suspect loose sight mounting system screws or fasteners, poor bedding, excessive barrel heat (due to firing too rapidly), or perhaps even a defective scope. This is assuming the problem is not traceable to a shooter who begins flinching as the effects of recoil accumulate. In addition, the entire matter often may be put to rest by simply tightening a few action screws. So, before deciding to tune a rifle that is shooting poorly, always be sure the problem isn't simply a dirty bore, loose screws, or a tired shooter.

Should a gun fail to feed, fire, or extract, most often the problem is dirt, grime and/or congealed lubricants. The working mechanism of a firearm needs to be kept meticulously clean for one hundred percent reliability. Cotton swabs, pressurized cans of gun cleaners and very tiny amounts of high grade lubricants are needed, applied as required, to maintain positive functioning. This is especially true with gas-operated semiautomatics.

As a rule, a centerfire bolt-action rifle should have the action and bolt cleaned thoroughly every 250 to 300 rounds. Be sure that brass shavings are cleaned from behind extractors, ejector holes, and plungers, bolt faces, and so on. Also, be sure to clean internal bolt surfaces.

Lubricate sparingly; lubricants attract dirt. Use only a drop or two as required for satisfactory smoothness in functioning. Moreover, when temperatures will be below 20°F avoid the use of lubricants entirely to prevent frozen or congealed

Look to the firearm as cause of difficulty only after shooter and ammo have been eliminated. (Courtesy: Fiduccia Enterprises)

lubricant problems. A few very high-grade synthetic lubricants will not congeal or freeze to temperatures of -20°F. or even lower. However, even these must be used very sparingly. And you must be certain that the stated claim for the lubricant is true. You can test by placing a few drops on a steel plate and placing it in your 0°F. freezer for a few days. Then compare the consistency of the lube with a few drops placed on a plate at room temperature. Naturally, you should be certain that any lubricant placed in your freezer does not contaminate foodstuffs.

Semiautomatic centerfire rifles should receive a complete strip cleaning every hundred rounds. Some may require such a cleaning after every use. One popular semiautomatic .223 rifle is prone to have its gas piston rust in place when it is stored for short periods, especially after use with specific propellants. At worst, the shooter will be unable to move the operating handle. At best, the operating rod will be sluggish enough to cause malfunctions.

Obviously, if you eliminate the lack of basic cleaning maintenance as the cause for malfunction or poor accuracy, the problem could then lie with the ammunition used. Not many factory loads will produce accuracy better than 1¾-inch to 2-inch at one hundred yards (five 5-shot groups), even from very accurate bolt-action rifles.

When using a bolt-action rifle, knowing that a two-inch group is a good one with run-of-the-mill ammo is an important aspect of analyzing a problem. It usually takes good reloads to get the 1½-inch or smaller groups we often hear about. Naturally, rare exceptions can occur. More on this later.

A few rifles will shoot poorly with one type of ammo and will do well with another. However, this oftentimes indicates a need for tuning, rather than ammunition superiority. Still, not every lot of factory ammunition is praiseworthy. Sometimes extremely poor accuracy, or even malfunctions, can be traced to a bad lot of factory ammo. Therefore, always check accuracy or functioning with an ammunition lot of known capability. A later chapter will discuss assembling ammunition of proven accuracy.

Semiautomatic functioning with specific lots of ammo can leave telltale signs if you are observant. If ammunition produces uniform chamber pressure, and, hence, uniform bolt velocity, ejection of the fired case will be in a predictable pattern. The point at which the ejected case typically first impacts with the ground should be uniform. That is to say, first impact for all fired cases should normally be within a five-foot diameter circle. After bouncing, cases will, of course, be randomly dispersed. Case ejection that results in the case's first point of impact being randomly dispersed over a wide area is often a sign of faulty ammunition.

If the cases are all landing in a close circle and the firearm is functioning poorly, the most likely area of fault is with the firearm. The exception to this is when the ammo being used does not generate sufficient energy (recoil or gas pressure) to properly and positively cycle the semiautomatic's action. This can often be indicated by cases first striking the ground quite close to the shooter.

Once you are certain that lack of routine maintenance, limited shooter capability, or poor ammo quality are not the cause of inaccuracy or malfunction, you can reasonably assume something is wrong with the firearm. You can then begin to look for problems of a specific nature.

Being familiar with cause and effect will, of course, assist in any determination as to what may be wrong. Indeed, reading through material presented later in this effort will help familiarize the reader with where to look for problem corrections.

In general, many problems are often the result of certain recurring defects. For instance, a certain firearm that is not feeding properly when manipulated as intended with the correct ammunition, will often be found to have bent clip ears, a broken cartridge guide, worn, damaged or improper receiver dimensions on feeding surfaces, a weak magazine spring, or a faulty follower—each, of course, as appropriate to the type of firearm involved.

For example, with many of the Marlin .22 bolt-action rifles which fail to feed, the first place to look is at the cartridge guide. This is a bent spring steel part mounted between barrel and receiver and protruding over the top of the chamber mouth. As another example, a semiautomatic pistol that fails to feed, should first be tested with a new magazine, as bent clip ears are the most common cause of malfunction on this type of pistol. Of course, the offending clip can be repaired.

Each problem with a specific firearm must be approached in an orderly fashion to prevent needless effort, which, if misguided, could make matters worse. It is important to be certain what type of repair work is required before moving ahead. It is the bad guess at what's needed that lies behind so many guns being ruined.

Some basic inspections should be routine for the serious-minded firearm owner. The first of these, an important one for safety (especially if reloads are used), is a headspace check. Using the appropriate gauge, headspace should be checked every one thousand rounds for centerfire metallic cartridge rifles. The same frequency would apply to handguns using magnum cartridges. Shotguns and standard caliber handguns should be checked every five thousand rounds. Quality rimfire rifles and handguns can be checked every ten thousand rounds.

Headspace gauges must be used delicately and the action should never be forced against the gauge. If a stripped bolt is used (no internal springs, firing pin, ejector or extractor), it will be much easier to feel the action closing on the gauge and insure that the action is fully seated without the forcing of parts. Naturally, if headspace should prove excessive, the gun should be taken from service until properly repaired.

Another inspection that should be made is the functioning of the action with dummy cartridges (no primer or powder). If you do not reload, have a reloading friend or a local gun shop make you up enough dummy rounds to fill the magazine and chamber of your firearm. Then, with crisp motions, function your firearm's action to insure that the dummy cartridges feed smoothly from the magazine and that the action closes fully on them. Check that proper extraction and ejection occur on the opening stroke of the action. Also check for any excessive damage that may occur to the case or bullet during the feeding cycle.

The same dummy cartridges used for routine inspection can later be used when doing repair work. Do be certain not to mix live and dummy cartridges together! Dummy cartridges should have a hole drilled through the case for easy identification—or paint them black. Moreover, remember that the use of dummy cartridges should never lead to careless firearm handling. Always handle firearms and dummy cartridges as though loaded ammo were being used. In this way, a mix-up will never cause a disaster.

Another routine inspection should be the visual review of the firing pin indent on the fired primer—or on the case if rimfire ammo is used. Shallow indentations are a warning of

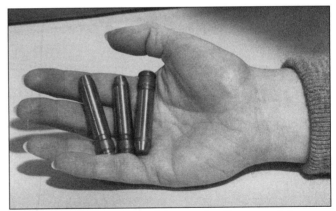

Headspace gauges are essential to routine firearm maintenance, especially if the shooter is a reloader. Headspace should be checked at intervals, the action never forced against the gauge.

future problems. They can be caused by dirty or gummed actions, frozen lubricant, weak mainsprings, and sometimes even a broken firing pin. Shallow indents can also be caused by excessive firearm headspace or reloaded cartridges that have been resized in a too-small sizing die.

Other inspections include the scrutiny of all unique

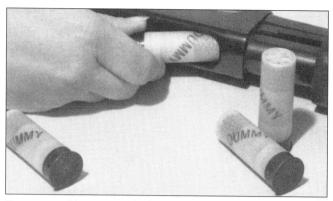

Dummy cartridges are useful for routine firearm inspection as well as testing repairs. But to insure that no mix up with live ammo occurs, they should be clearly identified.

Finding problems before they become major can keep gunsmithing requirements to a minimum. This small stock crack has not yet caused any accuracy problems. A bit of epoxy now will keep it from becoming a major split.

firearm features. Check the safety for proper functioning, making sure the chamber and magazine are empty beforehand. If the firearm is so equipped, check the half-cock hammer safety by applying pressure to the trigger with the hammer located in the safe position. Also, check such things as magazine releases, cartridge cut-offs and any other movable parts required in the proper operation of the specific firearm.

Inspect all wooden and synthetic materials used for stocks and handguards. Look for splits, cracks, or dents. Any such defects need prompt repair as delay may cause complete failure. Metal finish should also be carefully inspected.

A tad of surface rust is easy to remove and touching up the bluing on a small area is no special problem. However, once rust has started to pit the metal's surface, or it spreads over a wide area, easy corrective steps are no longer applicable.

Also, carefully check the crown at the muzzle end of the barrel. Nicks or any damage at the crown, which can influence the bullet as it leaves the barrel, will cause poor accuracy. Happily, such damage is easy to repair.

Generally, any firearm that functions in a less than perfect manner, or which displays any appreciable finish wear, is a candidate for the appropriate home gunsmithing. Simply keep in mind that it is self-defeating to attempt major repairs when only minor ones are called for. In addition, always be sure you know exactly what is needed before beginning a repair.

Specific details for many popular firearms will be discussed further along. For now, it is important only to realize that firearm knowledge; inspection, and maintenance are important aspects of any real gunsmithing program. Moreover, the extent of any repair undertaken should be in keeping with the magnitude of the problem.

2
CAN I FIX IT?

There are a great many repairs that the firearm owner can make. Equally, there are a number of repairs that should not be undertaken by anyone but a qualified gunsmith. Knowing the difference is imperative. Even then, some repairs are best left only to trained personnel at the factory of the firearm's origin. It is important that each owner carefully assess his capability before beginning any repair. The need to determine if all the necessary tools and parts are on hand is also vital. Nothing can make a job go sour quicker than improvising when a needed special tool or part is not available.

Headspace correction is one area that, in most instances, should be left to professionals. Often, the correction of a head-space problem involves the removal of the barrel from the action, the removal of a portion of the chamber end of the barrel, the contouring and re-threading of the chamber end of the barrel, reinstallation of the barrel and, finally, rechambering. Such an undertaking requires, at a minimum, a very exacting barrel vise with appropriate jaws, an action wrench, a really good lathe, chamber reamers, and headspace gauges. All but the last two are not apt to be available to the average firearm owner. In addition, the re-threading of the barrel will require a first-class toolmaker's knowledge. Obviously, then, headspace problems are not normally in the domain of the serious firearm owner or hobbyist gunsmith.

Rechambering any firearm, to a caliber using any cartridge other than the one for which it was originally chambered, should be approached carefully. The thinning of barrel walls

Most gunsmithing jobs are well within the ability of the careful firearm owner. But it is important to recognize those that are not.

can be dangerous if the person doing the rechambering is not thoroughly familiar with the requirements for maintaining adequate chamber-wall strength. Any work requiring welding, brazing, or heat treating is best avoided by the amateur. If not properly applied the use of heat on any firearm part can be disastrous. Total knowledge of what can happen if the job is done incorrectly is essential when using heat.

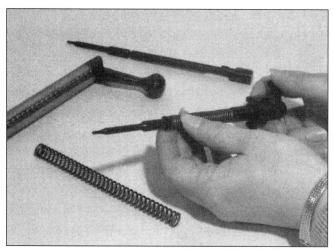

Parts replacements most often go quickly and easily, and are well within the scope of a home workshop.

The heating of a very hard receiver, to anneal a spot on it so that it can be drilled and tapped, can be ruinous to the receiver's strength. Too, softening a spot on the receiver to start a drill is, for most folks, the first step in breaking a tap off in that receiver. Very hard receivers should be drilled and tapped only by those with extensive experience. Taps are very, very tough to remove, without causing extensive damage, when they break off in a receiver or barrel.

Bolt handle heating, which enables bending for scope clearance, or welding on a replacement handle, requires very special care and knowledge if the strength of the locking lugs on the bolt are not to be adversely affected.

Barrels heated for the brazing of sight bases can wind up too soft or excessively brittle if the job is not handled correctly. I saw one revolver, that had been converted for the exclusive use of blanks, blow up. The cause was improper heating of the cylinder when it was pinned to prevent cartridges with bullets from being chambered. Even soft soldering jobs can lead to problems if the person doing the work is not familiar with all the potential pitfalls. Heating any firearm part is potentially dangerous if you are unfamiliar with all of the potential problems.

Any amount of heat, even from a soft soldering job, will discolor the metal surrounding the work area. Therefore, unless you are fully experienced and have the proper facilities for refinishing, the use of heat in repairs should be avoided.

In general, any repair that might compromise the strength of a firearm should not be undertaken by the amateur. Even

drilling holes in a barrel or receiver, while often a practical undertaking for the careful individual, needs to be carefully accomplished if the firearm's safety is to remain as it was prior to such work.

Needless to say, scopes should be repaired only by the manufacturer. Even if the owner could accomplish a satisfactory scope repair, the ability to replace the inert waterproofing gas in a scope is beyond the capability of most of us.

The making of firearm parts oftentimes is not practical due to requirements for heat treating in order to obtain the correct degree of part hardness. Few home gunsmiths have the necessary equipment to bring a part to the required temperature, to hold that temperature for the required time, or to allow for the necessary controlled cooling or quenching, let alone have the proper equipment to measure the results of the hardening process.

But, with few other exceptions, most other gunsmithing chores can be handled by a careful person who is able to use ordinary tools with the appropriate skill. For example, a firearm owner can replace almost any part of a firearm, except the barrel or receiver, if he has the correct part, necessary tools, and the know-how. Some factories do restrict the sales of certain parts to gunsmiths only. And a few parts are available solely for factory installation. Such restrictions are to protect consumers from potential physical harm and the factory from liability for that harm. Such parts often include barrels, receivers, bolts and trigger parts.

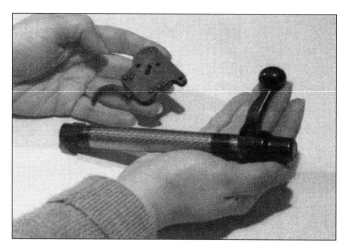

Some parts, such as this Remington bolt and trigger, are restricted to factory installation. Such restrictions are for the protection of firearm owners.

The restricted parts may require special tools and/or knowledge for correct, safe installation. Trigger parts, while easily installed, are restricted, in part, to prevent a too light trigger pull from being the cause of an accident. Besides unintentional discharge by finger pressure, over-light trigger pulls often prove to be the cause of a dropped firearm discharging. However, we will discuss trigger adjustment and replacement later.

Easily replaced parts include sights, stocks, firing pins, extractors, ejectors, and various springs. Other easy-to-install parts include cartridge guides, cartridge followers, magazine boxes, swivels, replacement clip magazines to convert box magazine firearms, replacement style floor plates and trigger guards, and other similar items. The careful workman can often replace such items as buttplates and custom style triggers, or add recoil pads, special scopes, and personal touches.

Naturally, each job requires certain, and sometimes, specialized knowledge. But each is a valid undertaking for the serious firearm owner who is willing to take the time to gain the bits of knowledge required, and to keep on hand those tools necessary to do such repairs.

While the refinishing of blued or anodized metal surfaces is best left to properly equipped professionals, or the factory of origin, wood refinishing is always in the domain of a handy firearm owner. And the simple touching-up of metal finishes, even plating touch-up on small parts, can be a practical undertaking for the average shooter or collector. But always remember that any refinishing, no matter how well done, does detract from the value of commercial firearms.

One possible exception is that sometimes careful refinishing of a custom firearm will not detract from its value. Another exception is the firearm that is so badly worn and/or that has little value. In this case, proper refinishing can actually add value to the firearm, as well as extend its useful life.

More often than not, poor accuracy can be corrected by the firearm owner. Recrowning of a barrel, rebedding of an action or barrel, or the glass bedding of the action and barrel are all practical home gunsmithing efforts that can greatly enhance a rifle's accuracy. Shotgun barrels can be altered to accept screw-in chokes. Complex firearms can be disassembled for needed cleanings and careful owners can adjust the trigger pulls on some makes and models to better suit their needs for accuracy. The list goes on. It is important to realize that you don't always require the services of a gunsmith to get the maximum potential from your firearm, or to repair it when it occasionally breaks down.

Deciding if a specific repair makes sense to do at home is a personal thing. The amount of experience you have, the type of tools on hand, and the degree of difficulty of the job must be considered. Do keep in mind that seemingly routine repairs do sometimes have safety aspects that need to be considered. For example, a firing pin replacement could cause problems if the new pin protrudes excessively from the gun's bolt or standing breech. Such a condition could lead to a pierced primer and allow hot gases to be dumped into the gun's action, possibly with disastrous results. Yet, many firing pins are made to very exacting dimensions and employ positive stops to forward motion. These are readily replaced.

Another consideration is the need of a firearm to be absolutely reliable after repair. For example, handguns used for personal protection must, above all else, be one hundred percent reliable. The improper installation or the improper alteration of something as simple as a trigger-return spring or mainspring could bring about a malfunction at the worst possible moment.

It is always necessary to consider personal experience and workmanship when deciding whether or not to undertake a repair. Avoid the temptation to over-estimate ability. For the most part, those repairs discussed in this effort are jobs that can be undertaken by any careful, mature-thinking firearm owner who is capable of following instructions and possesses a bit of patience.

Indeed, the repairs and alterations, as well as the detailed disassemblies and more advanced jobs discussed in this volume, are usually undertaken by the firearm owner, rather than a local gunsmith. Some of these tasks are obviously more difficult than others. Let your personal need guide your decisions to do, or not do, work.

Start with the easier undertakings and go slowly. Start your first repair efforts on guns which are not too valuable. Mistakes can happen, and you should be able to afford the error of a failed attempt. Yet, if you move ahead carefully, thinking out the job, using patience and, most importantly, if you proceed slowly and gently, you can grow to be quite

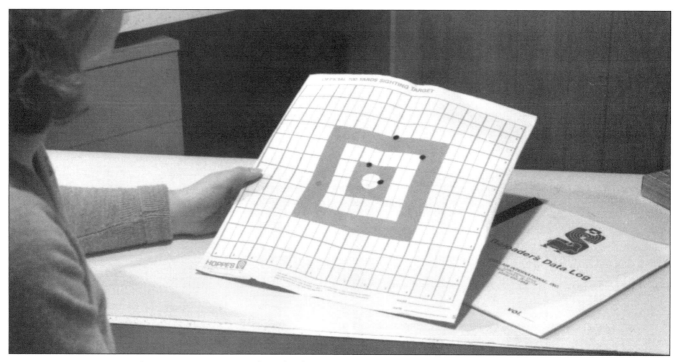

Accuracy got you over a barrel? Chances are you can correct the problem yourself.

proficient at gun maintenance and repair.

Chances are that if you feel confident about disassembly and reassembly you can repair most of the problems that might occur. Still, the following pages should help you to accomplish repairs or alterations that you might not have otherwise attempted.

Before starting any of the described undertakings, do read this entire book, then reread the pertinent sections. Be sure you have all the necessary tools, especially with respect to proper fitting screw drivers, drift punches, and other specialty tools, as required.

Remember, you can fix it if you are able to disassemble and reassemble the firearm without difficulty, if you have the proper tools, and if you are willing to proceed slowly—very slowly.

A few cautions: If your eyesight is such that corrective lenses do not supply good, crisp, close-up vision, any gunsmithing task should be carefully considered in the light of potential firearm damage that might occur due to vision problems. And do not proceed when you are rushed for time. Always leave plenty of time between a repair and the next anticipated use of the firearm. Repairs undertaken the night before a hunting trip, or shooting session at the range, very often go wrong. And before beginning any repair, do make certain that replacement parts are available should something unexpected result in the way of a broken or lost part. If extra parts are not readily available for your firearm, best consign the job to a pro.

3
HAND TOOLS

A workman's ability seldom exceeds the capability of his tools. The condition of his tools indicates a great deal about the ability of the workman. Gunsmithing, like many other undertakings, demands that the individual have a good supply of gunsmithing hand tools. A handful of carpenter's screwdrivers and a few chisels will not enable you to undertake satisfactory firearms maintenance or repair. Nor will a department store gun cleaning kit allow you to restore accuracy to an often-fired favored rifle. If you want results, you must use results-oriented equipment.

An assault on a firearm with just any old set of mechanics tools will probably bring about varying degrees of mutilation

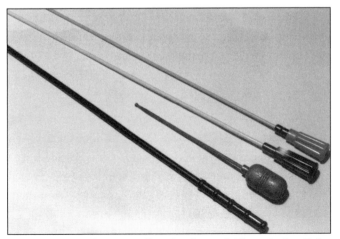

Nothing can replace a quality cleaning rod. These Parker Hales feature a spring steel core with an outer covering of bore protecting acetate.

to screw heads and other fasteners, or worse, result in small, fragile parts being broken. But, the ownership of the appropriate hand tools will not guarantee satisfactory results. Ownership without knowledge of proper use is a meaningless thing. However, the understanding of the proper use and selection of hand tools for gun maintenance and repair is easy to acquire if you proceed in an orderly fashion.

CLEANING RODS AND TIPS

Most firearm owners purchase an aluminum cleaning rod, either separately or in a kit. But consider, if you will, the softness of an aluminum rod. It bends easily and, if used with the essential snug-fitting patches and bore brushes, the rod is soon bent and warped. Then, as the rod continues to be used, sections of it bear firmly against the bore, resulting in bits of aluminum being shaved from the rod. The roughened rod surface then begins to pick up bits of grit, grime and dirt, which become firmly embedded in the soft rod. These are then rubbed against the bore's surface and, quickly, the cleaning process begins to do more damage than good. So why are there aluminum rods? Well, they are inexpensive and for a once-a-year shooter they could, perhaps, with good care, be used for four or five cleanings, thereby lasting that many years. But such rods are not very suitable for the serious firearm owner—and brass rods are not a heck of a lot better.

The minimum acceptable rod is a good, hard, steel one that is properly selected for size and correctly maintained. Because of its hardness, a steel rod is not easily bent, nor will it become roughened and abraded easily. Thus, it will not become a host for embedded particles of dirt, grime, and grit that could be ruinous to the bore. If a steel rod is disfigured, however, it can readily hold undesirable material picked up in cleaning or, worse, the hard rod's damaged portions can cause internal bore damage. Also, a bent or bowed steel rod can cause bore damage if the bowed portion rubs on the internal bore surface.

A rod should be notably smaller than bore size. Bore-sized rods are a serious hazard. Should a patch fall off the jag and get between rod and bore, a very serious jamming of the rod will occur. Often, the bore's surface will be damaged before the rod is freed. On the other hand, if a rod is excessively small in diameter it can be bent too easily. The rod should be from 0.03-inch below bore diameter, to perhaps as much as 0.10-inch below, the larger amount being practical on the larger bore diameters.

I once used a very nice stainless steel rod for cleaning a

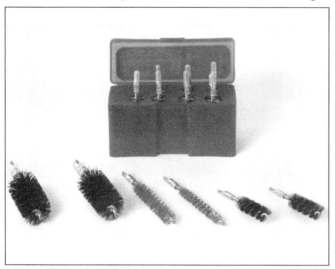

Proper fitting bore brushes of top quality are necessary for maintaining accuracy. (Courtesy: Battenfield)

specific rifle. However, the rod had a fair amount of flex when pushing a snug patch through the bore. If a cleaning rod guide was not used, the rod would bend considerably. One day, while in a hurry, I could not find the appropriate cleaning rod guide, but I commenced cleaning a .22-250 anyway. Well, the rod buckled enough in use to contact a sharp corner on the action which simply began shaving the steel rod with each forward stroke. The rod also took a slight set. Then I began to feel the

grating of the rod on the bore's surface. Luckily I stopped in time when I felt the first tinge of something wrong. But if I had not been paying careful attention to the feel of the rod's passage through the bore, I may well have ruined a $200 barrel rather than an $18 cleaning rod. Going slow and only when the right equipment is available is the moral of the story.

The best cleaning rods are, in my opinion, made of spring steel and are nylon coated. Because of the strength of the spring steel, such rods do not easily take on a set. And should they somehow take on a slight bow, the plastic covering will prevent barrel damage as the rod rubs the interior surface.

Naturally, the soft plastic covering of a coated rod is more easily damaged than the hard surface of a solid steel rod. However, I would rather risk such damage to the rod than risk damage to a barrel which may well cost ten times as much. Too, the soft plastic surface is very easily cleaned.

Regardless of the type of rod selected, it is important to wipe it clean every time it is removed from the bore. Wipe away any foreign material with a patch that has been lightly moistened with solvent. Then, using a dry patch, carefully run the patch along the rod, drying it and feeling for any abrasions.

Sometimes a damaged steel rod can be repaired by careful application of crocus-cloth. But keep in mind the relative value of the rod versus the barrel when being tempted to use a rod that's not just right. Using too long a rod will help cause the bowing that can eventually ruin it. A too short rod will see you banging knuckles against the end of the all important cleaning rod guide.

Ideally, several rods are required. If you attempt to use one rod for a number of calibers it is likely that its diameter will be too small or too large for some applications. One rod is required for .17 caliber, another can do for .22 through .26 caliber, and another for .27 caliber and on up to perhaps .40 caliber. Larger bores will require a hefty rod.

The tip used on the rod is an important part of this hand tool. One good style is the pointed jag that allows the impaling of a patch, to hold it in place, and also lets the patch fall free at the muzzle when the rod is withdrawn from the breech end.

The diameter of the enlarged section of the tip immediately behind the point is critical. If it is not of the correct diameter, the patch will not be snug in the bore. The user then will try to compensate by using multiple patches. This is wasteful and indicates that the right tool is not being used. A tip for every

Scope caps are an important cleaning "tool." They protect the scope lens coatings from harmful cleaning solvents. They also prevent the accidental jamming of a sharp jag into the lens.

Cleaning rod guides, which fit into the action, are basic and essential gun maintenance tools.

caliber is essential to insure proper patch tightness in the bore. Patches come in various sizes and are matched to the tip.

When using a cleaning rod it is important to be certain that scope lenses are protected by caps to prevent the tip from piercing a lens during a careless moment. A cleaning rod guide is essential to prevent damage to the interior action, chamber, or throat that could be caused by the sharp tip.

A useful alternative to pointed tips is the blunt jag which has the ability to hold a patch that is carefully placed over its end and wrapped around it. However, even when care is used, patches can fall off before the rod enters the bore, especially if a cleaning rod guide is not used.

The slotted tip is the worst possible choice as it invariably does not allow uniform patch contact with the bore. In some instances, the metal of a slotted tip can directly contact the bore as the rod is pushed through.

Rod tips must have threads that fit the rod with exactness. Sloppy threads may allow the rod tip to work loose and cause incorrect alignment in the bore.

Ideally, I prefer rod tips to be made of brass to prevent bore

or other surface damage if the tip inadvertently impacts with or is forced against the bore, chamber, or action surfaces. If a tip becomes damaged, due to the softness of the brass, knowing that more expensive damage to the firearm has been prevented.

Soft plastic tips are nearly useless as they first buckle one way and then another as they are used to push a snug patch through the bore.

Finally, any good rod needs free swiveling of its handle to insure that the patch can rotate in the rifling. Without a rotating rod, the patch would be forced to ride over the rifling and would not do a good job of wiping in the grooves. Ditto for any use of a brush.

A swiveling tip is fine in theory, but in practice you have no way of knowing if it's working or if the load placed on it is causing it to bind up. A good many swiveling handles do not rotate properly either. A quality rod is needed.

The most satisfactory rods I have used are the spring steel nylon coated, one-piece rods manufactured by J. Dewey Manufacturing Company and the Parker-Hale rods. Indeed, I own one Parker-Hale rifle rod that I purchased in the early

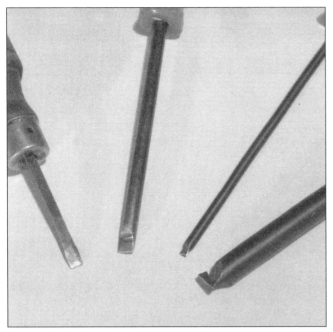

Tools like these poorly sharpened, bent and broken screwdrivers are signs that the owner is not up to routine tasks, at least not until he understands the basic care and use of such essential tools.

1950s and it's still going strong. The handle has been partially broken off, but it still swivels perfectly and its acetate coating is in near perfect condition. It has outlasted what would have been seven to twelve slightly more or less expensive rods.

SCREWDRIVERS

After cleaning equipment, the hand tools most often used are screwdrivers. They are also the most often misused and abused tools the average gun owner has on hand. Improperly selected and misapplied screwdrivers can cause extensive damage to screw heads and surrounding metal and wood. All this can be avoided if the firearm owner learns what a screwdriver is able to accomplish and how to proceed in obtaining the desired results.

Screwdriver bits are tough if a quality tool is purchased and the size of the tool is taken into consideration when it is used. For example, a screwdriver blade that is 1/8-inch wide and approximately 1/40-inch thick, has an average working strength equal to about fifteen inch-pounds of torque and an average breaking point of about seventeen inch-pounds. This means that the maximum working strength of this tiny bit will be easily reached by applying pressure only with the thumb and first two fingers. If you use a screwdriver with a bit of this size and attempt to turn up a screw with a grip taken with a closed fist, something is going to give. Either the blade will bend, twist, or break, or the screw head will be damaged or broken.

A full hand grip on a screwdriver will develop fifty inch-pounds of torque. That's enough to bring a screwdriver blade, with a width of 1/5-inch and a thickness of 1/25-inch, to its breaking point. The use of a T-shape handle or a ratchet wrench with a leverage length of 3½-inches will allow a force of more than a two hundred inch-pounds to be applied to the screw bit. This is sufficient to damage screw bits with heads measuring up to 3/8-inch width and 1/20-inch thickness.

Thus, it should be obvious that the users of a screwdriver must keep in mind the working strength of the screws and bits used to turn them into place. The table below shows the average working torque and the average breaking torque for screwdriver bits. These also apply to screws with corresponding slot sizes. Note that there is only a small difference in working torque and destructive torque, usually about ten percent.

SCREWDRIVER BIT LIMITS*

Blade Width	Blade Thickness	Working Torque	Breaking Torque
1/8-inch	1/40-inch	15 in. lbs.	17 in. lbs.
5/32-inch	1/32-inch	31 in. lbs.	35 in. lbs.
3/16-inch	1/40-inch	31 in. lbs.	35 in. lbs.
3/16-inch	1/25-inch	45 in. lbs.	50 in. lbs.
15/64-inch	1/25-inch	67 in. lbs.	75 in. lbs.
1/4-inch	1/40-inch	67 in. lbs.	75 in. lbs.
1/4-inch	1/25-inch	94 in. lbs.	105 in. lbs.
3/8-inch	1/40-inch	99 in. lbs.	110 in. lbs.
21/64-inch	1/32-inch	103 in. lbs.	115 in. lbs.
21/64-inch	1/25-inch	135 in. lbs.	150 in. lbs.
3/8-inch	1/25-inch	144 in. lbs.	160 in. lbs.
3/8-inch	1/20-inch	180 in. lbs.	200 in. lbs.

*Assumes chrome nickel molybdenum steel with hardness of Rc52 to Rc55.

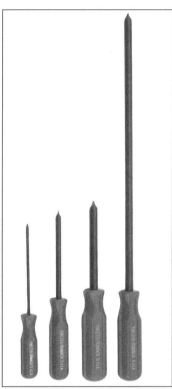

Screwdrivers are the premier gunsmithing tools. A few sets of good ones are essential. (Courtesy: Forster)

Obviously, the larger the screw the more torque that can be applied to a proper fitting bit. Generally speaking, use only the thumb and first two fingers to tighten screws that have fine-width slots and/or shallow slot grooves. Hand pressure can be used on larger screws such as those used for scope mounts. Normal hand pressure, or even a short 3½-inch T-handle, or a ratchet handle can be used for tightening large action screws.

All the foregoing assumes that the screwdriver handle is not more than one-inch in diameter. When a screwdriver with an overly large handle is used, special care must be taken to insure that you do not over-torque the bit or the screw.

When purchasing screwdrivers or bits keep in mind that extremely hard tips break abruptly and can cause severe damage to nearby metal and wood surfaces when breakage occurs. A tool that has some spring is preferable. If you should ever overstress a bit, its spring might give you ample warning to immediately stop the application of torque.

Use a screwdriver with a bit that exactly fits the screw head, both in width and thickness. Parallel sides on the bit are absolutely essential to insure full contact with the walls and the bottom of the screw slot.

A bit that is too narrow will bear only on the opposite ends at the outer edges of the slot. A bit that is not wide enough will not afford sufficient purchase to apply the proper amount of torque to loosen, or fully tighten, the fastener. And a tapered bit will bear only at the top edge of the slot and, because of its wedge shape, will cam out of the slot when maximum torque is supplied. All of these ill-fitting circumstances will cause damage to the screw and/or bit.

When using a bit with the correct shape and diameter it is essential to insure that it is positioned properly in the slot. If it does not bottom properly, or if it is not held plumb, then damage to the screw or bit is sure to occur.

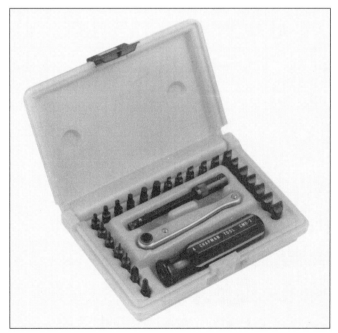

This Chapman gunsmith's screwdriver set allows ample torque to be applied without running the risk of breaking screws.

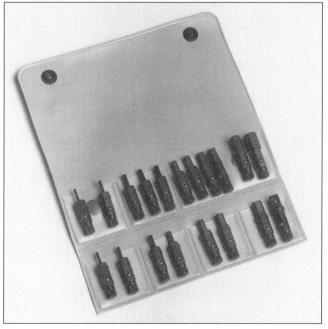

Accessory hex head drivers are also available from Chapman. (Courtesy: Chapman)

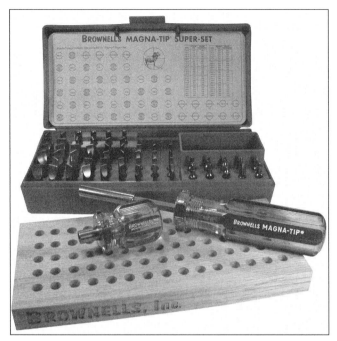

Brownells' Magna-Tip Super-Set will supply a screwdriver bit for almost any gunsmithing need, along with two different sized handles. (Copyright 2003 Brownells)

Using screwdrivers without damaging fasteners and nearby surfaces demands care and knowledge of proper application of torque.

Burred screws detract from a firearm's appearance and indicate that its owner is a tinkerer who doesn't really know what he is doing. Such screws should be replaced with carefully used, proper fitting screwdrivers.

Broken screws can become a major problem. Sometimes a broken screw can be removed by carefully attempting to rotate the screw with the judicious application of a pointed punch on the outer edge of the slot of the remaining half of the screw head. But a less than careful approach can mean even further disfigurement of the surrounding wood or metal.

Sometimes there is no way to remove a broken screw other than attempting to drill it out. Such efforts can sometimes be combined with an easy out. Other times, it means drilling and tapping for a larger screw and thread size. Still, on occasions, a broken screw can lead eventually to a ruined or greatly devalued action, barrel, frame, and so on. Proceed slowly and carefully when using screwdrivers. If you don't have a perfectly fitting screwdriver, wait until you can purchase one.

You can also grind an existing bit to fit. Take your time and be sure it's a perfect fit. When grinding a bit, be sure it remains cool. A bit can quickly reach temperatures of 400°F. or more when it is being ground. Such a temperature will

remove all the hardness of the steel, making further use of the screwdriver impractical.

Keep in mind the very small surface area and thickness of a bit when grinding screwdrivers. It takes only a few seconds against a grinding wheel to make the work area rise to 250°-350°F. A few more seconds and temperatures of over 400°F. will be generated. Keep work on the grinder for only three seconds and then quench in cold water. The quenching water should be at least a quart can. Small volumes of quenching water can be quickly heated if repeated quenching is involved.

When purchasing a selection of screwdrivers keep these points in mind. Purchase sufficient screwdrivers or bits to fit all of the various size screws on all of the firearms you are likely to work on.

Screwdrivers should be segregated by the thickness of the blade. Keeping all your blades and/or bits of a given thickness in one drawer or rack will enable you to quickly find a blade of the correct width once you have determined the proper thickness. By keeping blades segregated by thickness, you will prevent an accidental use of the wrong thickness.

HEX WRENCHES AND SCREWS

Originally, hex head screws found their way into firearms usage to prevent the mangling of slot head screws with poor fitting screwdriver bits. That was a good idea as, after all, many firearm owners frequently used poor-fitting bits. But the idea was not well thought out, or at least not put into fully effective application.

In my experience, most of the hex head screws used in the firearms industry are more easily damaged than the slotted types. This is due to a number of factors like the use of too small a hex, too shallow a hex, too soft a screw or simply poor dimensional tolerances on the hex or the hex wrench. The results of each and all of these is a hex hole that quickly has its shoulders wiped away, leaving a generally rounded hole. At this point the screw can neither be tightened sufficiently nor be removed for replacement.

But most of the hex screws normally encountered on firearms, scope base, and rings have proven less than up to the task–so much so that I go out of my way to find replacement slotted screws.

A word of caution when using hex wrenches and screws. Use a pressurized degreaser/solvent to clean out hex holes and wipe any grease from wrench surfaces to insure a dry, slip-free surface. Be absolutely certain that the hex wrench fits the screw snugly and that it is bottomed in the screw hex before attempting to turn it. Finally, use the hex wrench as intended. The long end goes into the screw and the short end is used for leverage. Using the long end for leverage guarantees that a hex hole will be quickly ruined. Yes, it's difficult to obtain sufficient leverage to adequately tighten a screw against recoil-induced movement when the wrench is so used. That's another reason to vote against hex head screws.

I have had many an individual bring a hopelessly ruined receiver to me. And all the trouble started with an attempt to remove a ruined hex head screw. With less than professional attempts to drill out the offending screw, the results have often been disastrous.

Keep in mind that the fit, hardness, and spring of a hex wrench is just as important to damage-free manipulation of hex screws as are the same qualities of a standard bit to be used on slotted screws. Even the best hex wrenches will wear out. When you note the sharp corners of your hex wrench becoming shiny and round, discard it and get a new one. They are inexpensive and even a large hex wrench can be purchased for less than a few dollars in a top quality version.

Hex head bits to fit standard, interchangeable bit screwdrivers are available. When combined with a one-inch diameter handle, these make the best possible tools for avoiding the hex-destroying excess torque that can be applied when the long end of a hex wrench is used as a handle. Such hex head bits are available for fine, custom quality screwdriver sets such as the one designed especially for gunsmithing chores and made by the Chapman Manufacturing company. Brownells also offers hex head wrenches in its Super-Set screwdriver kit.

PHILLIPS SCREWDRIVERS

The last type of screwdriver needed by firearm owners is the Phillips-head style. Phillips-head screws are often used on recoil pads and sometimes on buttplates. One of the advantages to Phillips-head screws lies in the usual shape of the matching screwdriver shank, i.e. rounded. A round-shanked screwdriver placed into a recoil pad will not chew up the recoil pad while the screw is being turned. Indeed, if done properly, such screwdrivers can be placed into a recoil pad and removed leaving little evidence of their passage. Only three or perhaps four sizes of Phillips-head screwdrivers are required for most gunsmithing chores.

Phillips-head screwdriver bits have a tendency to walk out of the screws' corresponding slots. Therefore, it is important to maintain adequate bit to screw pressure when using this type of screwdriver. And make no attempt to over-tighten!

Today, many gunsmith-style screwdrivers are manufactured with round shanks and parallel side bits. However, some fully acceptable ones are still made with flattened side shanks and semi-chisel points that have been "hollow" ground to produce the necessary parallel sides. The synthetic style handles stand up best when multiple mallet taps must be applied to the handle, but the wood handles give a better no-slip grip. Some of both styles are appropriate.

TIGHT SCREWS

While the practical torque that can be applied to a screwdriver is quite limited, it is often possible to loosen a severely tight screw, one that has slightly rusted in place, or one that has been set with Loc-Tite thread cement—without damaging screw or bit. When a screw refuses to turn loose with the appropriate amount of torque applied to the screwdriver, a slight tapping on the screwdriver may be the answer.

First, be absolutely sure that the screwdriver is bottomed in the slot and that it is not binding on the screw slot sides. If it binds, or if the screwdriver is not held plumb, then a broken screw might result. Now, with the firearm securely held and properly padded, try tapping the screwdriver handle squarely on top, with a few smart but lightly applied blows, using a small hammer or mallet. This procedure will often drive the screw threads downward into the mating threads sufficiently to create the amount of play necessary to start the screw out. Do not overdo the tapping as a split screw or stripped threads could result. Do not use wood handle screwdrivers for this purpose as they do occasionally split when tapped.

This same tapping procedure can be used to tighten a screw an extra tad to insure that a scope mount or sight screw does not work loose. Simply snug up the screw in the normal fashion with the appropriate torque. Then, being sure the screwdriver is the proper size and is held plumb, give the top of its handle two or three smartly applied, but light, blows with a small brass hammer. Apply the normal amount of torque to the screwdriver and you will often gain an extra small fraction of a turn on the screw. This procedure should be used only on screws that are never expected to be removed, because sometimes the screw will set up so tightly that later extraction is defied.

Many amateurs and professionals place a single drop of thread locking compound, such as Loc-Tite, on the screw before turning it into place, if it is intended never to be removed. Such applications have practical uses for the installation of scope mount bases or iron sight bases. Yet, tomorrow's needs are usually unknown. I have changed many a scope base or sight system for owners who decided to use a different sight system or scope base, or whose selection of a newer scope demanded that the iron sights be removed and/or a different scope mount base be installed. Thus, thread locking compounds need to be used judiciously. But when there's good reason to suspect the screw won't likely be removed, one drop of thread locking compound will insure that screw will stay tight. There will also be a 50-50 chance of satisfactory screw removal if the screw is lightly tapped by the small hammer and screwdriver method mentioned earlier.

BENCH VISES

Next to a screwdriver, a vise is the most often used hand tool when working with firearms. Because a vise frequently needs to be turned to correctly position the work, one that swivels is desirable. Additionally, if the jaws can be moved to both horizontal and vertical positions, all the better. But any swiveling vise needs to positively lock, without excessive jaw pressure, in whatever work position is selected.

There are many suitable vises, but perhaps the most universal in the firearms trade is the Versa-Vise made by the Gaydash Industries of Kent, Ohio. This vise swivels 360 degrees in either a vertical or horizontal jaw position. And it has a screw adjustment that allows automatic swivel locking when the jaws are closed to variable levels of pressure. This vise seems to be the ideal size for most gunsmithing chores. I have used the same one for more than thirty years for ninety percent of my gunsmithing and it is still going strong.

An overly large vise is not practical. It's simply too easy to cause firearm damage with a vise capable of delivering excessive pressure with modest tightening. Occasionally, there will be a need for a larger or smaller vise if you are to do a wide range of gunsmithing. The need for a larger vise has been limited to less than half a percent of all my work, whereas a small vise has been used for perhaps ten percent of my gunsmithing time.

A good bench vise is an indispensable gunsmithing tool. This one is the popular Versa-Vise.

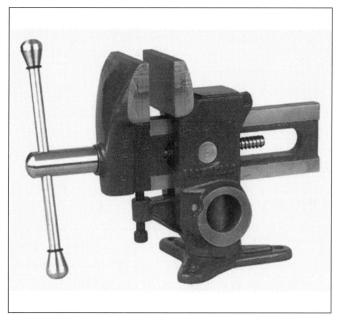

Vises come in many sizes and shapes. This one adjusts in every direction–horizontally, vertically, and can rotate 360 degrees in a horizontal plane. (Copyright 2003 Brownells)

A small vise like this one from Forster is often needed when working on small parts or sub-assemblies.

Small vises are irreplaceable when stoning or filing small parts, when working on small sub-assemblies or when trying to hold anything that's on the tiny side. A swiveling feature is also mighty handy, as well as jaws that allow for vertical or horizontal positioning of the part to be worked on. One perfect solution to the need for a small vise is the Forster Products Swiv-O-Ling vise. Others can be found, often in hobby shops or tool specialty houses.

The normal working vise should have a jaw opening of at least 3½-inch with a four-inch to five-inch opening being about perfect. The jaws should be three to four inches long. A 7/8-inch to one-inch opening is adequate for the small vise while 3/4-inch seems appropriate for jaw length. For a heavy duty vise, accept no less than a six-inch opening with jaws of equal length.

VISE PADS

Obviously, you cannot simply place a firearm (or some part thereof) into a vise and tighten the jaws without causing damage to the firearm. It is necessary to protect the firearm from the bare grip of the vise jaws. A bunch of old rags wrapped around the gun won't be much of a solution. Wooden vise jaw pads are essential and, at times, you may well require a set of commercial felt jaw pads, especially for the small vise. For rough work, a set of lead jaws for the medium and large vises are in order. A vise without the necessary protective jaws is not a suitable gunsmithing tool.

HAMMERS

Small hammers and mallets are other important tools. They are used for setting or freeing screws (in conjunction with the appropriate screwdriver), installing sights in dovetails, or removing drift pins (when appropriate punches are used), as well as a great many other chores. For the most part, the key to selecting hammers and mallets lies with their intended use.

For use with very fine drift pin punches, only very small and light hammers are appropriate or you may soon break the punch. Too, when driving sights in or out of dovetails with a heavy brass punch, a series of light taps are correct as opposed to a few heavy blows. Heavy blows can cause an improperly aligned sight or an ill-fitting one to quickly destroy the barrel's dovetail. For most work, hammers of one-half, one and two pounds should be all that's ever required.

For the one-half and one-pound size, a brass, flat-faced (both ends) style hammer is appropriate. Purchase only solid-head hammers with flat faces affixed to the handles in such a way so as not to allow the head to rotate on it. Do not make the mistake of purchasing a hammer with a head threaded onto the handle. These invariably work loose after a few wacks and severe part damage can occur when the head suddenly turns halfway around and your blow ricochets away from its intended application point. Screw-on plastic or brass hammer faces simply do not seem to work well either, as these frequently break off at the thread, again creating potential damage to the work.

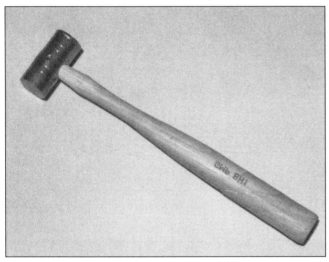

A few appropriately sized hammers will become essential.

It is safest to have a brass head for your two smallest hammers. This will prevent undue damage to any metal surface accidentally struck. For the heavier hammer, one rounded head and one flat head will prove most useful. The heavier hammer need not be brass; in fact, ideally, it should be steel, as its rounded head can be used for peening dovetails and similar efforts.

Another aspect to consider when selecting a hammer is to avoid a handle that is made of two or more sections threaded together. These threaded sections, when they become loose, can effectively cause the hammer head to rotate, which will damage the firearm.

To avoid hammer heads that will eventually rotate on handles that are press fitted, be sure the section of the handle entering the head is not rounded. A positive, non-round shape is necessary to prevent eventual head turning.

A good, solid leather mallet can, at times, be a useful tool.

An alternate would be a nylon or other plastic-type mallet. Such tools will allow blows to be delivered to delicate parts without harming them. Examples would be the tapping of a very tight shotgun magazine cap to free it for removal, or the tapping of a trigger assembly that is frozen in place.

Be sure never to use brass or steel hammers to apply blows to any aluminum part. Always use a leather or plastic mallet for such purposes. And use gentle blows only. Aluminum will bend or collapse easily.

PUNCHES

Punches are important gun maintenance and repair hand tools. They are essential for the removal of drift pins when assembling or disassembling firearms. When used to remove solid pins, punches can range in size from two-thirds to about nine-tenths the diameter of the pin to be removed. A tight pin will require as large a punch as possible to prevent bending or breaking of the punch.

When used to remove hollow or rolled pins, the punch should very nearly, but not quite, equal to the pin's diameter. If a punch that is too small in diameter slips inside a hollow (rolled) pin, it can freeze the pin and punch solidly in position. That can be a major problem. There are punches with raised centers on the end, which are designed specifically for hollow roll pins.

Use only hand pressure when punches are used to remove pins. Many pins are so loose and need only a slight amount of pressure to free them. When driving pins out of an aluminum housing, great care must be taken not to damage this soft metal.

The punch sizes needed will vary with the firearm to be worked upon. Generally speaking, if you have one each of 1/32-inch, 1/16-inch, 1/8-inch, and 1/4-inch, you will be able to handle most jobs. But there are some assignments, albeit just a few, that will require a smaller or perhaps in-between size punch.

Always be certain that the punch is held plumb to the pin to prevent damage to punch, pin, or surrounding areas. Use only light taps on the punch. Repeated light blows are to be desired over a few heavy blows. A heavy blow can cause a punch to slip from the rounded head of a pin and damage surrounding surfaces. Once a pin has been started sufficiently

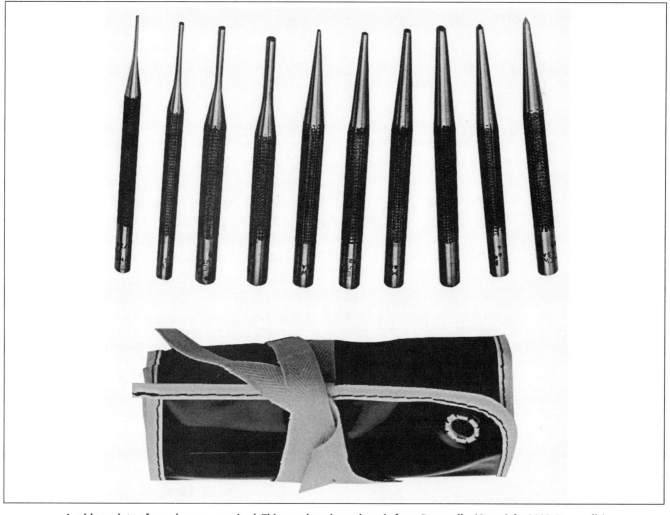

A wide variety of punches are required. This nearly universal set is from Brownells. (Copyright 2003 Brownells)

to allow the punch to be held below the surface, the temptation to use more forceful blows should be avoided. The punch still can damage internal parts that could well be unprotected due to an interrupted pin hole.

Most punches should, of course, have flat heads, that is with the exception of your center punch. Center punches are used for starting a drill bit, for peening metal, and for locating swivels, holes, and similar work. Ideally, the center punch should be on a 3/8-inch diameter shaft and should be quite hard. A shallow point is preferable to a long skinny one, which will deform easily.

Like screwdrivers, punches need to be kept cool should they need regrinding to repair a broken tip. Overheat them and they will soften. And a soft punch will peen outward, getting larger

at the tip and head with each hammer tap. This can create a difficult situation or a ruined parts housing. So be careful to keep punch temperatures well below 400° F when regrinding.

CHISELS

A good set of woodworking chisels is required for the rebedding of a barrel and/or action to improve accuracy. Such an undertaking is a common requirement. Chisel shanks need to be long enough to allow your hands to stay a comfortable distance from the work. Handles should be large enough for a comfortable grip. However, overly large handles can absorb some of the feel of the cutting which can lead to a poor job.

Chisels must be very sharp. All the cutting must be

accomplished by the chisel's keen edge rather than the strength of the hand, wrist, and arm of the person doing the work. If a chisel will not cut with a light steering pressure, it is too dull to do a proper job. Dull chisels lead to split wood or excessively large peels and gouges, which can easily ruin the job.

Chisels should be available in round, "V", and flat shapes. Angled blades, to the left and right, will also be required. Each shape must be available in a variety of sizes up to perhaps a 1/2-inch width.

Chisels can be sharpened preliminarily with a belt sander and then finished with stones of the correct shape. Use the belt sander sparingly to not ruin the temper of the very thin cutting edge. Naturally, if you do not have a belt sander the job can be done entirely with stones. If the sharpening chore is handled before the chisel becomes excessively dull, a stone alone will quickly return the needed sharpness.

When selecting chisels for gun stock work, I strongly recommend purchasing those offered specifically for gunsmithing. Many carpenter chisels are not up to the task. However, for rough work with a mallet on preliminary stock shaping, standard carpenter's chisels will do quite nicely.

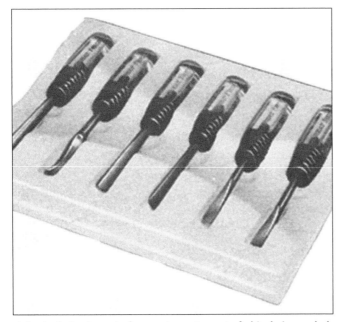

A basic, but adequate for most repairs, set of chisels is needed. More elaborate sets will be useful for any stock-making efforts. (Copyright 2003 Brownells)

RASPS AND FILES

Some rasps are needed to do the work that chisels alone seem too slow and tedious to accomplish. The basic shape of a stock, for instance, is best roughed out with a coarse wood rasp. Barrel channel rasps are quicker and easier to use than chisels. Finally, bottoming rasps allow the amateur to get good, flat surfaces and sharp angles.

As with chisels, rasps must be very sharp. Protecting their cutting surfaces is all that can be done to keep them in good shape. Don't throw a bunch of rasps in a drawer where they can be bumped and banged together. Properly cared for, a good rasp will last a long time. But once it becomes dull, throw it out rather than risk ruining a job in progress.

For most home gunsmithing efforts only a few files are needed. Their use is limited as any application will remove the metal finish and the surface hardness. Of course, the individual who desires to make a part will require a good selection of files.

Most of the applications for files in routine chores will be for shortening screws, fitting scope bases, removing burrs or perhaps cutting sight dovetails.

Keep in mind that files should never be used for trigger or sear work. Such applications would remove all or most of the surface hardness of such parts and allow them to wear rapidly in use, and create a potentially dangerous situation. However, files can be practical for fitting parts that have a uniform hardness throughout.

Files in triangular and flat shapes will prove useful. For most efforts, small sizes are most appropriate. Files with flats 1/8-inch, 3/16-inch, 1/4-inch and 3/8-inch wide will be the most useful. On occasion, there may be a 1/16-inch or 1/2-inch file required.

Files need care in the same manner as rasps. Don't store them en masse as bumping or banging together will quickly dull them. Store files and rasps so that they cannot come in contact with one another or any other metallic object.

Using files requires some thought. Coarse files are satisfactory for rough and preliminary work but fine-cut files should always be used for finishing steps. Soft aluminum will require a more open file than hard steel. Perhaps the best way to judge if you are using an appropriate file is the ease or difficulty of removing metal.

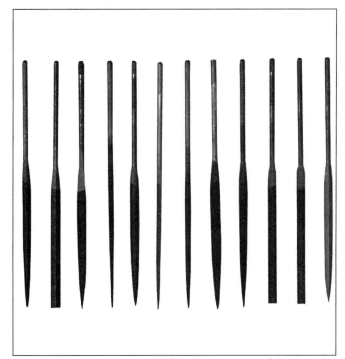

An assortment of gunsmith files are very useful. This set (Brownells) is suitable for almost any gunsmithing task likely to be encountered. (Copyright 2003 Brownells)

Files should not be applied in a strong arm method. Let the file do the cutting. If it does not cut easily, it is either the wrong file for the job or it is dull and should be discarded.

In some instances, you may encounter parts which are so hard that they defy effective filing. Consider this a good indication that the part should not be altered in any manner other than perhaps smoothing it out a bit with some hard stones.

POLISHING STONES

Stones are needed primarily for trigger work. They are essential tools for tuning many triggers. Trigger assembly parts should never be attacked with a file as the removal of metal can cause a trigger to fail (fire) when the gun is bumped or handled roughly. The surface hardness of trigger assembly parts should never be jeopardized. Any change to triggers, sears, firing pin surfaces that mate with sears, bolt stops, ejectors, extractors, safeties, hammers, locking surfaces, and similar parts, must be in smoothness or in dimensional changes measured in 0.0001-inch. Work on these parts should, therefore, always be done with appropriate stones.

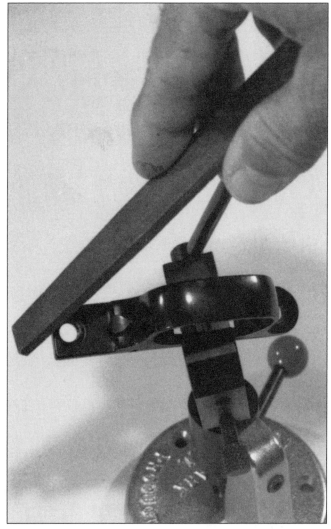

Files are often needed for gunsmithing efforts, but they should be sharp to insure clean, well executed work.

Stones are also useful for the final efforts of smoothing up work accomplished with files. For example, after cutting a 3/8-inch dovetail by hand into a barrel, for front or rear sight installation, it is always wise to smooth up the whole work surface with a triangular stone. This will allow the new sights to be driven into place without undue binding and the distortion of the parts that may follow if excessive force is applied.

Stones are extremely fragile and will shatter if dropped or if impacted by a heavy part. Since they are delicate and because the size, shape, and hardness of a stone needed for a specific job varies extensively, it is suggested that stones be purchased on an as-needed basis. The only stones that are

Polishing stones are effective ways of smoothing out rough spots without undue danger of taking away too much material. When stoning, always maintain original part lines and angles. Stones are the proper way to finish, shape, or sharpen jobs on screwdrivers and chisels.

routinely required are those used for chisel sharpening and screwdriver bit finishing after grinding.

The foregoing are all of the basic hand tools needed for routine maintenance. However, certain power tools and specialized gunsmithing tools and jigs will be required if any work past routine maintenance is to be undertaken.

4
POWER TOOLS

Most commercial gunsmiths could not survive for long without a full compliment of power tools which, in part, would include a very elaborate (and expensive) lathe, a floor model drill press, a power grinder, a belt sander, a flexible shaft grinder (for those hard-to-reach places) and even an electric checkering tool. But for basic repairs undertaken at home, none of these are essential. Indeed, most hobbyists have no power tools at all.

DRILL PRESS

On the other hand, the individual who is interested in somewhat more advanced techniques will find a drill press to be a minimum essential for drilling and tapping barrels and receivers for the installation of various style sights. A drill press will also prove useful for such basic jobs as swivel installation, skeletonizing magazines, and many similar tasks.

The drill bit must be held in an absolutely exact position and without movement when drilling sight mounting holes. This simply is not possible with a hand held and guided drill except by sheer chance. Even with the best of jigs used for drill bit alignment, a hand held power drill will lead to grief. It's just too easy to have a bit walk off its intended location or bend or break. Thus, a hand held drill is never adequate for drilling a firearm for the installation of sights.

Most gunsmiths use free-standing floor model drill presses. But a good bench-mounted drill, with a base that is perpendicular to its chuck, can be entirely satisfactory. Naturally,

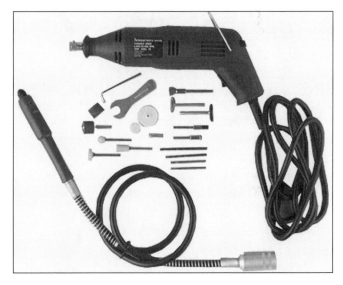

A portable grinders is handy and relatively inexpensive. It is useful for regrinding screwdrivers and rough-shaping chisels. (Copyright 2003 Brownells)

any drill press used will need positive and accurate adjustments to stop the downward movement of the drill at a precise and predetermined depth. This prevents barrels from being drilled more than half way through and prevents drill breakthrough on irregular inside receiver surfaces. The prevention of drill break-through is important whenever the drilled hole is located directly over any contoured or stepped inside receiver surface. A drill that breaks through on such a surface can "walk" away from its original axis and elongate holes. Oval holes simply aren't up to the task of taking a full thread.

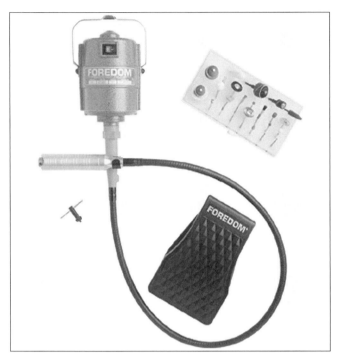

Small, flexible shaft grinders, like this Flex-Shaft Kit from Brownells, can make smooth going of some otherwise impossible grinding tasks. (Copyright 2003 Brownells)

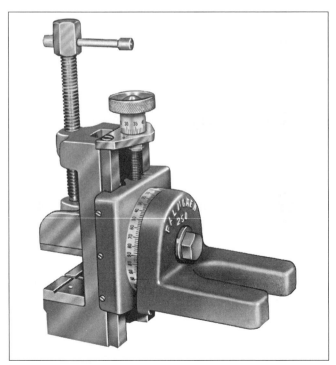

Milling attachments are available for drill press and lathe. They can be useful in making easy work of an otherwise difficult task. (Copyright 2003 Brownells)

LATHE

A small lathe can also be a useful home tool. The only way to obtain a proper barrel cut (when shortening) and accurate recrowning of the cut barrel is with certain a lathe.

A good lathe will also enable the serious hobbyist to turn smooth contours on stepped military barrels. However, no barrel turning should be attempted without also having the ability to straighten the barrel. Barrels that escape bending, due to the release of internal stresses during a turning operation, are very rare indeed.

A lathe will also be useful for making some small parts, such as firing pins. It is essential to any rebarreling efforts and is almost a must for any rechambering efforts.

GRINDER AND FLEXIBLE-SHAFT GRINDER/POLISHER

Of all the power tools that are handy in a home workshop, a small grinder is one of the most useful. This tool is useful for regrinding screwdrivers, rough shaping chisels, and shortening screws (though a lathe is preferable for this last task).

A flexible shaft polishing/grinding tool can be useful for slicking up feeding ramps and other similar chores. However, for the most part, its use will be limited to efforts on military surplus firearms.

A disc sander and/or a belt sander will see a great deal of use for the installation and trimming of recoil pads. Indeed, once the operator learns how to carefully install a recoil pad, he may be surprised at just how many pads he will find himself installing on personal firearms as well as on those belonging to acquaintances. Because recoil pads are a great asset on any rifle of .27 caliber or larger, and because

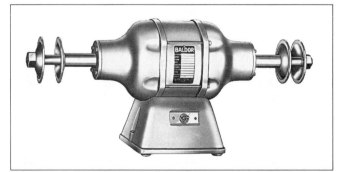

A good polishing wheel should be driven by a sturdy motor. Pictured here is a Baldor Buffer. (Copyright 2003 Brownells)

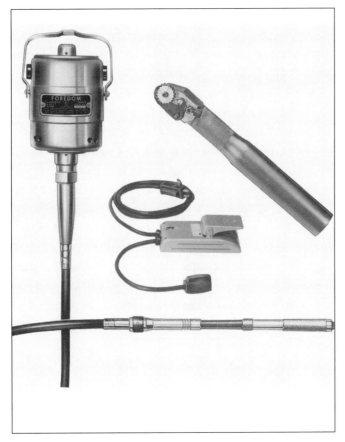

This electric checkering kit, from Brownells, is ideal for those who want to master the art of checkering. (Copyright 2003 Brownells)

of virtually unserviced market potential, these sanders will make the best possible initial area of investment in power tools.

The use of a hand-held electric drill is extremely limited in any gunsmithing effort. When clamped to a bench, they are useful for power scrubbing lead-fouled bores. But beyond this their use demands a careful hand and an exacting eye. Even a slightly misdirected bit can bring a lot of grief. It's best to consider a small bench-top drill press for drilling needs, as a hand-held drill is an accident about to happen.

POLISHING WHEEL

Polishing wheels need to be sturdy, large, and driven by powerful motors if they are to be practical for polishing firearms when preparing them for bluing or plating. Polishing is as much an art as checkering and few folks ever learn how to get a firearm as shiny as a new mirror without causing rounded edges, pulled holes, and the like. Thus, polishing wheels and their motors and fixtures have limited application for the home hobbyist. In addition, the ventilation necessary for safe polishing requires carefully engineered exhaust systems.

ELECTRIC CHECKERING TOOL

Almost all custom stockmakers these days use an electric checkering tool. It speeds up the work enormously and makes it far easier–in a physical sense. In terms of concentration, steadiness, and the need to be meticulously careful, it actually seems to make the work harder for some, at least until they have gained some experience in this delicate art. And an art it most certainly is. A mistake in design, a miscalculation, or the slightest slip of the hand, and a stock that might have been an object of beauty as well as a functional gem, can instantly become a "junker."

All the same, checkering, like any stock work, is fun, useful, extremely gratifying when done well–and potentially profitable if you become really adept. Read all you can on the subject, and begin my trying it on a cheap or battered old stock (preferable several of them) that you won't mind sacrificing if things go wrong. Also, start by copying or slightly carying simple patterns before creating your own or cutting very fine patterns that require difficult curves, borderless, no-runover edges, twenty-lines-to-the-inch, and so on.

WORK AREA SAFETY AND EFFICIENCY

Power tool installation should be based on considerations for safety, lighting, and work space. Except for the operator, there should be no traffic in and around the work area. Adequate shielding is necessary. For example, all grinding wheels should have adequate covers over the wheels (which can explode) and adequate means of vacuuming away the by-products of grinding. Eye protection and hand protection should be kept at the work station and used at all times.

Of course there are many other power operated tools that find their way into a gunsmith's shop. Yet, as stated earlier, their frequency of use will be extremely limited. The exception is when the gunsmith specializes in some particular job best accomplished, or at least most quickly accomplished, with the aid of a power tool.

For home enthusiasts, I would rate the general frequency of power tools, to as follows, from most use to least use.

1) Disc Sander (tie for first place)

2) Belt Sander (tie for first place)

3) Drill Press (table or floor model)

4) Power Grinder

5) Lathe

6) Flexible Shaft Grinder/Polisher

7) Polishing Wheel/Fixture/Motor

8) Electric Checkering Tool

9) Power Hand Drill

10) Miscellaneous Power Equipment (milling attachment for the lathe, and so on.)

For those who wish to equip a shop for the sake of having a complete one, the first five mentioned items are those that I would select. To broaden this would be wasteful, at least at the onset. Power tools are nice, but certainly not essential, especially once the first five items are on hand.

It should also be kept in mind that each power tool needs to be permanently mounted. A drill press or lathe that can "walk" about as it is operated will bring on a lot of grief. In addition, each power tool requires a special bit of knowledge to properly operate it. And while the operation of a drill press seems fairly straight-forward, running a lathe does require, at least at times, some special knowledge. This type of knowledge is beyond the scope of these pages. To learn more, attend a local high school or trade school's evening classes in machine shop practices. Or, perhaps take a home study course that would cover these topics. Another useful tip is to keep a good machinist's handbook in the work area.

5

WORK AREA & SPECIAL TOOL REQIREMENTS

Every hobby demands specific space requirements for the enjoyment of that hobby and gunsmithing is no exception. However, the gun crank's requirements for work space are modest and easily accomplished. Perhaps the most important consideration of any work area for gunsmithing is that it is free of all distraction when it will be used. Therefore, it makes good sense to select an area remote from normal household traffic. If you live alone this is no big deal. However, if there are children, young adults, or a spouse at home when you are working, it is best to select an area that is well out of the way. A corner in the basement or attic, or a small unused room can be a perfect place to set up shop.

The space selected must be well lighted; this point cannot be overstressed. Sometimes the ability to find out what's wrong with a firearm can boil down to being able to see a part that is rubbing or binding against some other part or portion of the firearm. The only clue you may have might be a very small, hard-to-see spot that has been rubbed bright as a result of friction.

Other efforts, especially the assembly or disassembly of intricate parts groups, require plenty of light reaching down into the mechanism. To accomplish this, many folks simply hang a good battery of fluorescent lights above the work bench. And often this can be a satisfactory solution to lighting needs.

However, if the ceiling above the work space is low, the normal moving about of a fifty-inch long firearm can create the hazard of broken glass should a barrel or butt stock bump into a long fluorescent tube. This is especially true when bringing a gun to the shoulder to check scope eye relief, when disassembling barreled actions from stocks, or even when using a cleaning rod. When low ceilings are present, I prefer to use standard bulbs mounted in out-of-the-way places. Two, or perhaps three, bulbs of 150 to 200 watts, combined with a spot lamp that can be swiveled to direct its beam where most needed, often make an ideal lighting team for the work area.

Avoid placing any bulb where it will be within three feet of the critical working space. Of course, if bulbs are adequately shielded with clear covers, which themselves are unbreakable, then light placement becomes less critical. It may be best to install lighting after the bench has been built, unless you are absolutely certain of your requirements.

Each work area selected will have specific lighting needs. Simply consider the risk of broken glass when working with long firearms and parts thereof. Also consider the need for

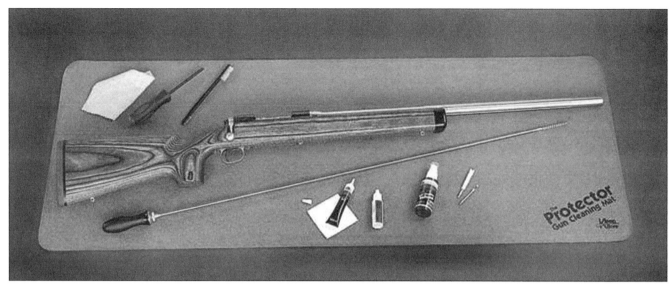

It is important to have sufficient room on your workbench so that tools and other cleaning equipment can be laid out without cluttering the work area. (Courtesy: Kleen-Bore)

plenty of light to be falling on the work area. Sufficient light will vary with the age of the gunsmith. Most of us require ten times more light at age fifty to see equally well, under a specific set of conditions, as we did when we were ten years old. Ever notice some parents nagging their kids to turn on the lights when reading, forgetting that the kids may see perfectly in one-tenth the light the parents need for effective vision? The point is, plenty of light for a twenty-five year old will prove entirely inadequate for a fifty-five year old. So, plan accordingly and prevent the grief that comes with not seeing well enough to properly position parts, or even to find the lost small one lying on the bench.

The bench itself is important. Through the years I've found that most folks err by building a bench too low to work comfortably with guns. You need to be able to get a bit closer to your work than other hobbyists. A bench top that is thirty-six inches from the floor is an absolute minimum and I find one between thirty-eight inches and forty-two inches to be preferable, depending upon the user's height. This range will be ideal for vise mounting also, with the extra height of the vise bringing work even closer to the eyes. A stool with the seat top twelve inches lower than the bench top works well for most of us. All the anthropometric data not withstanding, the important details of bench and stool height are that you are comfortable and the work is easy to manipulate.

It is important to have a sufficient work area to disassemble firearms in a space not directly in use as a work station. Tools and cleaning or other maintenance equipment should also fit on the bench without encroaching on the area actually used for working. A cluttered bench can result in firearms or parts being put down on top of tools, other parts, or what have you. When this happens, needless marring of the gun's finish can result.

I find an L-shaped bench to be most convenient, using one section for laying out the disassembled firearm and the other section for actual work and tools. I keep the section where the disassembled gun is free from all other items in order to prevent any possible damage to the firearm. The L-shape keeps the firearm and its various parts handier than if they were placed at the far end of a long, straight bench—and that can save a lot of time.

The actual dimensions of a bench top, regardless of its shape, should give you the equivalent work area of a twelve-foot length and at least a two-foot width. Any additional space on a longer bench will simply not be used, except perhaps as a junk accumulator. A wider bench, up to perhaps three feet, will be a nice plus. Any additional width, however, will be unused as it will be awkward to reach farther back. I prefer an L-shaped bench to be seven feet on the long length, with a five-foot shorter section.

I use the short end for storing the firearm and subassemblies not needed at the work station. I like my medium vise to be mounted at the extreme right front corner of the long section. The small vise is mounted just to the right side of the bend in the bench. I mount my large vise on a small three foot by three foot sturdy, but remote, bench.

Allow plenty of room under the short length of the bench for storage bins and drawers in which you will keep tools and parts. I do not like any shelving under the long bench section unless it is well recessed, so that I can sit comfortably with my legs under the work station.

While many folks will store tools, materials, parts, or gun cleaning equipment on shelves above the back edge of the bench, I do not do so. It's simply too easy to drop an item

being taken from, or placed on, such shelving, or to knock another item off the shelf. Falling items seem to always land on top of a stock or scope and damage or disrupt work in progress. I avoid the possibility of such grief by not storing anything above the bench. And I confess to having learned this lesson the hard way.

The top of any bench used for gunsmithing must be level. Small parts that roll off to vanish on the floor can be a real cause for lost time. The top of the bench must also be free from protruding bolts, lugs, or nail heads which can damage a firearm's finish. And, most importantly, the bench top must be solid. Any cracks, spaces, or holes will swallow up small parts.

Some gunsmiths assure themselves of a solid bench top by covering the bench with a sheet of Formica. This does take

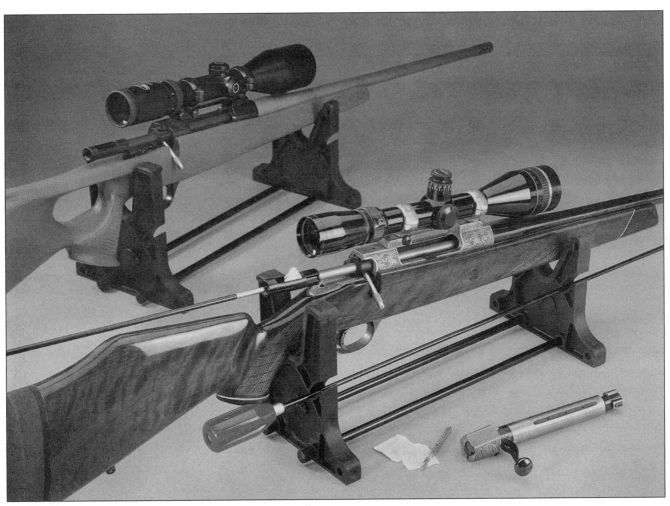

A good cleaning vise (shown are Stoney Points' Cleaning and Maintenance Cradle) will be essential for the frequent shooter. It will also serve as a work station for scope installation and many other jobs. (Courtesy: Stoney-Point Products)

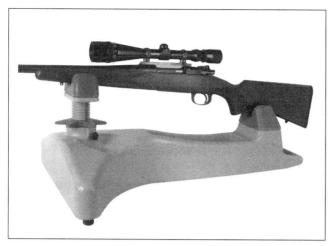

Left-handed cleaning vises are also available (for guns with cheek pieces positioned for left handed shooters). (Courtesy: Battenfield)

care of the problem of losing parts into spaces between top planks, but it creates another problem—a too smooth surface that will allow small parts to roll freely about and, sometimes, off the bench. A piece of slightly textured Masonite seems to be a fine compromise, though it may need occasional replacement.

Any bench used for gunsmithing must be sturdy. There can be no movement when work, which is mounted in a vise, is filed or rasped, or when a rear sight is driven into a barrel dovetail. If you are reaming a shotgun barrel for interchangeable choke tubes, or recutting a rifle's chamber, the holding vise and the bench must be rock solid. It follows, therefore, that the bench must be solidly constructed and firmly bolted to the wall behind it and/or the flooring. Anything less will lead to eventual grief.

SPECIAL TOOLS

Because of the uniqueness of firearms repair and maintenance, a number of specialty tools are essential. Some of these belong on every bench, others are needed only occasionally or for specialized work. Included are such items as a front sight pusher, drill and tap fixture, scope leveler, slave pins, bit brace, cleaning vise, headspace gauges, broken shell extractors for chambers and for reloading dies, collimator, various types of stock making screws, bore lights, plating kits, and a host of similar items. Many of these bear discussion as nothing makes a job go easier, or prevents it from going sour, better than the correct tool or fixture.

The most common gun maintenance chore, or at least it should be, is bore cleaning. Now, bore cleaning can be accomplished with the aid of the usual vise and properly padded jaws to hold the gun. Yet, the use of a bench vise for this purpose will sooner or later result in needless damage to a firearm. The padded jaws will slip, the gun will bump against the vise, the gun will slip in the vise, or the vise will be overtightened—these are just some of the possible accidents that can mar the finish of a firearm.

Bore cleaning can also be accomplished without a vise, simply by holding the firearm in hand. But this can lead to other problems. It takes two hands to start a cleaning rod straight, to guide it while brushing and swabbing and to prevent it from damaging surfaces while being placed into use. Those who doubt this will eventually regret their decision.

CLEANING VISE

A better solution, an absolute necessity to my way of thinking, is a cleaning vise. These cradles are properly padded

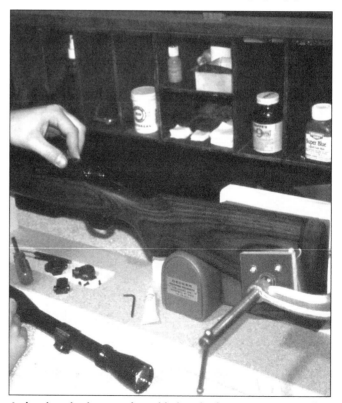

A cleaning vise is properly padded at the forearm support and at the butt-clamping area. (Courtesy: Mike Ahlman)

A good collimator and a set of spuds are essential to first class sight installations. A good one can be used for sight adjustment verification. (Copyright 2003 Brownells)

at the forearm support and at the butt-clamping area. A cleaning vise can make the chore of bore cleaning an easier task, but equally important, it can almost eliminate any potential for accidental firearm damage.

The Decker vise, because of its well thought out construction, has a good many uses. For example, it is a far better gun cradle for scope mounting chores than is a standard vise. The Decker vise completely eliminates the need to remove the stock of a rifle so as to solidly mount the action for screw tightening during scope mount installation. It is also the ideal vise for inletting chores, bore sighting and a goodly number of other jobs when the butt stock does not need to be removed. Once used, these vises will quickly fall into the category of "I wonder how I ever got along without it." And they are relatively inexpensive. The Decker vise's milled away base section is super handy for holding the small screws and parts often used during sight installation and other similar chores.

COLLIMATOR

A collimator, while not essential, can prove to be an extremely important tool when bore sighting or changing sights for different loads. It is useful for verifying that a sight is still adjusted properly, for example, when arriving at a hunting camp after a long trip, during which your gun case may have seen some overly vigorous handling by airline personnel.

Basically, a collimator allows highly accurate bore sighting (the alignment of bore and sights on a target) without the errors that can occur due to limited visual acuity or a less than rock solid rest. The collimator is used in connection with spuds that fit the bore exactly. These are slipped into the muzzle and protrude sufficiently to allow the collimator to be mounted to them. The spuds must fit the bore perfectly, as any canting will induce substantial error.

When properly mounted, many collimators will show an

X-type reticle on the collimating lens as viewed from the shooter's position. The scope's cross hairs are simply aligned to intersect the center of the X, or iron sights, and adjusted so that the aiming point coincides with the collimator's reticle center. The firearm is then correctly bore sighted. If your collimator is equipped only with a center reticle, its usefulness will then have been fully exploited. However, if you have a unit which is equipped with a grid, its usefulness will be greatly extended.

Because different rifles, even of the same make and model, will have variable points of impact (even when using the same lot of ammo), each rifle's sights will align with its bore in a somewhat different manner. By placing the grid-equipped collimator back into position, after actual sighting in at the range, and making a careful observation as to where the sights now align on the grid, you will have a reference that will enable you to readjust the sights at a later date if they are moved accidentally, or perhaps readjusted for a different load. Simply keep a very exacting record of the sight's intersection on the grid after actual range firing and adjustment with a specific load.

Double check the "repeatability" by removing the bore spud and checking collimator alignment several times. With some bore/spud/collimator combinations, repeatable bore sightings are not possible.

The point at which sights align on the grid can vary notably with any change in the lot of ammo used. One of my .30-06s has the sight reticle aligned 2½-inch graduations low and three graduations right when a Nosler 180-grain Partition bullet is used. Sighted with a Speer 150-grain bullet load, the scope's reticle is on the grid at 1/2-inch graduation high and 3/4-inch graduation left. When the scope is properly adjusted for a Sierra 125-grain bullet, the vertical cross hair aligns perfectly in the center of the collimator's grid while the horizontal cross hair is three graduations high. When switching loads, I install the collimator and adjust the cross hairs to coincide with these previously recorded positions and then I verify the setting by firing at a target, making any minor necessary adjustments.

You may not be able to bring the sights back to an exact adjustment due to the changes in stock bedding or due to the high improbability of being able to see the sights with reference to a very exacting position on the grid. You should, however, be able to adjust the sights so as to bring the actual point of impact within an inch or two of where it was when you last sighted in the firearm with a specific load.

The grid-equipped collimator's usefulness can be further extended. When I travel to some distant place to hunt, I always carefully sight in my rifle on my home range. When I'm satisfied that the sight setting is perfect, I install the collimator in the muzzle (always make sure its grid is not canted with reference to the rifle's scope). Then I make a very exacting observation as to where the scope's reticle appears on the grid. I also make a written note of this observation and stick it in the collimator's box, which is then put into my camera bag. When I arrive at my hunting camp, I can verify if my sight has been knocked out of its alignment during the trip to camp by merely installing the collimator and verifying the scope's reticle position on the grid against my written notes. If it is where it was when I started out, I feel confident in hunting with the rifle. If it has moved notably, I know that the rifle has seen some severe bouncing around and needs sighting in. Minor movement, of course, may simply be the result of less than perfect repeatability of the bore/spud/collimator combination.

When called for, I simply readjust the reticle back to its original position and fire a few rounds to verify the adjustment. A grid-equipped collimator used in this manner can prevent a hunt from being spoiled due to a missed shot. My Redfield grid-equipped collimator came in a well padded plastic box which protects the unit from damage and it has been a welcome piece of equipment on more than just a few hunts. I consider it an essential tool.

CROSS HAIR SQUARE

Another tool that is super handy is Stoney Point's Sight Lines Lens. Normally, shooters who want the cross hairs of a scope to be absolutely plumb and level with the rifle, mount the barreled action in a vise and use a level on the bottom of the action to verify it is level. Then the level is placed on the top of the scope turret, rotating the scope until it also appears level. All this requires removal of the stock and is dependent on a suitable flat on the action and another on top of the scope-adjustment cap. In short, it's a lot of work and the system is less than perfect.

All this can be avoided with bolt-action rifles by simply placing the Sight Lines Lens directly on the opened bolt of the gun. Slide the lens forward, against the scope's lens, and hold it in place with the stretch cord. Plumb and square the scope with the lens, then secure the scope in place with the ring screws. Simple, quick, and quite exacting.

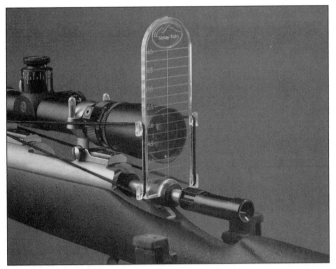

The Sight Lines Lens is designed for use with bolt-action, center-fire rifles. The engraved lines on the lens allow the scope's vertical crosshair to be plumb with the bore as it squares the horizontal crosshair. (Courtesy: Stoney-Point Products)

DRILL JIGS

If you mount a scope on a non-commercial sporter you may be required to drill and tap the receiver. These operations are critical and many receivers have been ruined due to less than careful procedures.

At the very least you should use a simple drill jig, such as the B-Square Pro-Jig, for the drilling operation. The use of a jig of this type will guarantee that all the holes are exactly positioned. This simple jig will insure that the holes drilled are truly perpendicular, that the recoil shoulder (if there is one) on the mount base will properly align with the mating receiver edge and that each hole will be the proper distance from the next hole. You must insure that the jig's flat base plate is at a true right angle to the drill bit. This is a passive step if a drill press with a level bed is being used.

The Pro-Jig, however, cannot be used for the drilling of scope-base holes in a barrel, or holes for open sight bases, or holes in a receiver's side for peep sight installation. Nor can it guarantee that the holes aligned centrally on the receiver will align with the bore's axis. If the barrel is not square in the receiver a problem could be encountered. But the Pro-Jig is a giant step ahead of any attempt to drill a receiver without some mechanical aid for positive alignment. The Pro-Jig cannot be

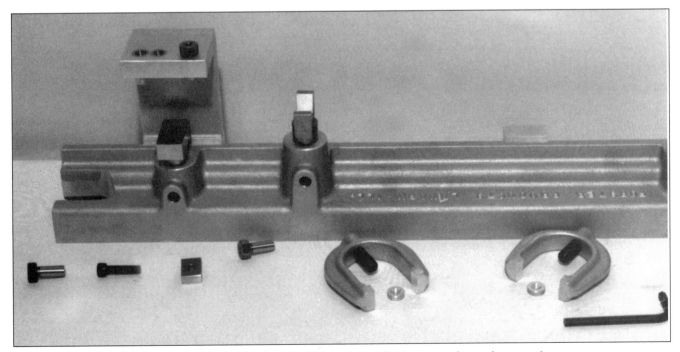

A drill and tap fixture, such as the Forster, is essential for more advanced gun repair.

used as a tap guide, but a separate tap guide can be purchased from B-Square.

In my twelve years of commercial gunsmithing, I found but one system one hundred percent satisfactory for the installation of scope bases, open sight bases, front ramps, and receiver sights. And if the holes to be drilled were on line with the bore's axis, even side mount scope bases could be installed easily with it. This system uses the superb Forster Universal Sight Mounting Fixture and a drill press.

Because the Forster Universal Sight Mounting Fixture uses built-in V-blocks to align all holes with the barrel, the drilling and tapping is always accurate, even if the barrel is badly aligned within the receiver. This jig will work with most rifles. The stock, naturally, needs to be removed. In the case of a rifle with a two-piece stock, only the forend need be removed. A rifle with a tubular magazine, or with a gas or slide-action system below the barrel, will require the removal of these appendages in order to be used with the Forster fixture.

The V-blocks of the Forster jig are adjustable for height as is the jig's action-support pillar. To prevent unnecessary disassembly there is a clearance cut in its base for the trigger group. Aluminum pads are supplied to protect the barrel from the mounting clamps. The leveling of the action, accomplished by the action-support post, is done easily and quickly. Hardened steel bushing inserts in the drill and tap support guide can accept interchangeable guides for the drill or tap sizes normally used (6-48, 8-40, and 10-32 thread sizes). A tapered point-locator pin is also supplied to insure that each hole drilled will correctly align with the base or sight to be installed.

There simply is no sight-drilling or tapping job that the Forster jig won't handle, even to the point of being useful for drilling and tapping when holes are not to be located along the bore's axis. If you anticipate sufficient need to justify the cost, this jig will prove to be one of the best possible investments you can make.

FRONT SIGHT PUSHER

A front sight can be difficult to install. The dovetail of the sight and the ramp must mate very snugly. But the usual pounding on the sight, even when a brass punch is used, can distort it, or the ramp screws can shear or strip when the sight is pounded into place. Such problems are not always encountered,

but just once is enough to make you wish for a better way. The only solution is a front sight pusher, as sold by Williams. This ingenious little unit will allow you to install or remove front or rear sights from any ramp or base without marring the sight, ramp, base or compromising the ramp-to-barre integrity. This tool is, in my opinion, a must for every gunsmithing bench.

HEADSPACE GAUGES

Headspace in a rifle, shotgun or handgun is critical. This dimension, from minimum to maximum, may have a total spread of only 0.006-inch. Headspace can increase due to the use of ammunition that causes slightly too much pressure or faulty gun parts. Headspace should be checked with routine frequency just like you check the oil level in a car. Unfortunately, few shooters perform this task even on a rare basis. But headspace gauges are essential. Regrettably, headspace gauges are not easily located. However, folks at Forster can help, as perhaps can others.

Headspace gauges most often are available in three sizes. These are sometimes referred to as "go," "no-go," and "field" (based on old military nomenclature). The go size is a minimum size over which the action should always fully lock. The no-go size is the equivalent of a maximum gauge over which the action should *not* fully close. The field

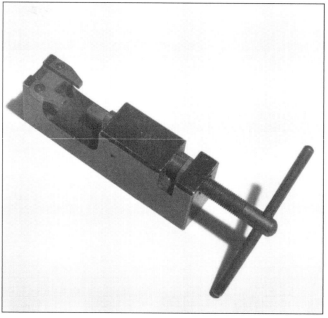

A Williams Front Sight Pusher is an essential special tool.

gauge is best described as a gauge to avoid. It has no real application for the serious hobbyist. In military application, if a gun in the field will close on the no-go, but not on the field gauge, it can, if required, continue to see use. However, the firearm's performance will be far from ideal. The suitability of reloading cases fired in a chamber that is beyond the no-go gauge is always hazardous.

BROKEN CASE REMOVER

Most of us who do our own gunsmithing are also handloaders. And if you make enough of your own ammunition, sooner or later you will tear the rim off of a case during resizing, leaving the case stuck in the sizing die. There are many products on the

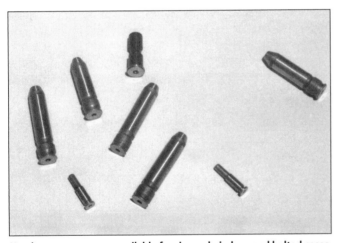

Headspace gauges are available for rimmed, rimless, and belted cases.

market that will remove the stuck case, after drilling and tapping the case head. However, there is another, far more practical and efficient way to remove a case that is jammed, even seemingly hopelessly, in a sizing die.

A stuck case remover, by RCBS, is exactly what its name implies. This is the best tool for the purpose, and it's inexpensive, too.

Broken-shell extractors for use in firearm chambers can be invaluable. These allow the removal of a broken shell from a rifle's chamber without much more effort than the manipulation of pushing a cleaning rod into the bore. These same broken shell extractors can be used if the entire head pulls away from the case body in a loading die.

Broken-shell extractors can make the very difficult and time-consuming task of removing a broken shell a simple,

two-minute effort. It's advisable to keep a broken shell extractor on hand for each of the popular bore sizes, i.e. .22, .24(6mm), .25, .26(6.5mm), .27, .28(7mm), and .30 calibers.

PLATING KITS

A small and inexpensive plating kit, such as available from the Texas Plating Supply Co., can be a useful tool. Plated screws or small parts can easily be refinished with gold, silver, nickel, brass, or chrome at a cost best described as surprisingly cheap. Firearms can also be given special aesthetic treatment by gold-plating all the exposed screws and so on.

OTHER TOOLS

Convenience tools such as swivel drill jigs, recoil pad trimming jigs, and bolt jeweling jigs are available. Each of these jigs helps simplify common tasks, making the job go quicker at an increased level of workmanship.

A good bit brace, some round steel stock for making slave pins, a bore light, and similar items will have varying degrees of usefulness. You can purchase such items on an as-needed basis or, if having a well-equipped shop gives you pleasure, they can be purchased at the onset of your shop set-up. The use of many of the tools and jigs I've mentioned will be covered in detail in the appropriate chapters to follow.

The Appendix lists various companies and other suppliers of special and not-so-special gunsmithing tools. Take the time to write, call, or e-mail these companies and compare their products before purchasing too many of your needs. Be sure to obtain a catalogue from Brownells as they are the industry specialist in supplying gunsmithing needs of all types.

Naturally, a good micrometer and/or vernier can prove essential depending upon the type of work you will undertake. These are available at outlets specializing in tool and machinist equipment sales, as well as gunsmithing trade suppliers.

As the need arises, look over the gunsmith trade catalogs for other special tools and jigs that are designed to make work go faster, more accurately, and without the cussing that usually accompanies certain nettlesome tasks.

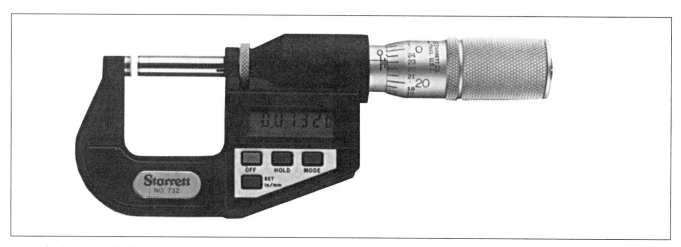

A good micrometer is often needed for gunsmithing chores. This American-made Starrett is an industry standard. (Copyright 2003 Brownells)

6

PARTS & SUPPLIES

arts are obviously an important part of any repair undertaking. But more importantly, having the right part on hand when it is needed is best described as a gunsmithing joy. The need to order a part can be needlessly complicated by minimum order requirements, long delays in waiting for the part (up to four months on some), or even by the total frustration of finding that no one has the part you so desperately need.

Obviously, the best approach is to keep a supply of parts on hand. One does not need to have a spare bolt or stock in the parts bin. But items such as firing pins, firing pin springs, extractors (with springs and plungers), ejectors (with springs), cartridge guides, and similar parts are all frequently needed. If you are gunsmithing for your own pleasure, one of each of these types of parts, as appropriate to the firearms you own, is a candidate for parts to be kept on hand.

Some discretion can be used, of course, depending upon the amount of money you wish to convert into parts to be kept on hand for an anticipated need, which may or may not arise. For example, if you have several Model 70 Winchester Featherweights in the long-action variety, you would reasonably need only one firing pin (and related firing pin assembly parts) to be kept on hand. If you have Ruger 77s in calibers .30-06, .280, .270, .25-06 and a custom .35 Whelan, you will need only one extractor as a spare because all of these calibers use the same part. However, you will need another extractor to fit any belted magnum cartridge, one for any of the .257 Roberts, 7mm Mauser, 6mm Remington or similar size, and one for the

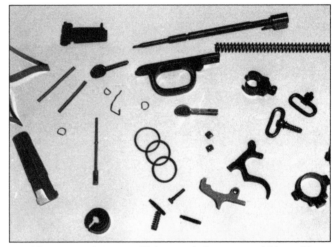

A wide range of parts will be needed as gunsmithing efforts broaden in scope. Having the potentially needed parts on hand before the job starts is an important aspect of keeping things moving smoothly.

short family of .243, 7mm-08, .308 or .358 cartridges.

Obviously, it will pay big dividends to learn which calibers use the identical parts. Interchangeable parts can include (but not always) extractors (along with springs and plunger), ejectors, firing pins, sears, cocking pieces, cartridge guides, magazines (with followers and springs), shell carriers, and a host of similar items. Referring to the manufacturer's parts list will sometimes help in determining part interchangeability. But as a whole, you will need to develop the knowledge of which cartridges have identical head dimensions (and, hence usually interchangeable extractors and ejectors), or identical lengths and basic shape (and, hence, usually interchangeable magazines, magazine springs, magazine follower and cartridge guide) to help determine the minimum number of parts to be inventoried.

It's useful to know which parts are most often needed. For example, during my ten years of gunsmithing, I replaced fifty Marlin .336 firing pins for every one Winchester Model 94 firing pin. Yet you may need several Model 94 cartridge lifters and never need one for a Marlin Model 336. And folks seem to have a real knack for breaking off cartridge guides on Marlin .22 rimfire bolt-action rifles. Darn few Remington 870 firing pins ever need replacing, but a fair inventory on Remington Model 1100 O-ring barrel seals might prove handy.

The specific firearms you own should be the guide as to what parts need to be kept on hand. If you gunsmith for others, you will need to know what models are popular in your area and what parts are most often replaced in these models. You can learn a lot by asking questions and doing a lot of lis-

Guard screws are a common replacement item, as many firearm owners have not learned the need for the use of an exacting fit and the working torque levels of screwdrivers. Even careful workmen occasionally goof and ruin a guard screw.

tening. Talk to firearms owners, gun shop proprietors, gunsmiths and, if you run into them, factory reps. Or call the manufacturers' customer service departments of the firearms you have interest in and ask them what you should inventory.

Owners of less popular rifles, or recently discontinued models, should keep in mind that parts for such firearms may be hard to obtain. And the situation could degenerate to impossible in the future. In these instances, my advice is to stock up now on any and all likely needs, in quantities matched to the anticipated useful life of the firearms involved.

Guns that were or are manufactured in the millions of units result in great stores of parts. Owners of Winchester Model 70s or 94s, Marlin 336s or Remington 700s, 870s, 1100s, and so on, should not encounter difficulty in finding parts. But if you own a Winchester Model 61 or 62 or a Remington 141, then a part may prove unobtainable, or nearly so, or cost a king's ransom. Planning ahead is always a worthwhile endeavor.

Parts are not always as sturdy or fragile as appearances may seem. In thirty-five years, I've only needed one Winchester Model 70 bolt-stop retaining pin, despite its rather fragile appearing profile. But I've needed heaps of Springfield firing pins.

Guard screws may occasionally get chewed up, even by a careful workman. And a selection of front sights of varying heights, widths, and styles always makes good sense, as does an extra set of scope mounting rings and several recoil pads of assorted sizes and thicknesses.

Experience will be the best teacher as to what's needed in the parts drawer. At the very least, keep one each of all the critical parts for those firearms used frequently.

The factory of origin remains the best possible source of parts for current production models. Sometimes they have limited parts for recently discontinued models. Some factories service customers' parts needs by return mail. Others see nothing wrong with keeping the customer waiting—sometimes for months. So get your parts ordered before you need them.

Discontinued parts are oftentimes available from specialized parts dealers such as Gun Parts Corp. and others. Some general manufacturers offer parts for specific firearms. For example, Williams Gun Sight offers firing pins (in kits) for a wide variety of single-shot and double-barrel shotguns, as well

Spare sights and scope rings, of all types, are commonly needed items.

as some specific parts for the Lee-Enfield rifles. The appendix section of this book lists the names and addresses of many parts dealers. Other parts dealers' names and addresses can be gained from such periodicals as Gun Digest, Shotgun News, and monthly gun magazines.

Some parts will be totally restricted, for reasons of consumer safety, or due to the degree of difficulty in fitting. Restricted parts are not available to the general public, but specific ones are sometimes made available to qualified gunsmiths.

While not always viewed as parts, such items as lubricating oils, lubricating greases, rust preventing grease, emery cloth, sand papers of varying grades, a wide selection of stock finishes, gun cleaning solvents, degreasing solvents, and similar items are best inventoried as parts. Get what's likely to be needed and well ahead of time to avoid delays or disappointments.

In the area of stock finishes, it's not unreasonable to keep

several years supply on hand. I learned this the hard way. I used one particular linseed type oil finish for eighty percent of my new stock finishing and perhaps fifty percent of my refinishing jobs. I usually kept six months supply on hand, but at one point I got down to a stock of two small jars. When I went to order several dozen jars, I found, much to my everlasting regret, that the manufacturer no longer supplied the product and that every distributor I dealt with had, months ago, exhausted their supplies. My reaction could best be described as going nuts. I have yet to find what I feel is a perfect substitute. And, worse yet, I have insufficient supplies to continue what once were easy touch-ups on many stocks that I have either finished or refinished in the past. Gloom is a feeling I get whenever I stop to think that what once was a simple touch-up effort, will now be a complete refinishing, undertaken for lack of a bit of stock finish inventory.

Some items, such as cold bluing touch up, should not be

While not exactly parts, a good inventory of oils, greases, cleaning solvents, degreasers, and similar items are essential on a day-to-day basis.

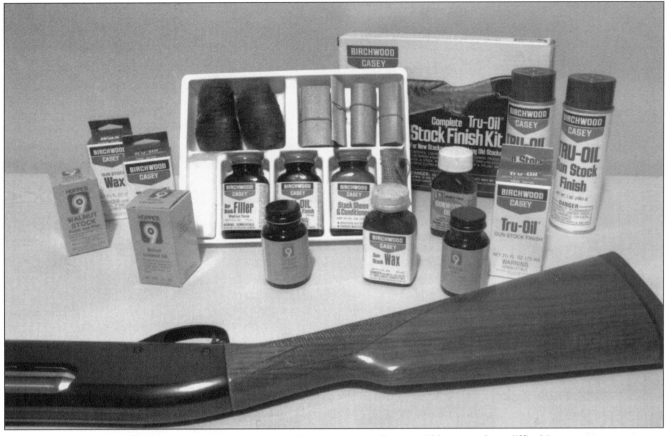

Stock finishes, in general, must be kept in adequate supply to avoid later touch-up difficulties.

inventoried in a great quantity as some of these seem to lose their potency with age.

Whether to repair a part or replace it sometimes is simply based on whether or not a spare part is available. Most times, it's a time saver, and a future aggravation preventor, to replace any faulty part with a new one. This, too, is a lesson most of us learn the hard way. I would rather special order a part, keeping myself or another waiting for a week or so, than spend three or four hours making a replacement which, with all best efforts aside, may not prove to be as durable as a factory-made replacement part. The reasons for this can include type of metal used, type of hardening required, type of manufacturing process best suited to the part, and so on. At least in the case of gun parts, handmade is not always best. Indeed, even the best handmade part can sometimes prove most inferior with respect to useful service life.

When stocking parts, always take into consideration the effect of long-term storage. Parts purchased a few years ago

and retrieved from the parts drawer in a hopelessly rusted condition, are inexcusable. Equally unforgivable is a drawer full of look-alike, but not identically performing, extractors and similar parts. A .257 Roberts extractor will prove satisfactory for a 6mm Remington or 7mm x 57 Mauser (at least most of the time), but may prove useless for a .30-06 cartridge.

When received, parts should be thoroughly degreased, cleaned and amply protected with a rust inhibiting grease. Then, they should be placed into accurately labeled envelopes or parts bins. This simple task can save a lot of confusion later, and deter the possibility of a good deal of money turning into a pile of rusted or unidentifiable scrap.

When labeling parts, include the manufacturer, model number, part number, and part name. When applicable, multiple applications should be noted. Also when applicable, make notes as to whether the part is an old or new style.

Time and experience will teach when and which specific parts lend themselves to repair. Also, the data contained in

Pressurized solvents and degreasers are some of the greatest time-savers ever devised for gunsmithing efforts, eliminating the need for time-consuming and complex disassembly.

Section III clearly indicate a number of suggestions on which parts can be reworked and which ones should be replaced. Keep in mind that surface hardness can play an important role in a part's operation. If you cannot duplicate a part's hardness, or if reworking would destroy the hardness of the original part, then the only course of action is to replace the piece.

Develop a system of replacing parts as they are used. Also develop a routine of checking that no adverse conditions are affecting parts in storage. Compare each replacement part carefully with the part to be replaced. Sometimes, manufacturers do change a troublesome design to improve on a part's useful- ness, life span, or to simplify manufacturing. If you note a design change, no matter how subtle, investigate whether or not the new part requires other modified parts in order to work in conjunction with its altered design.

When ordering parts, always state make, model, caliber and, whenever possible, the serial number or serial number range of the firearms in which the ordered parts are to be used. Some parts may require the possession of an FFL license in order to be purchased, so be sure to include a copy of yours with each order.

Finally, it's not a bad idea to mark the cost of a part on the package when you put it away for storage. If the part is installed in a paying customer's gun, or simply sold, it's often hard to remember that the cute little gizmo cost $30.00 and the big ugly one was only sixty-nine cents. If you wish to protect your costs from customer's eyes, code the packages. One simple code is to remember the word BLACKSTONE. In this code word each letter stands for a number–starting with one, proceeding to nine, and ending with zero.

If you purchase a part that cost you $13.00, the appropriate code would be BA. To keep customers from deciphering your code, use the letters XYZ as throw-in, meaningless values. For example, write $13.00 as BZAX. Naturally, any easy-to-remember ten-letter word, in which no letter is repeated, can be used for your pricing code. And any three non-value letters can be used so long as they do not duplicate your ten primary code values.

Outers Gun Blue Kit will restore the metal of any gun, with metal cleaner, deep blue-black gun blue, steel wool, applicator sponge, and polishing cloth. (Courtesy: Outers)

7

THINKING LIKE
A GUNSMITH

Commercial gunsmiths often become who they are based on extensive experience. It takes a lot of years and a lot of time spent working with many types of firearms to arrive at the point where one can earn a living by practicing the art and science of gunsmithing. But few have the opportunity to gain the vast amount of experience of a commercial gunsmith. However, this is not to say that with the proper attitude and approach one cannot be successful in undertaking many gunsmithing chores.

Long before I started to work as an apprentice gunsmith, I had a keen desire to know about firearms. To feed my curiosity I purchased, used, took apart, reassembled and occasionally repaired more than one hundred different models of firearms. I was young then, and not well off, so most of those guns were never in the gun cabinet in the company of more than a half-dozen of the others. I bought a few, learned what I could and then traded those for a few more. But even this approach is well beyond that which is necessary to be able to successfully complete a wide variety of gunsmithing tasks.

To properly approach the ownership of firearms, the user must possess a good deal of mature thinking. When hunting, shooting, or simply handling firearms, this mature thinking is what makes the use of firearms the safe hobby that it is. Firearms are potentially lethal, yet the low number of firearms accidents clearly indicates that most of us are capable of using guns safely. And it is this acquired ability that is the basis for developing gunsmith skills. To get started on gunsmithing projects or even a solid home firearms maintenance program, means that now you must build upon the original level of basic firearms understanding. You must also be willing to seek help, advice, and criticism as the need arises.

A firearm is considered by many to be a near indestructible commodity that has a very long useful life. But no firearm is forever. One should not anticipate that his great-grandchildren will be using one of today's favorite firearms. Barrels do wear, parts wear, even headspace slowly, if ever so slowly, increases. That each firearm has a finite life is something we should grow to accept. We need to understand that a firearm's finite life cannot be expressed in years. Rather, a firearm's life is a function of the number of rounds fired and the degree of care or misuse it receives.

Thinking like a gunsmith begins, or should, with understanding that firearms are mechanical devices that suffer from wear and quickly succumb to neglect. Also know that firearms must be able to withstand pressures ranging from perhaps ten thousand pounds per square inch to sixty-five thousand pounds per square inch, sometimes even a bit more. A 12-gauge shotgun shell producing ten thousand psi (pounds per square inch) is not actually producing only one-sixth the thrust against the bolt face as a sixty thousand psi centerfire cartridge. The actual total pressure applied to the bolt, or the chamber, of any firearm depends upon the actual surface area of the cartridge. Remember that pressure levels are per square inch.

For example, a 12-gauge shell has a head diameter of approximately 0.886-inch and, thus, a total surface area of approximately 0.196 square inch, while a .30-06 shell has a head diameter of approximately 0.473-inch and a total surface area of approximately 0.056 square inch. Therefore, the total approximate pressure applied to the face of the 12-gauge shotgun's bolt may be 6,162 pounds, while the total pressure applied to a .30-06's bolt face may be 10,582 pounds. Of course, wide variations can and do occur.

One needs to extend the development of thinking like a gunsmith to a willingness to learn and expand the store of knowledge, and to investing the essential time necessary to gain that knowledge. Before any attempt at repairing a firearm is made, a full understanding of that firearm's design, capability, and cycle function is essential.

Naturally, one does not need to know that carrier dog tolerance is critical when the job at hand is to install sling swivels on a semiautomatic shotgun. But, equally, one does need to understand that when the factory restricts the sale of specific parts, or recommends factory installation, such thinking is based on sound consideration of firearm integrity and shooter safety. If one tends to think that a factory's insistence of not supplying a trigger except for factory installation is due to greed, or a desire to inconvenience the firearm owner, then he certainly is not thinking like a gunsmith.

On the other hand, when one realizes the consequences of an ill-fitted trigger and understands that few people are qualified to install this part, then thinking like a gunsmith has begun. And when he begins to accept that there is no way for the average firearm owner to fit certain triggers, but that other triggers can easily be installed, and when he can accurately tell the difference between the two, then he is well down the road to routine gunsmith-like thinking.

For many, the mere knowledge that we cannot possibly know everything enables us to restrict our efforts to those tasks best suited to our ability. Thus, this book will not cover the building of a gunstock from a log of wood. Nor will it discuss the arts of checkering, carving, or engraving. Indeed, the execution of such tasks, in a quality manner, will remain beyond the skills of most firearm owners. Those who can excel in such areas will turn to literature dealing with these very narrow and highly specialized aspects of the gunsmith's efforts.

For our purposes we will deal with maintenance and repairs that can realistically be accomplished by most prudent firearm owners. Not every task outlined in this effort will be suitable for every reader. But at least some of those discussed will be easily accomplished by all readers. The ability to determine which jobs fit your skills is the culmination of thinking like a gunsmith.

The ability to think like a gunsmith is not related to the percentage of undertakings that you decide you can handle. Rather it is associated with the accuracy of your estimate with regard to which jobs you can handle. Thinking like a gunsmith may be accomplished by the most inexperienced person. Working like a gunsmith will come only with experience.

If you progress without an error, then you will know that your thinking is right. If you consistently have problems, ruin tools or firearms, then you need to rethink whether you should be attempting any gunsmithing at all.

A lot can be learned by reviewing material such as contained in Part III of this book. If you instinctively read material dealing with specific firearms that you do not own, you are, indeed, thinking like a gunsmith. If, due to inexperience, the text is less than one hundred percent clear, and you automatically refer to the firearm schematic drawing and parts lists to better understand what is being said—well, that's really thinking like a gunsmith. And if you can start to imagine how another firearm's function cycle is accomplished based on what you have learned about a similar type, indeed, you show great promise.

The real secret of any worthwhile gunsmith is his or her ability to carefully look over a firearm, repeatedly manipulate its action, and finally reach an accurate conclusion about how that firearm really works. To see all the built-in safeguards is to begin to understand the art of gunsmithing. No, it's not something easily assimilated, but neither is it overly difficult. It is attitude that will make or break a potential gunsmith. Sure, it will require more than the normal amount of patience, sharp eyes, and talented hands. But, above all, else it requires a good attitude.

There are several ways to gain a general overall understanding of what gunsmithing is all about. If you are a serious gun crank, perhaps the best way is to go to work as an apprentice. However, this route is highly impractical for most and very few would ever find it financially rewarding.

Another avenue of approach is to take a home study course. Depending upon your degree of knowledge, such a course may be quite informative or merely useful.

Typically, a home study course will include a study guide and quite a few lessons on a wide number of topics. Some of the topics may indeed be basic, like glossary coverage and ballistics tables. The student often receives such items as a bore light, honing stones, screwdrivers, trigger-pull gauge and shimstock. Lessons will often cover topics as varied as sporterizing military rifles, a subscription to a trade paper, and instructions on how to obtain a Federal Firearms License (FFL), as well as one or more parts and tool catalogues.

A home study course typically covers specific styles of firearm actions, such as single-action revolvers, double-action revolvers, and bolt-action rifles. Some persons will find usefulness in the instructions that may be included on such topics as trajectory charts, handloading information, instructions on using a micrometer, firearms history, or discussions on sight design. If you feel a home study course is of interest to you, be sure to examine a schedule of instruction and materials from several schools' courses, selecting the one best suited to your goals and current knowledge level. As in all fields, there are good and bad home study courses available.

There are several in-residence and correspondence schools throughout the country that offer courses in gunsmithing. Many are listed in the appendix. Thinking like a gunsmith involves a mature approach to solving practical problems of mechanics without violating any rules of safety or negating designed-in safety features. Many serious-minded gun owners will find that they have the basic qualifications. Starting with the easy tasks and progressing slowly should be something that comes very naturally, if you are indeed thinking like a gunsmith. The gunsmith thinking style means seeking advice when needed, working slowly, and stopping before fatigue or frustration results in a ruined part or worse. But if each added elevation of difficulty is approached with a sound mastery of the preceeding level of difficulty, thinking like a gunsmith will come almost effortlessly.

PART 2

BASIC MAINTENANCE AND REPAIR

8

BASIC FIREARMS MAINTENANCE

erhaps no single aspect of firearms ownership is more misunderstood or has more old wives tales surrounding it than the need for cleaning. Cleaning a firearm's bore has been suggested by some to be a needless waste of time. Others have stated that a firearm's bore is never adequately clean except prior to the very first shot fired through it. Both extremes are pure hog wash.

Firearm bores must be truly clean if they are to shoot as well as possible. Even the old adage about a .22 rimfire bore never needing cleaning is garbage. The fellow who dreamed up this proverb either never learned to shoot, had only inaccurate rifles, or purchased only junk ammunition. Or, perhaps all three conditions were present when his "wisdom" was first proclaimed. And any devotee of this type of thinking needs only to see the results that a truly clean bore will give with respect to accuracy. He will then quickly abandon any apostolic misconceptions.

Perhaps some of the thinking on bore cleaning has come to be simply because many folks do not realize what occurs upon the firing of a cartridge. When the bullet is pushed from case to muzzle, its extremely rapid acceleration causes a film

A muzzle that shows traces of "copper" coloring in the bore is an indication that a good cleaning is required.

of bullet jacket material to be wiped away and deposited on the bore's surface. Because this occurs under extremely high pressure and temperature, this film is deeply embedded into the microscopic pores of the steel barrel.

Following behind the bullet are the extremely hot gases

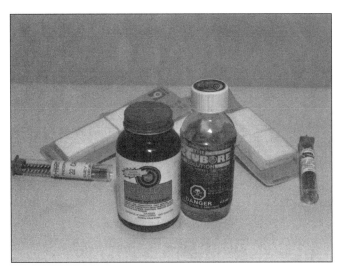

Shooter's Choice and Accubore are two effective bore cleaners.

generated by the burning propellant. The temperature of these gases, measured in thousands of degrees, causes a glazing and soldering effect on the fouling left by the bullet jacket. These gases contain a lot of combustion by-products which are left on the bore's surface in the form of grit and carbon.

When the next round is fired, the passing bullet forces the deposited grit and carbon into the barrel's surface and leaves another layer of bullet jacket material on top of it. It also leaves another coating of powder and primer fouling in the bore. And each succeeding shot results in still another layer of fouling. It's not difficult to understand that after not too many rounds have been fired, the barrel's interior is quite unlike its condition before firing began.

I have seen countless barrels that shooters have brought to me as being shot out. Indeed, looking into the bore from the breech showed that the rifling lands were very nearly the same level as the rifling grooves. It doesn't take long to fill up a groove that may be only 0.004-inch deep (or less) with copper fouling if it is not removed frequently. A quick peek into the muzzle of these barrels always revealed the telltale copper coloring that was left by bullets with jackets containing a high percentage of copper. Barrels that use many lands and very shallow grooves sometimes foul up even more quickly.

The exclusive use of lead bullets does not eliminate fouling problems. Indeed, the smear of lead left on a bore's surface can be equally difficult to remove, builds up faster and has even greater effect on accuracy.

Velocity is a major contributing cause of metal fouling in the bore. The higher the velocity, the greater the fouling. With very hard lead bullets, the problem becomes severe when velocities approach or exceed 1,800 feet per second. With soft lead bullets extensive leading may occur at eight hundred feet per second. When using copper jacketed bullets the problem usually begins to get severe at about three thousand feet per second.

Because velocity is a major factor in the build-up of heat caused by friction, rimfire barrel fouling often is at its worst at a point between sixteen to twenty-three inches from the breech (the distance at which the bullet reaches its highest velocity). Centerfire rifles usually have the worst build up of fouling right at the muzzle.

But the degree of roughness in a bore's surface is also equally contributory. The rougher the bore, the quicker metal fouling builds up. This is why barrels that have undue surface

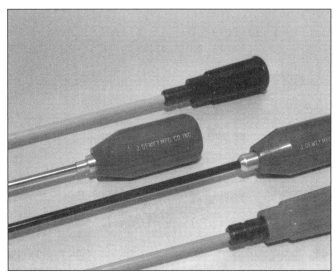

Swiveling handles, as on these Parker Hale and Dewey spring steel, plastic-coated rods, are important to proper barrel care.

roughness, or pitting caused by rust, seldom shoot accurately for very many consecutive rounds. It is also why a barrel may consistently foul most severely at one particular point.

Barrels that have seen extensive use develop a very rough surface due to erosion caused by the hot gases of combustion. This roughness can escape detection except under a microscope. Thus, barrels having extensive use will foul more quickly than those with less use, all else being equal, of course.

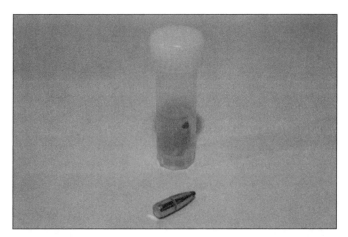

Comparative testing of a bore cleaner's ability can be done by placing a jacketed bullet in a bit of the solvent and letting it soak for a long time.

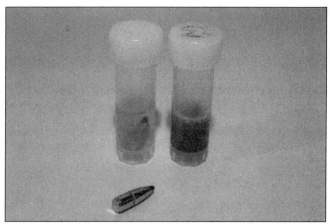

The effective solvents will rapidly change color and cause a surface deterioration of the bullet's jacket and lead nose.

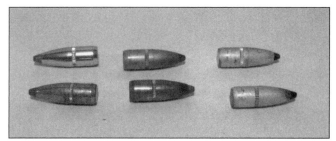

The differences between an ineffective solvent (right bullet) and a highly effective ones (middle and left bullets) are shown.

Sometimes a new barrel will have a somewhat rougher surface than one that has seen limited use. This is due to surface roughness left by machining. This roughness is quickly polished away by bullet passage. It takes only about one hundred rounds of centerfire ammo to rid a bore of this roughness. About five hundred to one thousand rounds of rimfire ammo will accomplish the same task.

Because new bores do foul quickly and because accumulated fouling becomes more difficult to remove with each succeeding shot, knowledgeable shooters clean new bores very frequently. When velocities of 2,800 feet per second or greater are standard, cleaning after every fifth shot is not unreasonable for the first twenty-five to fifty shots. Then cleaning after every ten to twenty rounds, until a total of one hundred rounds has been fired, is a good practice. Thereafter, clean the bore thoroughly every fifteen to twenty shots to maintain peak accuracy. For velocities of two thousand to two thousand eight hundred feet per second, the cleaning frequency can be extended to perhaps cleaning after twice as many rounds have been fired.

When rimfire lead bullets are used, cleaning every five hundred rounds thereafter seems about ideal. Centerfire lead bullets will demand varying frequencies of cleaning based on the hardness of the lead. The rule here is to clean as soon as the first smears of lead can be detected in the bore.

Besides the lack of understanding on how fouling builds up in a bore, the lack of knowing how to clean a bore, what bore cleaners to use, and how to determine if the bore is really clean, also have resulted in a lot of misinformation. A barrel is not clean if you can see fouling by looking into the muzzle (or breech) end of the bore, or if the use of a truly effective solvent leaves traces of copper or lead fouling on the wiping patch.

SOLVENTS

Many shooters use bore cleaners that are not capable of removing deeply embedded barrel fouling, though many will remove the fouling that is lying loosely on the surface of the bore. Some cleaners simply stop working after five or ten minutes and extensive soak periods have no benefit.

Still, other bore cleaners are slightly abrasive and while they will remove fouling, their abrasive action also works on the barrel's steel, thus shortening the potential accuracy life of the barrel. I used one such cleaner in an experiment, side-by-side with a proven satisfactory one. Both were used in identical .270 Winchester Model 70 Featherweight hunting rifles, shot with identical ammunition and an equal number of times under nearly identical conditions. The bore used (carefully, mind you) with the ever-so-slightly abrasive cleaner had a useful accuracy life of just over 2,500 rounds. The bore used with the non-abrasive cleaner maintained useful accuracy for more than five thousand rounds, and it is still being used.

Bore cleaners that promise rapid cleaning without soak periods can be justifiably suspect. However, in instances of serious bore fouling, an abrasive cleaner might be the only way to bring things back to normal. But such cleaners should never be used routinely, except perhaps in rough bores that foul badly with just a few shots. Accuracy life will then be short, but this is the lesser of two evils—as a badly fouled bore has no accuracy. Obviously, abrasive cleaners have a specific niche.

The very first step, if beginning with a brand new barrel, might be to have the bore hand-lapped using a lead slug and extremely mild polishing compound or a slightly abrasive bore cleaner. However, because this is a task safely completed only by an expert, it's best left undone unless you know someone eminently qualified to do the job.

The Dewey cleaning-rod guide, which replaces the bolt, being used in a Remington action to protect the chamber and throat from damage.

The second step is to insure you have a suitable cleaning rod, brush, jag, patches and solvent. The use of an aluminum rod is an unforgivable error and has been discussed earlier in the chapter dealing with hand tools. Brass generally is a no-no for cleaning rod material. A solid steel rod is also less than ideal, although it is a grand step forward. The best rod is a spring steel one with a plastic, nylon, or similar coating. And a good rod always has a swiveling handle.

While a number of bore cleaners may prove satisfactory, I recommend Shooter's Choice for those occasions when fouling is very heavy. For normal cleaning chores, Shooter's

Choice or Accubore cleaner will prove effective. For lighter duty cleaning Rig 44 or Hoppe's No. 9 solvents work well.

Because of the strength of Shooter's Choice and Accubore cleaners, I do not suggest their use with a bronze wire brush. These will deteriorate any brush with a high copper content. Of course, either can be used with a stainless steel brush, but such brushes should be used sparingly.

Steel brushes are extremely hard and can be erosive on the bore unless used only when absolutely necessary, and then quite sparingly. Nonetheless such brushes can be useful in removing fouling from severely neglected bores or ones with rough surfaces. When brushing, use a solvent such as Rig 44 or Hoppe's No. 9.

To test any bore cleaner for potential copper fouling removal, drop a bullet into a plastic or glass vial that can be sealed. Place only enough solvent in the vial to cover nine-tenths of the bullet. Every few days, agitate the container. When a number of solvents are tested simultaneously, the test results are most impressive.

Some solutions will simply show a separation of the "polishing" compound from its oil-like carrier. Others will exhibit no reaction at all with the bullet. Still others will display a discoloration of the solvent as it slowly dissolves the copper on the bullet. After several weeks or so, the best will produce a definite change in the bullet's color and appearance.

It is possible to actually measure the difference in bullet diameter after a period of time, if the solvent is a very effective one. (This difference will be perhaps 0.0002-inch to 0.0006-inch.) Naturally, each bullet will need to be carefully measured before the soak period. You will note that some solvents soften and even begin to dissolve the bullet's lead tip.

Always use a rod tip that allows the patch to fall free after it has been pushed through the bore. To drag the patch back into the bore will only allow the grit on it to be reintroduced to the bore and increase the risk of scratching or the accumulation of crud in the locking-lug recess.

Always use a good cleaning rod guide to protect the receiver end of the gun from the sharp jag and also to protect the rifle's throat from damage. These are inexpensive and simple to use. They replace the rifle's bolt and allow the cleaning rod to align properly with the bore.

Wipe the rod's surface with a *lightly* oiled patch before

beginning the cleaning operation in order to remove any grit or foreign material. Carefully inspect the rod's surface for nicks that might cause barrel damage. And remember to wipe the rod off before every insertion into the bore.

Always put the rod into the bore from the chamber end to protect the muzzle from excess wear or damage. The last few inches of barrel are extremely important to accuracy and wear or damage caused by a cleaning rod can quickly ruin any hope for accuracy.

There are two suitable types of jags for your cleaning rod. The sharp, pointed style allows you to spear the patch, push it through the bore, and then let it fall off at the muzzle when the rod is withdrawn. The other suitable type is the cleated style, which allows the patch to be securely held by simply wrapping it around the jag's cleats. These also allow the patch to fall off at the muzzle, most of the time, anyway.

For firearms that cannot readily be cleaned from the chamber end (many semi-autos, pumps and lever actions), great care must be used when inserting the rod into the muzzle. Always use a slip on brass fitting to prevent the rod handle from bumping into the muzzle. Use care to guide the rod by hand as accurately as possible, in order to prevent undue contact that could damage rod or bore. In these instances, it is preferable to use a cleated jag that will hold the patch on the rod in order to prevent it from falling off into the action or chamber at the end of the stroke, unless it is easily retrieved.

Keep in mind that it is always beneficial to push a patch only one way through the bore even if it means removing the patch by hand. Patches are for removing loosened fouling—they do not do the cleaning as is so often assumed. Patches must fit very snugly if they are to wipe the bottoms of the grooves. Naturally, the fit of the patch depends greatly on the diameter of the jag being used.

Begin the cleaning procedure by pushing a thoroughly soaked patch through the bore. Repeat this operation again,

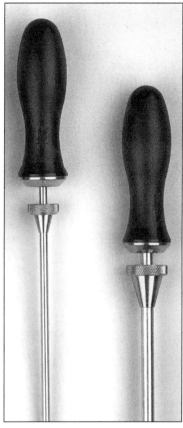

Brass "bumpers" used on cleaning rods will help prevent muzzle damage. (Courtesy: Kleen-Bore)

being sure that you can observe an excess of fluid exiting the muzzle in front of the second patch. Then pass two dry patches through the bore. This will remove all loose fouling and, in particular, any grit or grime.

Then pass another soaked patch through the bore. Remove the jag from the rod and install a bronze bore brush of the correct size. Soak the brush in solvent and push it through the bore allowing it to exit the muzzle (or chamber) and then pull it back through the bore until it exits the chamber. Repeat this in-and-out brushing operation once for each shot fired since the last cleaning. Then run a dry, clean patch through the bore.

Now push a soaked patch through the bore. Follow with another soaked patch, being sure excess solvent exits the bore in front of the second patch, and then set the firearm aside in a horizontal position, with the muzzle down perhaps just a tad to keep solvent from running into the action. Allow the bore to soak a minimum of thirty minutes, three to four hours is better. Keep in mind that this advice applies to solvents that continue to work so long as the barrel remains damp.

At the end of the soak period, run a dry, clean patch through the bore. Repeat until the bore is dry. Proper bore cleaning always demands repeated applications of solvent over a period of time.

After the soak period, begin the same process over again, omitting only the brushing step. The brushing can be repeated if fouling is severe. If, at the end of the second soak, the cleaning patches come out heavily stained, consider a third soak period being extended to twenty-four hours. Keep repeating the process until the dry patches used at the end of the soak period come out without any green stain. It is counterproductive to allow a soak of more than twenty-four hours.

It may take three to five day-long soak periods (using a strong solvent) before all the fouling is removed from a smooth barrel that has been fired fifteen to twenty times.

A greater number of soaks will be necessary if the bore is rough or if a greater number of rounds have been fired. That's right, it can take a week or more to get a barrel really clean!

Don't be tempted to stop the cleaning process too soon. If you fired the rifle twenty times and remove the fouling from only fifteen shots, think how much fouling will be left in the barrel when it has have hundreds of rounds fired through it. Then you may never be able to get it truly clean.

If the barrel is truly clean you will not be able to see any traces of copper-colored fouling, when looking at the rifling near the muzzle. A gray-colored appearance after cleaning is normal and is not connected to fouling, but is rather the steel with the bluing worn away.

Does all this pay dividends? You bet and big ones at that. I have done enough experimenting to know that rifles that routinely shoot 1½-inch groups with "cleaned" bores can actually shoot groups as small as 1/2-inch to 3/4-inch when truly clean. And rifles that appear to be inaccurate, shooting at best two-inch or three-inch groups (five shots at one hundred yards), can often be restored to a useful accuracy level of 1½-inch to 1¾-inch groups after a thorough bore cleaning.

Immediately wipe up any spills or splashes that get on the stock during cleaning procedures. Any solvent that can effectively attack copper fouling, lead fouling, plastic residue (from shotgun wads), powder fouling, and primer residue can and will attack stock finish if it's given time to do its work. Those that are harmless to stock finishes are, at best, weak cleaners.

Remember to keep scope caps in place during cleaning procedures. More than just a few scopes have had the eye piece lens pierced by a wayward cleaning jag. If you have not bumped a scope cap (or worse, a scope lens), you simply either do a minimum of cleaning or are one of those few persons who are truly careful all of the time. And even if you don't run the cleaning rod through a scope lens, scope caps will keep powerful solvents from destroying the surface coatings on your scope's lenses. I bet I've banged into scope caps dozens of times in my thirty-five years of gun cleaning.

After bore cleaning, it is imperative to get all solvent out of action recesses. Solvent left in a bolt lug recess could eventually work its way down along the action screw, contaminating the stock or bedding material. If this happens a stock's bedding could eventually be ruined. Special cleaning apparatuses, such as those made by Sinclair International, are available to make the chore of cleaning lug recesses go more easily then might otherwise be possible. But a few bent cotton swabs on a flexible stick (such as Q-Tips) can do a satisfactory job of removing solvent, grit, and sludge from the lug area.

Generally speaking, simply wiping all remaining action surfaces with a solvent-soaked cloth, and then drying them, cleans the metal satisfactorily. Bolt faces may need to soak a bit before drying to remove all traces of brass accumulation. Use a solvent-soaked toothbrush to reach hard-to-get-at spots. When finished, a few drops of oil should be sufficient to coat the entire working surfaces of any action.

Caution: After cleaning and before firing, always visually inspect the bore with care to insure that no patch, piece thereof, or excess fluid remains in the bore. Firing a gun in such a condition could wreck the gun; maybe even the shooter.

STRIP CLEANING

After approximately every eight hundred rounds, consider dismantling the entire action to rid it of accumulated oil, dirt, combustion by-products, and other foreign material. A complete strip cleaning is also in order any time the firearm is subjected to immersion, or very heavy rain, sleet, or snow. A few drops of moisture, left to do damage, can rust internal parts and surfaces beyond repair.

Normally, most actions do not need to be stripped of every part in order to be thoroughly cleaned. In fact, it is best to avoid unnecessary dismantling, especially of triggers, ejectors, and extractors. Also, note that retaining pins, clips, springs, and plungers wear with each stripping and these parts are easily lost and sometimes easily broken or damaged during disassembly and reassembly.

Once an action is free of the stock (with the bolt removed), most surfaces, even those deep inside sub-assemblies, can usually be cleaned with a pressurized cleaner. However, I do not suggest this procedure for bolts that should always be separated into two pieces (the bolt body and the assembly consisting of firing pin, spring, and cocking piece). This two-piece takedown of most bolts will suffice for proper cleaning.

There are a number of pressurized gun cleaning products. It is important to select one that is non-gumming, that will displace moisture and remove all foreign material, and one that dries without leaving any residue. A product with sufficient viscosity to flow smoothly is essential to insure that all of the cleaner drips free of the various mechanisms. A blast of dry air (such as canned air available at photo shops) can help remove all the cleaner. Do not use compressed air of the gas station variety as such air can contain a great deal of moisture. Keep your eyes shielded with glasses whenever using compressed air or pressurized cleaners. The cleaner that I like best is Birchwood Casey Gun Scrubber.

Parts cleaned with a pressurized cleaning solvent should be set aside to allow ample time for complete draining of the cleaner, usually overnight. Shaking parts before positioning for good drainage will help rid the parts of a lot of the cleaner. I do not like to use cleaners containing oils or preservatives as these tend to attract dirt.

Naturally, all parts should receive a light coat of friction-reducing and rust-preventing oil after cleaning. But I hasten to point out that oiling is often overdone. When correctly used, oil cannot be seen and almost cannot be felt on the parts. To use more oil than this usually causes crud to accumulate. Apply a drop to your fingertip and wipe all parts carefully. A one-third drop applied to hinge joints and moving parts is adequate. Spread the oil over these parts by working the action repeatedly. Because oil should be used sparingly, I usually avoid pressurized cans. Be sure it is non-gumming at low or high temperatures. Any oil that freezes can render your rifle useless causing misfires and worse.

If a rifle is used in extremely cold weather (10°F or less), I prefer not to use any oil at all. However, a rifle used extensively without lubricant will suffer unnecessary wear. This seldom applies to hunting rifles, since only a few shots are taken when afield.

Remember to keep exposed surfaces protected from the elements. A good coat of gun wax will work as well as a light application of oil and is not messy. One product I have been using that seems very well adapted to protecting smooth finishes from rust, if applied after each use, is Rust Guardit (manufactured by Kleen-Bore). Others are available and many auto waxes also work well.

STOCK PROTECTION

Stocks should be protected from the ravages of weather, perspiration, and plain old wear and tear. A good coat of Simonize auto and furniture polish works very well. Wax that

Pressurized cleaning solvents and degreasers can speed cleaning chores and avoid unnecessary dismantling. (Courtesy: Birchwood Casey and Kleen-Bore)

gets into checkering or hard-to-reach places can be removed with a soft toothbrush. Commercial gun stock waxes can also be used for effective protection. Because waxes behave differently under varying conditions, if one does not prove satisfactory, try another until you have found one that seems to best suit your needs.

DEGREASER

For severely gummed actions, a pressurized degreasing fluid will be useful. After cleaning a firearm that will be used in an extremely cold climate, spraying it with a pressurized degreaser, such as Rig 3, so every trace of cleaning solvent has been removed. A degreaser will also be necessary for other gun maintenance chores, like touching up bluing scratches.

COLD BLUING

Before cold bluing is applied the surface needs to be prepared by removing any burrs or deformed metal. This can be done usually with a careful application of a fine file and/or crocus cloth. Be extremely careful not to remove bluing from surrounding areas. Keep your repair confined to the damaged metal. When the surface is properly smoothed (simple scratches or bluing rubs require no pre-polishing), the area should be sprayed with short blasts of a pressurized degreaser to prepare it for application of the cold blue. Then wipe the area dry with a clean cotton patch before applying the cold blue.

The bluing used for touch-up is available in liquid and paste forms. With a cotton swab, the liquid blue is easily applied to only that area to be touched up. I find the paste far more difficult to use.

Some touch-up bluing solutions have the propensity to adversely affect the original blue of surrounding areas. For this reason one, of the bluing pens (ball point pen-like applicators) which allows the application of the bluing to an extremely exacting area, can be advantageous. In any case, always test any cold bluing on the same part to be touched up, but in an area that cannot be seen. Naturally, do this sparingly. If you want to touch-up a barrel, be sure to test the solution on part of the barrel. Checking on another part, (such as the receiver or bolt handle), may not tell you what you want to know as these may be made from a different type of steel and, hence, react differently to the touch-up bluing.

Another application of pressurized degreaser is to remove oil from screws and screw-hole threads when mounting sights. But this will be covered in a later chapter.

ROUTINE CHECKS AND DISSASSEMBLY TIPS

Proper gun maintenance means more than cleaning. All screws and fasteners must be periodically checked to insure that they are doing their intended jobs. Check each one by the proper use of the appropriate screwdriver or other hand tool.

It is important to realize that fasteners, by their physical size, require very specific degrees of "tightness." Attempts to exert undue pressure can result in broken screw heads, stripped threads, or ruined hand tools. Failure to keep fasteners adequately tightened can cause inaccuracy or malfunctions. Specifics on the proper amount of effort to be applied have been covered in the chapter dealing with hand tools.

In general, proper firearms maintenance should be undertaken after every shooting session. At this time, bore cleaning is always appropriate. Also, all fasteners should be checked.

When checking fasteners, do not attempt to increase the torque previously applied to the fastener. Simply apply enough torque effort to insure that the fastener has not worked loose.

Further cleaning should be extended to include a dismantling of the firearm into basic component groups whenever it has been used in inclement weather that has resulted in water penetration into the action or between metal and wood. When a firearm has been exposed to salt-water spray, the cleaning needs to be started as soon as possible, certainly within a few hours of the end of the hunt.

A strip-down to basic sub-assemblies should also occur after every use of most semiautomatic centerfire firearms which has resulted in the firing of one hundred or more rounds since the last complete cleaning. Rimfire semiautomatics should be stripped to basic sub-assemblies about every one thousand rounds or so. The use of pressurized cleaning solvents on sub-assemblies is suggested in lieu of disassembling complex part groups. Such cleaning can result in a perfect job without the danger of lost, broken, or mutilated small parts. And the job will go much faster.

Bolt-action guns should have the internal parts separated from the bolt body when cleaning. But do not attempt to remove extractors, ejectors, or reduce the firing pin assemblies into component parts. Doing so will enhance the possibility of needless wear and will add nothing to facilitate cleaning of the gun. Clean all the internal surfaces that can be reached with swabs.

Do not further disassemble a bolt gun because every time a rifle is removed from its stock and is reassembled, it will need a sight adjustment or at least verification of previous point of impact. Of course, if you suspect that moisture has gotten between the stock and metal parts, or that moisture has penetrated to the trigger group, it will be necessary to disassemble the rifle.

If disassembly is necessary, help minimize the possibility of a point-of-impact change by tightening action screws in the reverse order of their removal and do try to duplicate the same amount of torque on each that was present before disassembly. A bolt gun is usually rugged enough to last its entire accuracy life without a complete strip cleaning, if it does not get wet internally. And accuracy will be extended if extra rounds are not being used to check sight adjustment after disassembly.

Semiautomatics are a different nature. These will need to be stripped for cleaning after every one hundred rounds or so. The exact frequency of strip cleaning needs to be flexible. If you are using a light, clean burning target load in a semiauto shotgun, you may be able to go five hundred rounds or so. Use common sense based on how dirty the gun actually is when you first strip clean. Needless take-aparts will cause needless wear. However, if your semiauto seems excessively dirty because of the ammunition used, or other factors, then a more frequent cleaning schedule is appropriate. If you experience malfunctions caused by accumulated dirt, combustion by-products, or unburned propellant in the action, then obviously your cleaning schedule is not nearly frequent enough.

Pump and lever-action firearms do tend to get a bit dirtier than bolt guns. Yet, complete disassembly of these action types is seldom required. Indeed, due to the complexity of many firearms, shooters often do not bother to disassemble these types of actions until there is a real need to do so. This is an acceptable avenue of approach if the shooter pays close attention to such warning signs as an action that is getting a bit more difficult to operate or one that does not seem to be functioning as smoothly as it could.

It is important to remember that strip cleaning, as referred to in normal firearms maintenance, never means the disassembly of sub-groups, complicated gas systems, mainspring housings,

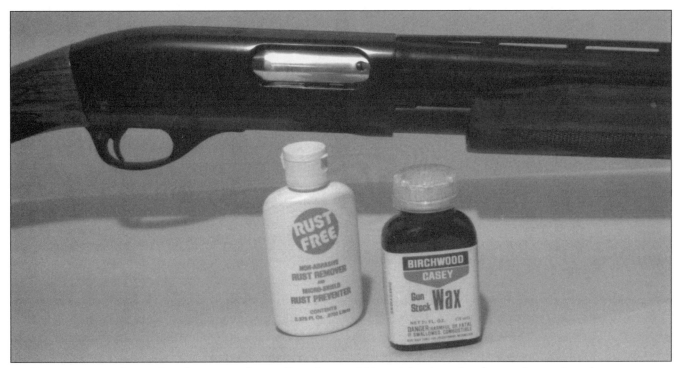

Dry rust preventatives and stock waxes work as well as oils on outside metal and wood surfaces and are not nearly as messy.

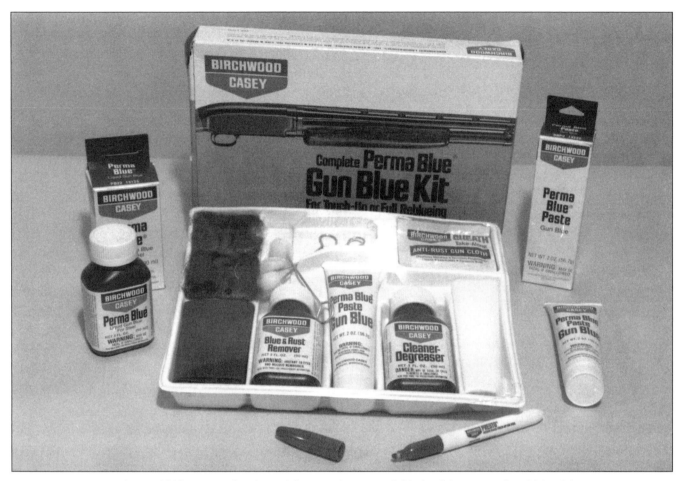

Touch-up cold bluing can often be satisfactory. Kits are available for doing a complete bluing job.

firing pin assemblies (particularly on bolt-action firearms) and so on. I cannot overstress that the disassembly of such part groups should never be undertaken except to replace worn or broken parts. Even after total submersion in salt-water such assemblies can usually be cleaned effectively with repeated applications of pressurized solvents, degreasers and oils.

PARTS REPLACEMENT

Other routine maintenance might include replacement of extractors, ejectors, or springs and plungers relating to the operation of these parts.

When a firearm begins to close hard on cartridges, the cause may be a rough extractor face which is binding as it attempts to slip over the cartridge rim. A gun that begins to eject weakly may need a new extractor, a new ejector, or a new ejector, plunger and spring; that is assuming these parts and

related working surfaces have first been checked for proper operation after a thorough cleaning. Such replacements are easily accomplished. But be careful as small springs, plungers, ejectors, and extractors are easily lost when they escape under compression and subsequently bounce about the work shop area. Because of firearm variations, the replacement of these parts will be covered in the sections dealing with specific models.

HANDGUN MAINTENANCE

Revolvers and semiautomatic handguns do need special attention, especially when lead bullets are used. Lead build-up on the front of a cylinder and the back edge of a revolver barrel can very quickly become a cause of difficult cylinder rotation in guns having minimum barrel-to-cylinder gaps. If left to accumulate, such build-up can be extremely difficult to remove.

Lead in handgun bores can sometimes be quite severe. It is not wise to continue using lead bullet ammunition that causes excessive leading. Nor is it wise to shoot lead bullets in a handgun whose bore is rough and therefore leads excessively. Nonetheless, leading is a facet that needs to be dealt with, even in good bores using good ammunition.

Normally, a bronze bore brush, soaked with solvent and vigorously applied, will rid the bore, cylinder face, rear of barrel, frame area at rear of barrel, and the outside diameter of the cylinder of accumulated lead. This method is preferred over all others as it is not harmful to metal surfaces and will not cause any noticeable blue wear.

Lead-removing cloths are not suggested for blued or plated surfaces as these cloths quickly wipe away finishes. Such cloths, torn to patch size, can be useful in bores, but their performance level is only about on par with a solvent-soaked brass or bronze wire brush.

POWER CLEANING

In cases of really stubborn or very heavy lead deposits, cleaning time can be shortened drastically by motorizing the brushing operation. Simply mount a cleaning rod shaft (no handle) in an electric drill, preferably one with a variable speed. Then screw a solvent-soaked brush to the rod. Run the motor at medium speed and slowly push the barrel over the brush (or across the leaded surface). This procedure will quickly brush the leading free of the metal surfaces.

Be careful with any brushing, whether by hand or power, to allow only the soft brass or bronze wires to contact the bore or metal surfaces. Any contact by the rod (or power drill chuck) can cause accuracy-destroying or finish-marring damage.

Brushing, even with a power drill is not particularly beneficial to remove copper fouling. Soaking with a copper dissolving solvent is effective for removing this type of fouling. Avoid any inclination for excessive brushing to help rid a bore of this type of fouling.

Power brushing can sometimes be useful to clean up severely leaded shotgun bores or remove excessive plastic residue. However, great care must be taken to keep the long cleaning rod from contacting the bore. Some older shotgun barrels are quite soft and should not be subjected to power brushing.

The soft steels sometimes used in .22 rimfire barrels should never be subjected to any form of power brushing. Even the relatively soft copper or bronze wires used for brushes can be damaging to such barrels.

Generally speaking, avoid using steel wire bore brushes when hand brushing and never use such brushes for power brushing or on outside finished surfaces.

Avoid firearms that require excessive amounts of routine maintenance. For most applications, a bolt-action rifle will prove completely satisfactory, be as accurate as possible, and require minimum maintenance. But, if you choose an autoloader because of personal preference, remember its special requirements for routine cleaning. Keep in mind that some autoloaders will prefer light applications of a high-pressure grease, rather than a few drops of oil, to maintain reliable function. Lever and pump-actions may be appealing, but these require more complicated maintenance procedures. There are exceptions, of course. The Marlin lever actions, for example, are as simple to maintain as any type of rifle.

SCOPE MAINTENANCE

Don't forget your scope when doing your cleaning chores. After the gun is clean, remove the scope caps, and examine the lenses for dirt, grime, and smudges. As needed, apply a single drop of camera lens cleaner to a lint-free lens cleaning tissue (never directly to the lens). Start at the middle of the lens and proceed by cleaning in a circular pattern from the center to the edge of the lens. Repeat with a dry lens tissue and the job will be done.

Remember that not all lens cleaning tissues are lint free. Those that leave a dusty lint on the lens are near useless. Good tissues have a crisp feel rather than a soft textured one.

Keep oil, grease, solvents, and any cleaning compounds away from scopes. The gaskets used to keep scope lenses tight and scope bodies waterproof can be adversely affected by different chemicals. Use only a clean silicon-impregnated wiping cloth on the scope tube. Avoid contact with lens surfaces when wiping the tube.

OTHER REMINDERS

When performing routine maintenance, keep in mind each different firearm's specific requirements. A trace of oil needs to be present on a revolver's ratchet, hand (pawl), front

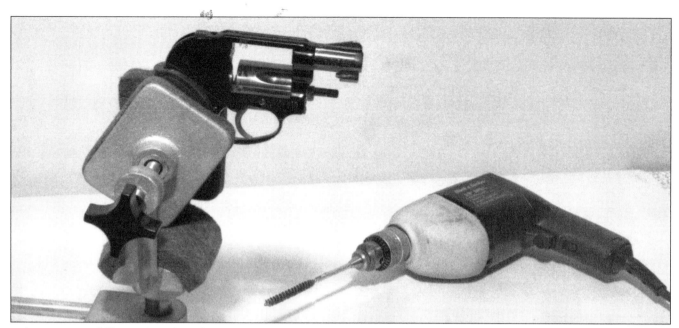

Using a power drill to spin a bore brush at moderate speeds is an effective way to rid a handgun bore of extremely heavy lead deposits.

and rear lock-up points, and on all the surfaces around which the cylinder rotates. Tubular magazines, which have accumulated interior moisture, will rust horribly if they are not cleaned as needed. The same applies to the inside surfaces of detachable clips. Revolver ejectors need special attention to insure that no action-stopping crud builds up underneath or around them. Some gas-operated semiautomatics build up unbelievable deposits in and around the gas port and piston.

Knowing what is needed should start with the simple act of reading the owners manual. And knowing what is needed should also come from getting quite familiar with a firearm's individual characteristics. Routine maintenance, carefully and slowly performed, will provide a great deal of insight into the special requirements of individual firearms. One thing is for certain, the more complex a firearm's design, the more parts it will have, and the more maintenance it will require.

9
ACCURACY
HOW TO FIND PROBLEMS AND CORRECT THEM

Every shooter cherishes an accurate rifle or handgun. However, individual definitions of accuracy vary so widely that one person's inaccurate firearm may be another's treasured favorite. Technically, accuracy, as applied to firearms, has two distinct meanings. In one, accuracy means the measure of a firearm's ability to shoot a very small group. After placing three, five, or perhaps ten shots into a single group, the acceptable level of accuracy will vary with shooter and application. Shooters generally agree that a big game rifle producing an average group size of one and one-half inches, for five five-shot groups fired at one hundred yards, is quite accurate. Some will use three three-shot groups as a criterion, albeit such limited shooting will not precisely reflect a rifle's true capability. Others, those really into accuracy, will use the average group size of five ten-shot groups for a measure of accuracy. Obviously, if a rifle's individual group size varies greatly, the average group size may not truly reflect the firearm's field capability.

Serious varmint hunters will demand that the average group size be one-inch or less before a rifle is considered

"Accuracy" can differ depending upon the shooter's application of firearm and ammunition. This hunter's definition of accuracy is one-inch groups for ten shots at seventy-five yards. (Courtesy: Stoney-Point Products)

For ultra long-range varmint shooting most hunters will settle for no more than 3/4-inch groups for ten shots at one hundred yards. (Courtesy: Stoney-Point Products)

satisfactory. However, dedicated benchrest shooters will junk a barrel that shoots only half-inch groups, while a rimfire squirrel hunter will be looking for one-inch capability at seventy-five yards. Accuracy also means placing one group at the intended point of impact today as well as tomorrow, next week, and even next year. To a hunter, it is perhaps more important to have a consistent point of impact than it is to be able to shoot small groups. A hunter correctly reasons that a small group at the intended point of impact today, followed by a small group that is two inches to the left tomorrow, followed by a small group that is six inches low next week or next season, is not something to brag about. A hunter needs to be able to place shots at the intended point of impact whenever he shoots, and would gladly accept two-inch groups that always print where intended, rather than one-inch groups that randomly wander about the target with the passage of time.

ACCURACY VERSUS ACTION STYLE

Accuracy is related very closely to the type of firearm used. In general, bolt-action rifles, and some single shots, are the most accurate. Surely any of these that could not group under two inches or less at one hundred yards, after tuning, is not a particularly good specimen. Semiautomatics tend to be less accurate, with two and one-half inch to three and one-half inch groups (again at one hundred yards) considered good. Pump guns are often slightly less accurate than the semiautos.

Compared to other types, accuracy with lever-action rifles tends to be the poorest. Lever guns grouping four to six inches are often considered typical.

Of course, exceptions with any action type do occur. Indeed, I have shot more than a few Marlin .336 lever-action rifles that were fully capable of consistent two and one-half inch groups and, occasionally, even better. And I have fired a few other lever guns that would not average six inches regardless of what was done with them.

When evaluating a rifle's performance, it is necessary to consider the type of action being evaluated. Equally important is the performance of similar models of the same make or style. For instance, a Remington 700 or a Winchester Model 70 that cannot be made to shoot one and one-half inch groups, or less, would be a rare exception and worthy of all the non-affectionate terms often applied to a gun with poor accuracy.

Yet, another bolt-action rifle model, of which I have shot a great many, is just as apt to turn in one-inch groups as it is two and one-half inch groups—even when tuned to perfection. I won't use a rifle that's not more predictable than that. But many folks do, and then they want to have a magic formula that enables these guns to shoot one and one-half inch groups. Frequently it's just not possible to obtain their goals.

Bolt-action rifles are most often the most accurate types available. (Courtesy: Browning)

AMMUNITION AND ACCURACY

Ammunition plays an important role in accuracy. Factory ammunition is seldom capable of better than two-inch groups—and then only when fired from a very accurate bolt-action rifle. Sure, there are exceptions; some mighty fine lots of ammunition have been produced. I have gotten groups as small as one-half inch with factory ammo. But, such lots of ammo are the exception rather than the common occurrence. I continue to look upon two-inch accuracy from factory ammo as exceptional and two-inch to three-inch groups as normal.

Thus, if a rifle's accuracy is to be truly evaluated, the shooter must have ammunition that performs somewhat better than average. A discussion of this requirement will be undertaken later. In this chapter, however, it will be assumed that the shooter has previously established that any ammunition used for accuracy testing is of sufficient capability to be useful for the purpose.

BEDDING

The first few shots with a rifle can tell you much about its potential. For example, if a rifle strings shots vertically on the target, perhaps covering four to seven inches between the highest shot and the lowest, while the left and right spread is minimum, one can reasonably suspect that the bedding of the rifle is at fault. It would be safe, on most such occasions, to assume that the upward pressure of the fore-end against the barrel varies considerably from shot to shot.

The cause may be as simple as a barrel expanding as it heats and, thus, creating additional contact between it and the fore-end. If this is the case, allowing the barrel to cool completely between shots should result in a notable shrinking of the group size. But the problem can be due to a barrelled action that shifts its position in the stock under the stress of recoil.

If groups string left and right but are small over the vertical measurement, one can assume that the barrel is being influenced by contact with the stock on one side or the other, for the reasons just stated, rather than contacting it at the bottom of the barrel channel.

Not surprisingly, most serious shooters have long ago abandoned all the various wood contact bedding methods for hunting rifles, and accepted a free-floating barrel (one with no fore-end barrel contact, even when the barrel is hot) as the best solution to a consistent point of impact and small group sizes. When a barrel is free-floated, changing points of impact, due to the fore-end warping, are eliminated. And it has been my experience that ninety-eight percent of all hunting rifles will group best when the barrel is free-floated.

Yes, there are the rare rifles that will shoot OK to ho-hum groups with a pressure-bedded barrel, but when free-floated do not do as well. There are even rarer hunting rifles that shoot very well with pressure-bedded barrels and then do poorly with a floated barrel. For the most part, these represent rifles that simply are not right to start with, and in which the pressure point, just by chance, helped correct a barrel stress or other problem.

Sometimes, such rifles suffer from poor receiver inletting and the barrel/fore-end contact is all that gives the gun half a chance of shooting. When the barrel is floated on such a rifle, the barrelled action is then free to wander about in the ill-fitting receiver mortise as each dose of recoil is applied, making accuracy about as bad as it can get.

In most instances, these problem rifles can be corrected by insuring that the action is correctly bedded in the receiver. The surest way to accomplish this is to bed the offending rifle's action in some form of epoxy. This procedure will be discussed in detail further on. For the remaining few rare rifles that simply favor a stock pressure point against the barrel (or several such points), I'll go on record as stating these are best used for trading stock. A rifle that depends upon a pressure point in the barrel bedding will need its point of impact checked frequently as the stock warps with seasonal changes. Indeed, such a rifle sighted with a dry, moisture-free stock could have its point of impact so altered, after being exposed to several days of heavy rain, as to cause a missed shot when hunting. While my condemnation of pressure point bedding is strong, it is based on years of hunting experience. Unless a synthetic stock is used, pressure bedding has no place on a hunting rifle.

Rifles with synthetic stocks are free from any problems caused by moisture. Without the water absorption problems that occur with wood (even well-finished wood), these stocks hold their point of impact quite well. But even with synthetic stocks, I find pressure bedding usually results in less accuracy than that which can be obtained with a free-floating barrel.

Those who shoot only three-shot groups may never detect the difference; but if you are deep into accuracy, especially ten-shot groups, a free-floating barrel will correct a great many problems or simply make a good rifle better. To determine the type of barrel bedding on a rifle, fold a dollar bill in half and, with the rifle supported in a cleaning vise, attempt to slip the folded bill between the stock and forearm. In a correctly floated barrel, the bill will slide easily, from the tip of the fore-end to the receiver, without drag. If you notice any drag or resistance, the barrel is contacting the fore-end, or will do so when hot, and thus, it intentionally or unintentionally has pressure bedding. This test should be done first with a cold barrel and again immediately after firing a five- (or ten-) shot

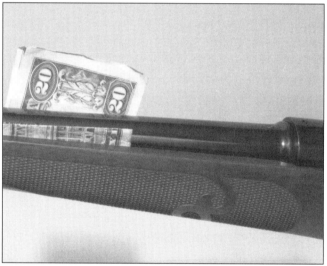

Checking a barrel to determine if it's free-floating is easily done with a folded bill. If the bill binds when slipped from fore-end to receiver, the barrel is not properly floated.

group. Heated barrels sometimes expand notably and may contact the stock when hot, though they did not do so when cold.

Additional checking of a rifle's bedding needs to be made if accuracy is a problem. A free-floated barrel will make such inspection easier. The rifle should fit into the receiver exactly. The back of the recoil lug should bear firmly against the corresponding stock mortise. Also the bottom and the side of the recoil lug should locate with uniform contact in the recoil lug mortise. If, with the action screws removed, you can detect any front to rear movement or lateral twist (when the recoil lug is fully seated into its mortise), the rifle's bedding needs work.

Usually it's possible to correct any such problems with the use of an epoxy (often called "glass") bedding compound.

When the recoil lug mortise has been properly bedded, then contact at other parts of the action can be checked using lamp black or other inletting highlighter. This is discussed in detail in the chapter dealing with glass bedding. It is important that the action be properly supported at each point an action-retaining guard screw is employed. Any twist or bending of the action that occurs as guard screws are tightened, will cause varying levels of inaccuracy. Additionally, the guard screws must be free of any contact with the stock material. Keep in mind that improperly bedded actions, or guard screws that contact the stock, can not only destroy accuracy, but can also be the cause of stock splits and repeated loosening of guard screws when shooting. The stock inletting should also be checked to insure that any moving action parts are free of stock contact over their entire movement range. This also applies to the bolt handle on bolt-action rifles.

When the bolt handle is locked fully into place its base should contact only the steel portion of the corresponding receiver cut. If the bolt contacts the stock, accuracy can suffer. If such contact is excessive, it may be difficult to operate certain style safeties.

FOULED BORE

Accuracy problems can, obviously, have their causes traced to other difficulties. One of the most common problem is a fouled bore. Do not eliminates the possibility of a dirty or fouled bore until you are certain this is not the problem. As noted in the chapter on maintenance, a bore cannot be cleaned properly with just a few passes of a bore brush and some cotton swabs wetted with a weak solvent. If you are in doubt, re-read the maintenance chapter from time to time.

POOR CROWNS

Poor rifle accuracy can also be traced to a defective barrel crown. The barrel crown is the radius or undercut at the muzzle that insures the bullet's simultaneous release around its entire circumference as it exits the muzzle. The barrel crown also helps prevent any minor nicks, dings and burrs, that occur at the muzzle, from interfering with the uniform and non-damaging release of the bullet. However, the crown cannot always prevent damage that can adversely affect accuracy.

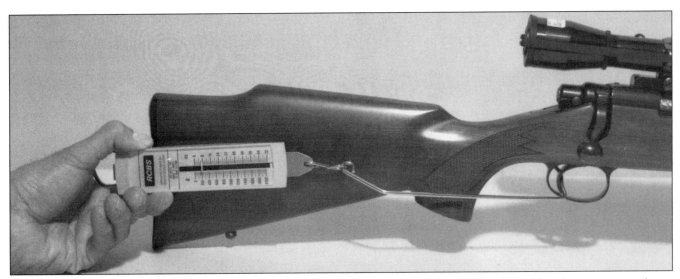

A uniform crisp trigger pull is essential for getting the most out of a rifle. Accuracy will suffer with a heavy, creepy trigger. A pull of about two and one-half to three pounds is right for most shooters.

The muzzle needs to be inspected for any dents, nicks, burrs, or other abnormalities that encroach on the all-important junction of the bore's actual termination and the crown of the muzzle. Damaged areas that do not encroach on the bullet's exit will, of course, have no affect on accuracy. If a crown has been so damaged as to cause poor accuracy, repair can be made easily with the use of a lathe and a crowning cutter as discussed later in this effort.

BORE WEAR

Worn rifling can, of course, create accuracy problems. Improper cleaning of the barrel is as often the cause of rifling wear as is repeated firing. Generally speaking, a bore reaches peak accuracy capability shortly after being placed into service (one hundred or so rounds). This peak accuracy may last four thousand to five thousand rounds on lower intensity cartridges (.222 Rem., .30-30 Win., .35 Rem.) On cartridges of normal intensity, such as the .30-06, .270 Win., .308 Win., peak accuracy will last perhaps three thousand to four thousand rounds. With higher intensity cartridges, such as the .264 Win. Mag., 7mm Rem. Mag. and .300 Win. Mag., peak accuracy may last only two thousand rounds or so. Bore wear, with respect to cartridge intensity, is very real.

Heavier powder charges cause more rapid bore wear. Also longer bullet-bearing surfaces cause greater bore wear. The higher the chamber pressure the greater the bore wear.

Cartridge intensity describes bore wear-producing conditions that add to the total amount of heat (calories) produced in the bore and the maximum temperatures reached, as well as all other erosive or friction-inducing conditions. But even when a bore has passed its peak accuracy it may provide a satisfactory useful accuracy life for several thousand rounds more, depending upon the needs of the shooter.

TRIGGER

Equally important to accuracy is a good, clean, crisp trigger pull of about three pounds. A trigger that has a creepy or jerky movement will cause a great deal of deterioration in the shooter's ability to obtain maximum accuracy. A heavy trigger pull is self-defeating when accuracy is tantamount. A pull of two and one-half pounds is about right for an experienced shooter under target shooting conditions. The same shooter may find a trigger pull weight of three pounds right for most big game hunting. An inexperienced shooter would be best off with a three and one-half pound pull.

Keep in mind that too light a trigger pull can cause unintentional discharges. Such firings can occur when attempting to use the firearm with cold hands, gloved hands, or in haste. No trigger should be adjusted so light that it fires when the gun is bumped or dropped. A trigger that fires the gun by breaking clean, like a glass wand, always makes it easier to shoot accurately than one that is spongy, creepy, jerky, or has

When looking for accuracy, the flat, no-slip surface of a rubber buttplate is preferable to all other styles.

considerable after-travel (movement after the sear has been released). Anything less than a good pull and the shooter will not be able to realize the firearm's full accuracy potential.

BUTTPLATES

Accuracy is also related to the ability of the shooter to hold the gun motionless, or very nearly so. A gun with a smooth metal or plastic buttplate, especially if it is curved, is difficult to hold steady. Even from a bench rest position, this type of buttplate tends to slide and slip about on the shoulder, making it very difficult to get even a modicum of accuracy. On the other hand, with a flat, checkered, metal, or plastic buttplate it is far easier to control the firearm. And a gun with a flat, no-slip rubber butt or recoil pad will be easier to hold steady.

SIGHTS

Accuracy problems can often be traced to loose or improperly mounted sights. A sight (and its base) needs to be solidly mounted and free of all play. Each screw used should be checked to insure that it can be fully turned up without bottoming in its hole. A screw that comes to rest against the bottom of its hole cannot do an adequate job of securing a sight or base. To check for this problem, install each screw in the appropriate hole with all other screws removed. When the screw is snugged up, check to see that it is holding the sight or

base very tightly. Then remove that screw and try another and so on. If any screw bottoms and won't hold the part tightly, shorten it a bit using a small file. Work carefully so as not to damage its threads.

When inspecting sights be sure that beads, or other aiming surfaces, are tightly positioned in the front sight. Also be certain that any folding leaves, adjustable leaves, and other moving parts of open rear sights, are all held snuggly in position. Remember that most shooters have difficulty in maintaining three-inch groups with open iron sights.

Inspect any aperture (peep) sight, its parts, and its mounting to locate any loose parts or screws. As a whole, two-inch groups with a peep sight (at one hundred yards) can be considered about as good as can be had by most shooters.

SCOPES

Scope rings and bases need to be very snug. Inspect each screw for bottoming as mentioned earlier. A drop of Loc-Tite, a screw locking liquid, applied to base screws will help prevent screws from loosening under recoil. This same compound applied to metallic sight base screws will help prevent problems.

When checking for poor accuracy do not forget to inspect the scope. A scope with an objective bell resting against the barrel can be problematic. Also, be sure that manipulation of the firearm's action does not cause any part to impact the scope, (such as a bolt handle or ejected cases). In addition, the scope's internal parts and optical system can cause inaccuracy. One of the most frequently encountered problems with inexpensive scopes are optics or other internal parts that actually move about under recoil. The number of times I've found a poorly constructed scope to be a problem are uncountable. But such problems are not easily isolated. The best investigative technique is to replace a suspect scope with one of known quality and proven performance.

One can determine if the scope has excessive parallax. Parallax is a term for an optical condition in which the target image does not fall on the same optical plane as the cross hair. When this condition is present, the reticle will move about on the target as the eye moves behind the scope.

To check for parallax, aim the scope at a bullseye one hundred yards away, using sand bags or a similar rest to hold the gun and scope in alignment. Make sure that when the eye

Using a scope of known quality and performance is an important aspect of accuracy testing. (Courtesy: Leupold & Stevens, Inc.)

is held in the center of the eye piece, the reticle of the scope aligns precisely with the center of the bullseye. Then, without moving the gun and scope, shift your eye left, right, up and down while looking through the scope. If the reticle moves about on the target, then the scope has a parallax condition.

If the reticle moves a maximum of only a half-inch or less, with extreme eye movement, the parallax condition can be ignored as it is not great enough to detrimentally affect grouping. However, if the cross hairs move an inch or more about the center of the bullseye, it will be difficult to shoot good groups, unless the eye is held precisely in the same position, in relationship to the scope eye piece, for every shot. I have examined scopes with as much as three inches of parallax at one hundred yards and, unfortunately, such scopes are not rare.

One scope brand is designed and built by the manufacturer to be free of parallax at one hundred yards. Another is designed to be parallax free at one hundred fifty yards. Either is fully acceptable. But some scopes, when inspected for parallax, are so inferior as to make it seem the manufacturer was unconcerned with the problem. Higher power scopes, meant for very precise shooting, are oftentimes equipped with an adjustable objective (front) lens. By turning the sleeve at the front of the scope, the user can select the range at which he wishes his scope to be free of parallax.

This adjustment range is often from twenty-five yards to four hundred yards and even to infinity. But poorly made scopes, even with adjustable objectives, sometimes prove less than satisfactory with respect to providing a parallax-free sighting picture. And worse, some very expensive scopes are not much better. Checking a scope carefully for parallax can be an important part of correcting an accuracy problem. I have found scopes with loose objective lenses. This problem, surprisingly, is not at all uncommon. In some instances, the movement of this front lens can be detected with the finger tip. Other times, the problem evades easy detection. When doubt exists, do use a scope of known worth to check the firearm's accuracy.

There are a few scope mounts that are totally unsuitable to the task. If, with the firearm firmly supported, the scope can be moved about when it is grasped at both ends by hand, the mount should be replaced. Brackets or rings that also can be moved are not conducive to accuracy.

SUMMARY

Sometimes the cause of accuracy problems can be difficult to determine, especially in unusual instances. But for the most part, if you consider the following points you will be able to quickly isolate most accuracy problems.

The points to cover are:

1. Shooter capability (flinching or lack of experience). Some shooters' ability to shoot well fluctuates daily. Several trips to the range may be required.
2. Barrel condition (fouled, worn, eroded crown).
3. Looseness (sights, screws).
4. Poorly designed buttplate.
5. Poor mount not offering stable base for scope.
6. Trigger pull (should be crisp and clean).
7. Reasonable accuracy expectations (based on action type).
8. Barrel bedding (a free-floating barrel is best).
9. Receiver bedding (action should be correctly supported and firmly held in position).
10. Moving action parts should not contact wood (bolt handle does not touch stock when locked).
11. Scope problem (parallax, loose internal parts).

Experience teaches that accuracy problems can sometimes be related to a great many other things, some of which are not so easily uncovered. In semiautomatics the gas system or recoil system needs to afford a uniform operation of the action. Unduly fast or slow cycle times can bring on grief. Firearms with two-piece stocks (such as lever-actions, pumps, semiautos, and some bolts) seldom shoot as well as one-piece stocks. Heavy, stiff barrels sometimes shoot better than light ones. Action screws that protrude into the receiver deeply enough to contact the bolt, or similar problems, all can destroy the potential for fine accuracy. When the problem occasionally goes beyond the listed trouble areas, you will need to proceed very slowly to find the difficulty.

Sometimes nothing will work short of a barrel replacement. But this is an expensive undertaking, so first rule out all other possibilities. If good records on firearms usage have been kept and they indicate five thousand or more rounds have been fired, then barrel replacement may be a likely candidate to correct accuracy.

Never forget that excessive headspace can cause some accuracy problems. Use a "no-go" gauge and if a stripped bolt closes fully on this gauge, the gun needs corrective repairs.

As you become experienced in accuracy problems you will quickly learn to detect all the abnormal conditions that can destroy accuracy. But with only limited experience, careful checking of those problems discussed in this chapter will lead to their correction.

10

CROWNING A BARREL

The crown of a barrel must be just right if it is to accomplish its two-fold purpose. Its first function is to help prevent the damage of bumps, bangs, and dings from causing an irregular surface at the junction of the rifling and the outside mouth of the barrel. The crown's other purpose is to help insure a very exacting and uniform release of the bullet as it emerges from the barrel, thus giving the bullet its final assist in accuracy.

Barrel crowns come in many styles including heavy radius, shallow radius, and recessed flat. Perhaps the most common are the radius, as found on most hunting rifles, and the recessed flat, as found on many target rifles. Regardless of its configuration, the crown is intended to protect the junction of rifling and muzzle by recessing that junction somewhat below the highest point of the crown. In this way, if the end of the barrel is inadvertently run against a stone wall, or what have you, any damage occurring will most often not involve the vital-to-accuracy area of the bullet's release from the muzzle.

The crown must be absolutely perpendicular to the bore to insure that the entire circumference of the bullet is released from the bore simultaneously. If the crown is so shaped that a portion of the bore bears on a portion of the bullet, after it has been nearly released by the bore, accuracy will be abysmal. For this reason, except for emergency repair, a crown should always be formed, or repaired, with the use of a good lathe and the appropriate cutting tools.

Whenever a barrel is shortened or whenever a burr, ding, or dent occurs at the crown/bore edge, or when a new barrel is made, the barrel will need to be crowned.

It is easiest to crown a barrel before it has been installed on a receiver. However, it makes no sense to attempt to remove a barrel from a receiver solely to crown it. A barreled receiver can be carefully chucked up in a lathe, in a manner that will prevent any imbalance of the receiver from causing wobble in the barrel as the lathe chuck spins. It is important that the lathe chuck jaws be tightened securely against the barrel. Therefore, unless the barrel is properly padded it could be damaged. It will be difficult for the lathe chuck to maintain a secure and continuous purchase on the barrel if the padding is not appropriate. Leather strips of adequate thickness make ideal pads for chuck to barrel contact.

I prefer to use a live center on the lathe's movable tail stock when setting up the barrel. This insures that the bore, at the muzzle, is running true to center as it turns. Once everything is as it should be, the live center and tail stock are moved away from the barrel.

If the barrel is to be shortened before crowning, a parting tool can be mounted in the lathe's tool post and the barrel cut off at the length desired. However, many gunsmiths will simply use a hacksaw on the spinning barrel, cutting it about 1/8-inch to 1/4-inch longer than the desired finished length. While the hacksaw treatment does work, care must be taken to

Good crowns vary in configuration but all insure an exacting simultaneous release of the bullet's entire circumference as it emerges from the barrel. The general configuration of a crown also helps protect the junction of rifling and muzzle from nicks, dings, and bumps.

prevent a chattering saw or broken blade from damaging the outside of the barrel surface. The use of a parting tool is the best route to follow when shortening a barrel.

The actual forming of the crown is conveniently accomplished with a cutting tool pre-shaped to the radius desired for the crown. When the cutter is mounted securely in the tool post and moved slowly inward over the muzzle end of the barrel, the crown will be formed without a hitch if the cutter is properly aligned with the barrel. I prefer a cutter that is so shaped as to place the front end of its edge inside of the bore and the back end of its edge beyond the outside edge of the barrel. A properly shaped cutter will allow a wide range of barrel diameters to be crowned with a single tool. But don't make the mistake of trying to use a too small or large cutter. Grind a new cutter when faced with extra small or large barrel diameters.

As the crown cut is completed, decrease the speed of feed of the cutter to almost nil. Then allow the cutter to dwell a moment before backing it away from the barrel. This will give a very smooth cut. After cutting, the crown will need to be polished to a high gloss in order to prevent rust from forming and to give the appearance associated with first class work.

If the barrel is not to be reblued, polishing will have to be done with great care so as not to remove any bluing from the barrel itself. Only the crowned area should be polished. This is not as difficult as it sounds, and a small piece of crocus cloth, stretched over a fingertip and carefully placed against the bore, will result in the crown surface being nicely polished as the barrel spins in the lathe.

Caution: Be certain there are no sharp edges on the barrel that could cut through the crocus cloth and cause personal injury.

Depending upon how well the cutter was aligned with the barrel, the use of only a very fine polishing grade of crocus cloth will be necessary. If multiple grades of paper are needed to produce a very high polish, you can bet the cutter wasn't properly shaped, sharpened, or aligned.

Press the finger, with a piece of crocus stretched over it, into the bore, as though you intended to plunge your finger through the barrel. With pressure, slowly manipulate your finger in a manner that causes the polishing action to move outward around the crown's radius. Don't get any polish beyond the crown's edge (the outside diameter of the barrel).

Caution: It is always best to remove any front sight and any detachable front sight ramp before attempting to crown a barrel. Spinning front sights and/or ramps can cause serious personal injury and property damage.

To effect the stepped flat crown common on target rifles, a straight cutter blade is used. However, the blade is not used to attack the barrel flat end to flat end. Rather, only the tip is used (such as when turning a piece of metal to a smaller diameter). Begin by cutting a single flat across the entire surface of the barrel. Then proceed to cut a deeper flat, beginning at the bore's center and progressing outward. The second flat should be deep enough to give ample protection to the crown/bore edge. The second cut looks best, to most folks, when it is made to equal one-half the barrel's diameter. Finally, to add a professional touch, break the sharp corner of the edge of the barrel with a small, very small, cut.

A flat crown, such as described, is very difficult to cut smoothly. And it must be very smooth since this type of crown does not lend itself well to any after-polishing. Some skill in the use of a lathe is essential to insure that a properly shaped cutter is used and that it is placed at the proper angle of attack to the metal. A person who is experienced in turning smooth outside diameters will have no difficulty and will realize the need for a very slow feed rate and a properly shaped cutter. Others would be best to use the easy-to-do radius crown.

Great care must be taken in all crowning efforts and after-polishing to insure that the rifle crown junction maintains a very sharp edge. Any reduction of the lands at the end of the crown will result in reduced accuracy capability.

Sometimes barrel crowns can be damaged when rifle and shooter are a long way from anything that even looks like a lathe. Yet, some sort of repair may well be called for if the crown has been heavily damaged. In such instances a vise, brace, and a ball-shaped grinder point bit may save the day. With the barrel firmly mounted in the vise and a grinder ball mounted in the brace, carefully position the ball grinder in the muzzle. Rotating it uniformly may accomplish a satisfactory temporary crown repair. It won't look like much but it will be, if carefully done, a much better performer than a badly damaged crown.

When attempting a crown repair by hand, realize that it is an emergency procedure only. The shape of the grinder ball is not critical because you are trying only to get a uniform and perpendicular parting line between bore and crown. Naturally, any emergency crown repair should be properly redone, on a lathe, as soon as possible.

Caution: Always carefully wipe the bore free of chips and grit immediately after crowning. Firing a gun with any kind of metal chips, polishing compound, or bits of a grinding ball in the bore can ruin the accuracy of the barrel or cause a catastrophic failure of the barrel in the form of a burst muzzle.

11

TEN EASY GUNSMITHING PROJECTS

There are many popular firearms that see extensive use by millions of shooters. Because of the great quantities of these firearms and the frequency of their usage, certain repairs have become comparatively commonplace. There are minor modifications, such as the need to replace basic sighting equipment, or to add basic accessories, such as an aperture sight, that fall into the category of easy-to-accomplish tasks.

The purpose of this chapter is to deal with the more common repairs and alterations. These are the tasks that should be among those first attempted by firearm owners. Perhaps you will recognize several of the firearms covered as being identical to ones you currently own. But do not skip reading those sections dealing with firearms you do not presently possess. The general knowledge contained in this chapter will be useful later on, and is essential to the overall effort of understanding basic firearm repair.

The jobs covered in this chapter are:

1) Replacing Marlin .22 rimfire cartridge guides.
2) Replacing open iron sights.
3) Replacing Remington 870 trigger groups with an adjustable unit.
4) Repairing and improving Ruger Mark I .22 magazines.
5) Winchester Model 70 bolt disassembly.
6) Plating small parts.
7) Removing broken cartridges from chambers and dies.
8) Measuring headspace.
9) Installing a detachable clip in the Remington 700.
10) Installing aperture sights.

JOB 1
REPLACING MARLIN .22 RIMFIRE CARTRIDGE GUIDES

There are more than nine million Marlin .22 caliber rimfire rifles in the hands of firearm owners. Many of these rifles employ a uniquely shaped spring steel cartridge guide which ensures that cartridges being stripped from the

The Marlin bolt-action .22 has a cartridge guide that can become broken or damaged.

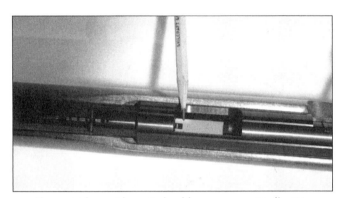

The cartridge guide as it should appear on a Marlin .22.

magazine will enter the chamber smoothly. When present in their original condition (see photo), these guides seldom are given a second's thought. However, when they are broken off, their absence may not be detected by the uninitiated. When broken away or severely distorted, the cartridge guide cannot do the job for which it is intended. Then, attempts to feed cartridges into the chamber will invariably result in cartridges jamming against the end of the barrel. Replacement of this Marlin cartridge guide is quite simple.

Begin the Marlin cartridge guide repair by removing the clip, bolt, and stock.

To begin the repair, remove the bolt, clip and stock from the rifle and be certain, naturally, that the chamber is unloaded. Next, drive out the pin that holds the barrel and receiver together. Do so by firmly supporting the barrel, right up to the receiver, in a well-padded vise. Use a moderately heavy hammer and a large diameter pin punch to drive out the retaining pin. Next, separate the barrel and receiver. If barrel and receiver do not separate easily, consign the job to a person familiar with the correct procedures or return the gun to the factory.

You will note that a portion of the original cartridge guide will still be in the retaining groove at the rear top of the barrel. Remove the broken part and replace it with a new cartridge guide. Reassemble the barrel to the receiver and reinstall the retaining pin. Be certain that the hole in the barrel and the receiver align perfectly before driving the pin into place. It may be beneficial to stake the end of the pin hole, on the receiver, to ensure that the pin does not come loose.

Prior to reassembling the barrelled action to the stock, give all the metal surfaces a light coat of rust preventing oil or a good application of firearm wax. Check the clip retaining screw, as well as the safety mounting screw, for tightness.

JOB 2
REPLACING OPEN IRON SIGHTS

Front and/or rear sight replacement can become necessary for a number of reasons. A sight may be broken, lost or simply does not allow for enough adjustment to properly sight in. In any case, the replacement of these sights is easy.

Front and rear open iron sights generally will be attached to the barrel either with one or two screws, or a dovetail arrangement. Oftentimes, a front ramp may have one screw hidden beneath a dovetailed front bead or blade.

Never attempt to drive out a dovetail front or rear sight if it is dovetailed to a screwed-to-the-barrel base or ramp. To do so could cause the retaining screws to shear or strip their threads and leave you with a headache you hadn't planned on. To remove a sight dovetailed to a screwed-on base or ramp, always use a tool such as the Williams Front Sight Pusher (it works well on rear sights, too). This tool is also essential when adjusting such sights for windage when sighting in. Always remove the sight by pushing it from the left side out to the right.

Front or rear sights dovetailed directly to the barrel will have to be removed with a brass punch and hammer. Again, always remove from left to right.

When replacing front sights be sure to use the appropriate style to match the rear sight. Round beads should be matched to U-notch rear sights, while a blade or post is correct for a square rear notch. The bead or blade size should always be small enough to be seen with adequate light on both sides when viewed through the rear sight.

If the front sight is being replaced to correct a deficiency that prevented proper sighting in, remember a lower-than-original front sight will cause the gun to place its group higher on the target, while a higher front sight will cause the point of impact to be shifted lower on the target.

If a gun is equipped only with open sights, do not use a rear sight that can be folded down. Sooner or later that is the position it will be in when a quick shot needs to be taken. Rear sights with large ears (buck-horn style), should be avoided too. These are slow to use, hide a lot of target, and will give varying points of impact under different light conditions. Select sights that have shallow aiming notches of good proportion and flat tops.

Always drive replacement rear sights into position from the right side to the left. If a replacement sight is not tight in

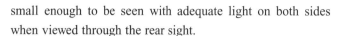

Remove dovetailed open rear sights by driving them from left to right using a brass punch and hammer.

Remove base or ramp-mounted dovetail sights only with a Williams front-sight pusher. Hammering on these sights might shear off the screws that hold the base or ramp to the barrel.

Loose dovetails can be peened a bit with a punch (or ball-peen hammer) to tighten up the raceway.

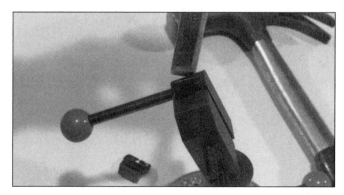

A sight's dovetail can be enlarged a bit by using a cold chisel to broaden its dovetail base.

the dovetail, remove it and peen the edges of the dovetail slightly with a ball peen hammer or a punch and hammer. Do so carefully, bending over just the edges of the dovetail no more than necessary to insure a tight-fitting sight.

If there still is excessive play between the sight and slot, the sight's male dovetail can be enlarged slightly. This is done by using an old cold chisel and setting a long crease in the base of the dovetail that will parallel the edge of the sight along the dovetailed edge. Naturally, the sight will need to be properly supported and a very healthy blow is required to move the metal outward. The chisel should be held very close (approximately 1/16-inch to 1/8-inch) to the edge of the sight if this procedure is to be effective.

Rear dovetailed sights will require movement left and right during sighting in. Therefore, do not make the dovetail fit so tight as to prevent movement when a brass punch and light hammer blows are used for adjustment.

JOB 3
REPLACING REMINGTON 870 TRIGGER GROUPS WITH AN ADJUSTABLE UNIT

The Remington 870 has been sold in million of units and, for the most part, shooters are generally happy with its non-adjustable trigger. However, those who use smooth slug barrels or rifled ones, as well as the serious clay bird shooter, may desire a cleaner, crisper pull for improved shooting performance. Happily, for 12-gauge 870 owners, there is an easy-to-replace trigger unit available.

Hastings and Timney have cooperated in developing an all-steel trigger assembly that offers a very clean, crisp trigger pull. The weight of pull is adjustable within reasonable limits, as are any take-up or backlash. All the parts are machined steel, an improvement that proud 870 owners might like to make, even without the advantage of a trigger that will rival those in many bolt-action rifles.

Remove the original trigger group by driving out the two retaining pins and lifting the entire trigger-plate assembly free of the shotgun. The replacement Hasting/Timney trigger unit should be adjusted for an appropriate trigger pull before installing the unit in the shotgun.

The spring that clearly shows in front of the trigger (near its top) has a threaded screw and two lock nuts in front of it.

Remove the original trigger group by driving out the two retaining pins and lifting it free.

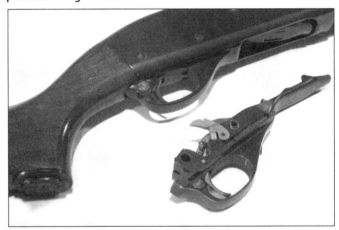

The Remington 12-gauge 870 trigger group can be replaced with a fully adjustable Hastings-Timney trigger.

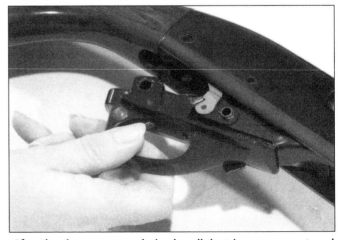

After the pins are removed, simply pull the trigger group outward and away from the receiver.

The replacement trigger should be adjusted to the desired pull before it is installed.

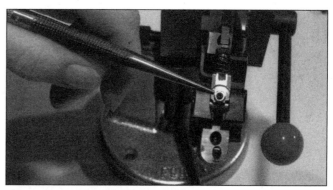

This screw and its lock nut control the amount of trigger travel (take up) before the sear is released.

After-travel (backlash) is controlled by the screw located in the rear top of the trigger guard.

It may be necessary to remove some metal at this point if the cartridges do not properly feed from the 870's magazine after the installation of the replacement trigger group.

By moving the lock nuts toward the trigger, the weight of pull will be increased. Conversely, moving the lock nuts away from the trigger will lighten the weight of pull. Generally, the trigger pull weight can be adjusted from 2¼ to 4½ pounds. A pull of approximately three pounds will be about right for most shooters.

The adjustment for take-up is located on the top of the trigger. Simply loosen the lock nut and turn the screw (hex head type) inward to decrease take-up. Do not reduce take-up excessively. Ample sear engagement must be maintained to insure the gun will not fire if bumped or dropped. Be certain that both the weight of pull and engagement adjustments are locked up tightly.

Backlash is adjusted at the rear top of the trigger guard. Simply insert the appropriate hex wrench into the adjusting screw and screw it in one-quarter-turn at a time, checking for proper trigger release. Keep turning this adjustment in until the trigger will not release the hammer. Then back out the

screw one full turn and the adjustment is complete.

Caution: Do not allow the hammer to move forward violently during testing of trigger adjustments. This can damage the unit. Prevent the hammer from flying forward by holding your thumb in front of it. Recocking is easily accomplished by pressing the hammer rearward with the thumb.

After the trigger has been adjusted for a clean, crisp three pounds, install the entire trigger-plate assembly into the shotgun and make a final test of the adjustments. It may be decided to remove the trigger-plate group for a final adjustment.

Important: After completing the adjustment and installation of the Hastings/Timney trigger, the shotgun must be checked for proper feeding. Do this by loading dummy 12-gauge shells into the magazine and cycling them through the action. If the shells do not fully escape from the magazine and up onto the shell carrier, then further fitting of the unit is required. Remove the trigger-plate assembly and mount it in a well-padded vise by grasping it in the area where the rear retaining pin passes through the assembly. Grasping the unit in a vise at any other point may irreparably damage it.

Next, lift the cartridge follower into its uppermost position. Now carefully remove a small amount of material from the top front edge of the trigger-plate assembly, in the area that is contacted by the carrier when it is in its full down position. Be careful not to remove material from the rearmost portion of this area as doing so will bring your file in contact with the piano wire spring that lies across the trigger guard.

Remove only enough metal to allow the carrier to drop low enough so that shells emerging from the magazine will clear its edge and lie fully rearward on top of the carrier. This is a trial and repeat process. Remove only small amounts of metal at a time. It should not be necessary to ever remove more than one sixteenth-inch of material in total. Reinsert the trigger group into the shotgun and check feeding each time you make three or four cuts with your file. Check that the cut you make is carried far enough back into the trigger guard to allow the follower to fully drop onto the cut.

Also be certain to carefully wash away all metal filings with a good solvent so they run off the forward edge of the trigger-plate assembly, never into the unit.

Properly installing the steel replacement unit will enhance the durability and beauty of any 870. And its bluing can be easily touched up if ever required—something not possible with the original aluminum unit. The clean, crisp trigger pull may well mean better slug groups or, perhaps, more broken clay targets.

JOB 4
REPAIRING AND IMPROVING RUGER MARK I .22 CALIBER MAGAZINES

Ruger Mark I pistols are available in a number of model variations, including fixed-sight versions, adjustable sight models, long and short barrels, as well as heavy bull barrel variations. Each of these share the same common magazine. If there is any area of fault common to the Mark I pistols it is that mutual magazine. After extensive use, reliable feeding will be impaired and the pistol will begin to jam. Also, the Mark I magazine (unlike the Mark II models which are not interchangeable) will not leave the bolt open on the last shot. This

The Ruger I semiautomatic pistol bolt will not stay open on the last shot if a standard magazine (left) is used. But a specially converted magazine (right) will cause the bolt to be held in the open position when the last shot is fired.

can lead to needless dry firing of the pistol if the shooter does not carefully count his shots. But the feeding (and resulting jamming), as well as the bolt not staying open on the last shot, are easily corrected problems.

The feeding problem manifests itself when the two ears of the clip (one located on each side near the mouth of the clip) lose their inward bend. This is a natural occurrence caused by repeated loading and feeding of ammunition through the clip. Each loading and feeding cycle results in the two small ears being flexed outward and then relaxed. Eventually, they do not return to their original position. This allows the cartridge to raise up unduly high as the rim of the case clears the turned-in portion of the clip and, in turn, the cartridge's bullet impacts

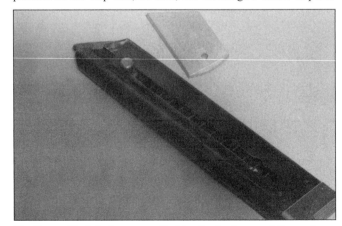

The Ruger Mark I clip as supplied by the factory and the replacement follower which holds the bolt open.

The replacement cartridge follower in the Ruger Mark I clip will protrude far enough into the receiver to interrupt the bolt's forward motion when the last shot is fired.

the rear of the barrel, over the chamber, causing a jam.

To correct the problem you will need a pair of thin needle-nosed pliers. Pull down on the thumb piece, making the cartridge follower withdrawn into the magazine. Then insert a punch through the slots in the magazine, above the follower. Slowly release tension on the thumb piece so that the follower bears against the punch. This will keep the follower in a withdrawn position. Then, using needle-nosed pliers, carefully bend the two clip ears inward.

Note: The ears are that section of the magazine (approximately one quarter-inch wide) at the open end of the clip, lying between the permanently shaped front and rear sections. Do not bend in the front section of the clip (this actually has a slight outward flare). The ears should be bent inward so that they are positioned about 1/16-inch inside of the magazine walls. Excessive bending can cause irreparable damage. I reommend using a plier with a rounded inside nose to help

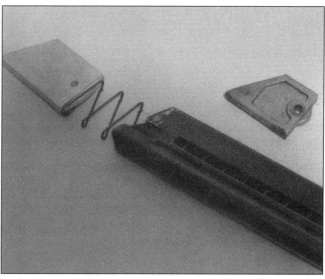

The replacement follower is simply seated on the magazine spring and the magazine is reassembled.

prevent a sharp crease in the magazine ears.

Compare any clip-causing jams with a clip that is working properly. It is an easy matter, then, to bend the ears of the faulty clip to match those of the working clip.

Converting a Ruger Mark I clip to hold the bolt open on the last shot requires the magazine follower to be replaced by one that will protrude sufficiently from the magazine to engage the bolt on the last shot. This type of follower can be built duplicating the original follower dimensions, but instead, make the replacement exactly 3/8-inch longer at the front edge and 1/2-inch longer on the rear edge. Or, you can purchase a new follower.

If you decide to make your own follower, use only a fine

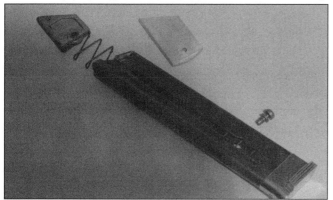

Removing the thumb pin on the Ruger clip (with the follower completely depressed) will allow the follower to be withdrawn from the magazine.

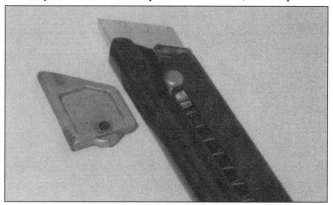

The bolt hold-open follower will protrude significantly from the magazine.

grade aircraft aluminum. This will prevent damage to the bolt face and give it maximum follower life.

To remove the old follower, fully depress it into the magazine using a suitably sized screwdriver. Don't bend any part of the clip's open end. Fully depress the follower so that the thumb piece may be withdrawn from the left side of the clip. You may have to slightly reduce pressure on the follower to align the thumb piece exactly with the enlarged area of the cut in the side of the magazine. Then slowly release the pressure on the follower. Make sure that it or the spring does not fly free.

Remove the follower from the magazine and work the follower spring carefully back into the magazine. The spring will tend to get caught on the clip's ears. But by pushing each segment of the wire spring fully to the rear, you will be able to work it under the bent-in ears. Insert the new follower, compress it fully to the bottom of the magazine and insert the thumb piece into the left side of the magazine. Be sure the

thumb piece retaining step slips up along the inside of the clip as you release tension on the follower.

The new follower will pop up in front of the bolt face when the last shot is fired, preventing the bolt from closing.

Because the bolt is now bearing against the clip follower, under tension of the return spring, the clip sometimes cannot be dropped free until this pressure is removed. Do so by fully pulling the bolt rearward while simultaneously applying the safety. This will lock the bolt open and allow the magazine to be withdrawn. Some firearms will allow the magazine to be withdrawn without this step, but the bolt will close as the follower clears the bolt face. In this case make certain there is no cartridge left in the chamber.

This altering of the Ruger Mark I clip will reduce the magazine capacity by one round–from nine to eight. This is a small price to pay for a major improvement.

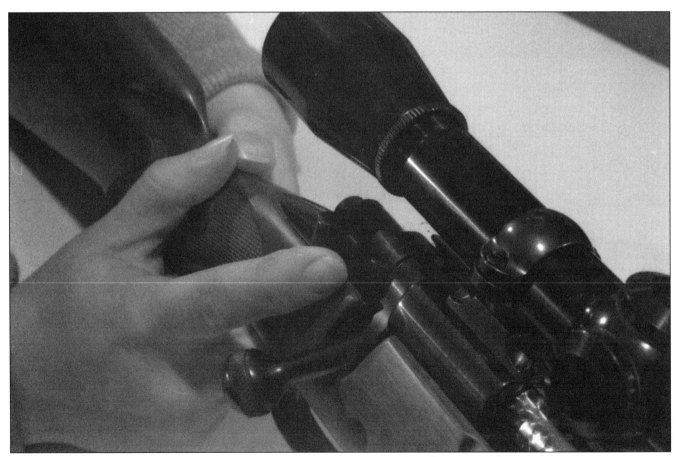

Before removing the Winchester Model 70 bolt, move the safety to its mid-position.

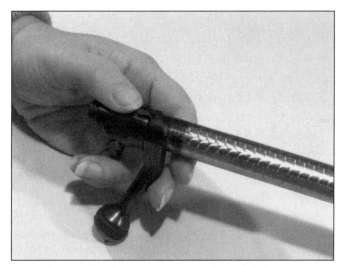

Begin disassembly of the Winchester Model 70 bolt by depressing the spring-loaded plunger on the left side of the bolt wile simultaneously unscrewing the entire cocking assembly.

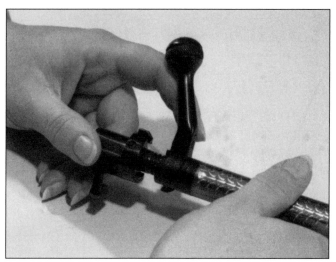

The entire cocking assembly can be withdrawn from the bolt body; then the inside of the bolt and the cocking assembly can be cleaned with pressured solvents and degreasers

JOB 5
DISASSEMBLY OF THE WINCHESTER MODEL 70 BOLT

Proper cleaning of any bolt-action means that occasionally the bolt body will need disassembly. The Winchester Model 70 bolt lends itself easily to such disassembly.

To begin, cock the firing pin by raising and lowering the bolt handle. Then move the three position safety to its middle position—sticking out at right angles to the bolt body. Next, remove the bolt from the rifle by depressing the bolt release button at the left rear of the action while simultaneously pulling the bolt handle rearward. The bolt will slip effortlessly from the receiver.

Now depress the spring loaded plunger on the left side of the bolt (between the bolt body and the cocking piece) and, while holding it inward, unscrew the cocking piece assembly by rotating it counterclockwise. The plunger needs to be held in only for the first full turn of the cocking piece. Completely unscrew the cocking piece and withdraw it from the bolt body. With it will come the firing pin and firing pin spring as a complete assembly.

For most purposes complete cleaning of the bolt mechanism can now be accomplished with a pressurized solvent.

Further disassembly can, if needed, be accomplished as follows: Push the safety to its forward most position. Then carefully compress the firing pin spring rearward. Do this by

inserting a tool designed for the purpose between the spring and the retaining washer and clip (located at the front end of the spring). With the rear of the firing pin resting against a table, compress the spring sufficiently to allow the retaining clip to be slid off to the side. Then lift off the retaining washer. Now allow the the heavy spring to gradually relax.

Caution: the firing pin spring is very strong and if care is not taken, the retaining clip and washer, as well as the spring itself, can escape to become lost or possibly cause personal injury.

With the spring and retainers removed, the screw through the cocking piece may be taken out, allowing it to be separated from the firing pin.

The safety can then be removed by wiggling it upward and away from the cocking piece. However, it is seldom necessary to do so. In that the safety spring and its plunger are easily lost during disassembly, it's best not to remove it unless necessary.

There are a few variations on the Model 70 bolts. Some use a firing pin retainer that requires rotation of 180 degrees before can be slipped forward from the firing pin. Others use a pin to hold on a bolt cap over the end of the firing pin. Other minor variations are sometimes encountered. Though each requires a somewhat modified disassembly, each change will be obvious.

To remove the extractor from the bolt, push a fine punch into the hole in the extractor and slide the extractor out of its groove. Take care not to lose the spring or plunger.

To remove the ejector, hold the bolt in a padded vise. Compress the ejector slightly and drive out the retaining pin. Then slowly release the pressure on the ejector. Withdraw it and its spring from the bolt.

Because extractor and ejector parts are easily lost during disassembly, it's best not to attempt their removal unless replacement parts are on hand. Reassembly is easily accomplished in reverse order.

Earlier Model 70 Winchesters used a Mauser type extractor and ejector. To remove the extractor from the bolt, rotate it out of its retaining groove (at the front end of the bolt) and push it forward off the bolt and its retaining collar. On these earlier models the ejector is mounted to the rifle's receiver.

JOB 6
PLATING SMALL PARTS

There is often a need to refinish small parts. A screw that has been burred due to the use of an improper screwdriver can often be saved by careful reshaping with a file. But it then needs to be refinished. Or a lost screw may be replaced but the blue finish on the replacement (if it has any) may not match. Too, small parts that have been made or repaired will require finishing.

Often it is simply not practical or convenient to reblue a small part in a hot bluing salt bath. And the cold blues, while a bunch better than nothing, seldom match the color desired and seldom last more than a brief period before the color fades or the part begins to rust.

The simple solution to all these and many other difficulties is to plate the screw or small part. Indeed, many firearm owners feel that plating all of the screws on a revolver adds a personal touch to an otherwise look-alike gun. Others plate the slides of semiautomatic pistols or the floor plate of a rifle and so on to add a bit of distinction to their firearm. Best of all its super easy to plate small parts.

The real secret to successful plating is in the preparation of the steel parts to be plated. The finish of the plating will reflect the degree of polish the part receives before the plating.

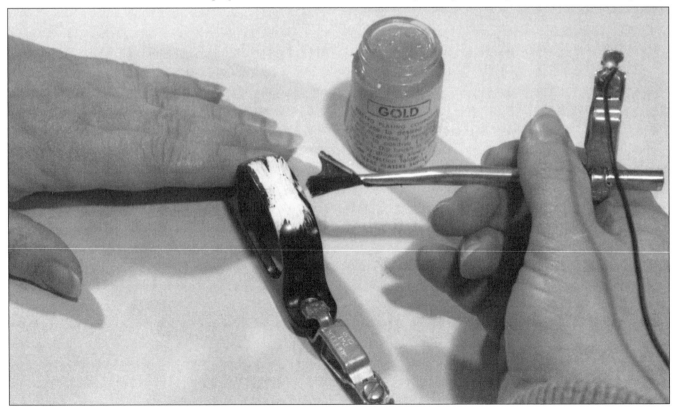

Plating small parts is easily done with a plating kit, a few dry-cell batteries and plating solution.

If you want a bright, lustrous finish the metal will have to be polished to a mirror reflective level before plating. This may be done by hand or it can be done with the use of professional polishing wheels. It is essential that all old bluing be removed, along with any rust or foreign material.

The part must then be completely degreased. This is easily accomplished with the use of one of the commercial pressurized solvents. All traces of oil and grease must be removed. If you attempt to plate over oil, grease, dirt, rust, old blue, or anything else, then plating will turn out tarnished.

After degreasing, wipe the part carefully with a clean, soft cloth to remove all traces of the solvent. You are now ready to plate.

The best small part plater I have used is the simple unit sold by Texas Platers Supply Co. Their plating solutions are tops and their small brushes and clamps are entirely adequate for the purpose.

You will need a source of electric current. Depending upon the size of the part and its make up, a three volt direct current will be minimum and a 4½ volt D.C. will be near perfect. This current can be obtained from the use of two or three fresh, dry cell batteries (No. 6 size) of 1½ volts each. Connect the batteries in a series.

For two batteries, connect one battery's plus (positive) terminal to the other's minus (negative) terminal. Then connect the unused minus (negative) terminal to the work to be plated. The unused plus (positive) terminal is then connected to the plating brush.

In a three battery hook up, connect the first battery's negative terminal to the second's positive terminal. Then connect the third battery's positive terminal to the second's negative terminal. The unused positive terminal of the first battery is then connected to the plating brush. The unused negative terminal of the third battery is then connected to the work to be plated.

However, it is more cost effective to use a battery charger or battery eliminator of the proper D.C. voltage. Depending upon the composition of the metal to be plated it may sometimes be useful to use higher voltage, as much as six or eight volts. Keep in mind that three volts will prove adequate only when plating a part with a total surface area of less than four square inches. For larger surface areas, 4½ volts would seem about right. More voltage will speed up the work, but also necessitate far more careful brushing. Always connect the positive lead to the brush and the negative lead to the work to be plated.

Begin by dipping the plating brush into the plating solution, being certain that all the bristles and the underside of the anode (the metal hood portion of the brush which covers a portion of the bristles) are well covered with solution. Then apply the plating to the work area using very short circular motions. The anode area of the brush must always be on top of the bristles and pressed lightly against them. The brush must be kept in constant motion while plating. Dip the brush frequently into the plating solution to renew the supply of metal. Each square inch of work must be plated for thirty seconds minimally for a light plating. Longer periods of time will be required for a heavier plating.

Copper, nickel and brass platings can be applied directly to the steel work part. If you wish to plate gold or silver you will first have to apply an undercoat of copper plating.

All white metals (except thin coats of nickel), as well as gold, will have a foggy appearance when the plating is finished. Immediately after plating, wash the part with running water and wipe dry to improve the appearance. Then lightly polish to a bright finish with metal polish. Great care must be taken to avoid excessive wear on new plating whenever you attempt to polish it.

A complete plating outfit will include ample supplies of gold, silver, nickel, copper, and brass, along with brushes and some wiring. Such an outfit will enable you to do a variety of jobs, perhaps even an entire handgun. But do gain some experience by working on practice parts before attempting to plate a valuable part or handgun.

JOB 7
REMOVING BROKEN CARTRIDGES
(FROM CHAMBERS AND RESIZING DIES)

It's not often that a factory case will separate into two pieces during firing. Indeed, such an occurrence would be quite rare or be indicative of excessive and dangerous headspace. But when an overzealous reloader uses a case once too often, it's not uncommon to have the rear of the cartridge case extract and eject, leaving behind the front half of the cartridge case.

It may seem like a monumental gunsmithing task to

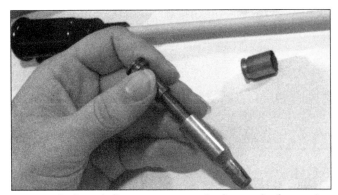

A proper broken shell extractor can make fast work of removing the front half of a broken cartridge from any chamber. A cleaning rod is also needed.

Shells firmly jammed in a resizing die can be quickly removed with the aid of a tool like the Stuck Case Remover (from RCBS).

The first step in removing a shell jammed in a die is to remove the decapping rod and expander button.

After the decapping rod and the expander button have been removed, it is a simple task to knock out the jammed cases with one of the supplied steel rods and a hammer.

remove the broken half of the shell, but it is a simple operation to do. You will need an Alex cartridge extractor and a strong cleaning rod.

Begin by removing the bolt and setting it aside. If the firearm's bolt does not remove easily, simply lock the action open. Then insert the broken shell extractor into the chamber. Make certain before doing so that the sliding extractor portion of the broken shell extractor has 1/4-inch of free travel. This is adjusted by screwing in (or out) the base portion of the unit on the central shaft.

It is important to fully seat the broken extractor into the chamber to insure that the claw section of the extractor enters deep enough to pass the end of the case. Now point the barrel upward and push the cleaning rod into the barrel. Gently tap the rod until you feel the claws engage the front end of the cartridge case. A moderately sharp blow on the cleaning rod will now drive the shell extractor and broken case free of the chamber.

Do not attempt to use the bolt to push the shell extractor

into position or to withdraw it and the broken case from the chamber. Doing so can damage the bolt face, especially its extractor and ejector.

To remove a broken shell (one in which the rim has torn off) from a reloading die is almost as easy. In the past, reloaders have drilled and tapped the broken case and used a large screw to withdraw the case from the die. This process was slow and often not effective, especially if the case was tightly stuck. There is a better way.

The one special tool required for quick, simple removal of a case jammed in a resizing die is the Stuck Case Remover (available from RCBS). This tool will work with all RCBS, Bonanza, Forster, and similar type reloading dies and will not damage the die in any way.

The sizing die should be screwed tightly in the press. Begin by removing the lock nut and the adapter nut (through which the decapping rod screws) from the top of the die. The screw-in top portion of the stuck case remover unit should be turned all the way in. Place the case remover over the die's threaded decapping rod.

Now place the supplied washer over the decapping rod so that it sits on top of the case remover unit. Then install the original die adapter nut, in an upside down position, onto the threaded decapping rod. Screw it onto the threaded decapping rod until it rests solidly against the washer. Then install the die's original decapping rod lock nut and bring it firmly against the upside down adapter. This must be a tight fit as the decapping rod stem must not turn during the next step.

Holding the bottom of the case remover unit with an appropriate size wrench, unscrew (counterclockwise) the top half of the unit using another appropriately sized wrench. This will cause the entire decapping rod to be moved away from the die, drawing the expanding button free of the case. When it has been freed, remove the entire unit from the die.

Using the supplied knock-out rod (use the largest one that will fit into the die), drop it into the top of the die so that its end rests on the bottom of the stuck case. Now apply a few smart blows to the rod with a hammer and the jammed case will pop free of the die.

The whole process can be accomplished in four minutes or less, and without the drilling or tapping normally associated with other methods of removing a stuck case from a sizing die.

If a case separates in the die with the head end coming away with the shell holder, first remove the decapping rod as described. Then use the method and tool described for removing a similarly broken shell from a firearm chamber.

JOB 8
MEASURING HEADSPACE

The headspace dimension on any firearm is critical. If there is too little headspace, a cartridge may be encountered (or many of them) that will not allow the action to close over it. If there is too much headspace, a cartridge may fit dangerously loose in the chamber and could rupture upon firing, possibly causing havoc with the firearm and/or the shooter.

The headspace dimension is that dimension which insures that there will be neither too little nor too much space between a fully seated cartridge and the bolt face. Basically, there are four common ways of obtaining this dimension.

A headspace gauge is a vital tool for firearms maintenance, reloading, and verifying ammo quality. (Courtesy: Forster)

In the instance of rimmed cartridge cases (i.e. .22 Long Rifle, .38 Special, .30-30 Winchester and .45-70 Government and shotshells), the headspace dimension governs the chamber area that houses the cartridge case's rim. Thus, the distance from the face of the bolt to the bottom edge of the rim recess becomes the headspace dimension.

Belted magnum cases do not have a rim per se. For these style cases (such as the .224 Weatherby Magnum, 7mm Remington Magnum, .300 Winchester Magnum and the .375 Holland and Holland Magnum), headspace is measured from the bolt face to the bottom edge of the chamber area containing the cartridge's belt.

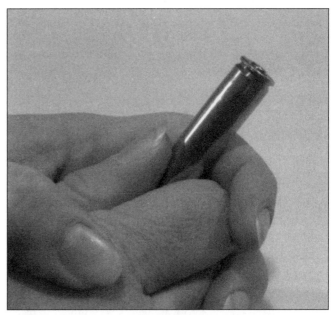

A backed-out primer is a good reason to check chamber headspace. Be sure to strip all working parts from the bolt before inserting a gauge in the chamber.

Headspace is measured differently for cases that have no rim or belt. In the instance of rimless cases with a shoulder, headspace is measured from the bolt face to a datum point (of given diameter per each cartridge) on the chamber's shoulder area. This method is used for cartridges such as the .222 Remington, .270 Winchester, .30-06 Springfield and the .358 Winchester. The fourth common method of headspace measurement is the distance from the bolt face to the end of a chamber for a straight case (the case mouth). This is the type of system used for cartridges as the .25 ACP, .380 ACP, 9mm Luger and .45 ACP.

The only practical method for measuring a chamber's actual headspace is to use headspace gauges of the correct caliber and size. The use of shim stock applied to the back end of a case can lead to a great many errors as the case will be of unknown dimension and vary among any given case selection.

As mentioned earlier, headspace gauges are available in three different sizes commonly called "go" gauge (minimum), "no go" gauge (maximum) and "field" gauge (very dangerous). These names have their roots in military origins. The chamber's acceptance of the "go" gauge indicates that the chamber is of sufficient depth with respect to headspace measurement to accept a cartridge that has a maximum headspace dimension. The chamber's acceptance of the "no go" gauge would indicate that the chamber's headspace measurement is excessive and that the firearm should be removed from service because of potential hazard to firearm and user.

The "field" gauge was one designed for use in the military field where presumably every firearm was needed. Firearms that accepted a "no go" gauge could be retained in use on an as needed basis. But a firearm that accepted the "field" gauge was promptly removed from service as it posed a very real and immediate hazard to its user and bystanders.

Thus, for general purposes, only the "go (minimum) and "no go" (maximum) chamber headspace gauges have a practical value.

Generally, there is a difference of 0.006-inch in length between a minimum and maximum gauge, depending on the specific caliber. The military "field" gauge was another 0.004-inch longer. Thus, it can be seen that there is very little difference in the size of a chamber large enough to be acceptable and one large enough to be considered potentially dangerous.

More importantly, a firearm's headspace dimension is not an absolute for all times. A firearm that sees abuse in the way of reloads loaded to a pressure only slightly higher than normal can, after an indefinite amount of use, slowly develop an increasing headspace measurement. This is caused by the locking lugs being repeatedly driven against the mating receiver surface under great pressure. Eventually, enough metal will be displaced to allow headspace to gradually increase. If the original firearm headspace dimension was midway between minimum and maximum, it will take a change of only 0.003-inch to change headspace from safe to dangerous. Compare this to the average thickness of a human hair which is 0.002-inch.

However, checking headspace is not merely a matter of dropping a headspace gauge into a firearm and closing the bolt or action. Headspace gauges are made of very hard steel and the rim area is not designed to necessarily allow for extractor clearance. Because checking headspace demands a very accurate feel of the firearm's bolt interaction with gauge and chamber, the presence of a spring-loaded, bolt-mounted ejector will interfere with an accurate appraisal of head space dimension. Headspace cannot be accurately gauged or felt if the firing pins under spring tension are left in the bolt and so on.

Caution: It is possible to permanently damage a bolt face, extractor, or ejector when using a headspace gauge. This is especially true of the smaller, lighter-dimensioned extractors used on many modern firearms. Therefore, before attempting to measure headspace, strip all working parts from the firearm's bolt. This includes extractors (with springs and plungers), extractor collars, bolt face contained ejectors (with springs and plungers), cocking pieces, firing pins, and firing pin springs.

Carefully clean, oil, and grease any residue and foreign material from the chamber and the headspace gauge. Ditto for the bolt lugs and their matching recesses in the receiver. Finally, clean the face of the bolt.

Drop the "go" headspace gauge into the chamber, gently closing the action. The action should fully close without any felt interference from the headspace gauge.

Now drop in the "no go" gauge. Gently begin to close the action. The action should never close fully on the "no go" gauge if the gun is to be considered safe for use. The degree of action closing will vary with the specific dimensions encountered in the individual chamber.

Make careful note of how far you can close the action. In this way, when headspace is again measured, you will be able to determine if the headspace dimension is growing larger. This can occur with extensive use or with ammunition that produces above-normal pressures.

Handloaders will do well to measure firearm headspace every one thousand rounds or so. Users of factory ammunition might be content with measuring every five thousand rounds. If a problem is suspected, check it immediately. Some of the warning signs that would indicate the need to check headspace are: Primers that partially back out of the case upon firing; cases with bright circumferential rings after firing; cases that give evidence of incipient splitting and so on.

Just as chambers must be within a very narrow range of headspace dimension, so must ammunition. If ammunition has too much headspace length it may not properly fit into the chamber of a firearm, preventing the action from being closed, or closed only with difficulty. If a cartridge has too little headspace it will be too short to be supported by the chamber and may rupture in the chamber when fired. With factory ammo, headspace of the cartridge is verified before it is packaged. However, with reloads, the ammunition you make should be carefully checked, except in the instance of rimmed or belted cartridges. Rims and belts are not dimensionally altered by the firing and reloading process, hence there is no need to be concerned with case headspace.

However, rimless cartridges, both bottleneck and straight styles, can have their headspace dimensions altered by firing and reloading. Cases stretch in length as they are repeatedly fired and reloaded. In the instance of straight rimless cartridge cases (Such as .32 ACP, 9mm Luger, .45 ACP), the case will stretch continuously until its headspace (measured from base of case to mouth of case) has become so long as to prevent proper chambering. To avoid this problem, a reloader will trim his cases back when they reach or exceed the suggested maximum length. And so long as he does not make the cases too short, headspace will be maintained. The only tool needed to check headspace dimensions on straight cases is a vernier or dial indicating caliper.

But for rimless bottleneck cases (such as .223 Remington, .243 Winchester, .270 Winchester, or .30-06 Springfield), headspace dimensions are from the base of the case to a specific datum line on the case shoulder. Headspace on these cartridges can be dangerously reduced by a resizing die of improper dimensions, a too thin shell holder or a combination of both. In that it takes only several thousandths of an inch to create a problem, it is best to carefully measure the headspace of all rimless bottleneck case reloads. This is easily done with a cartridge headspace gauge such as the one made by Forster.

Cartridge headspace gauges are chambers into which the loaded round is dropped. The rear of the chamber is finished in two steps. The lower step is a minimum headspace step. The loaded round should never drop below this level. The upper step is maximum headspace and a loaded round should never extend beyond flush with this step. The mouth end of the same die is used for gauging minimum and maximum cartridge length.

Every shooter should have firearm headspace gauges for each caliber rifle he owns. Some gauges will do double duty. A .30-06 gauge also works in a .270 Winchester, while .243 Winchester gauges are suitable for the .308 and .358 Winchester rounds. Every reloader should have a cartridge headspace gauge for every rimless bottleneck caliber for which he loads. Headspace gauges are among the most important gunsmithing tools and should be used frequently.

JOB 9
INSTALLING A DETACHABLE CLIP ON THE LONG-ACTION REMINGTON 700

The Remington 700 series bolt-actions are the single most popular rifles of type. Millions of owners have been quite satisfied with their 700s. However, there is a large number of owners who long for quick loading and unloading of a clip model rifle. Such hunters are often those who frequently change locales during a day's hunt. Popping a clip in and out of their rifle would be a welcome luxury.

It's not difficult to convert any long-action Remington 700 rifle, originally chambered for the .257 Roberts, .25-06 Remington, .264 Winchester Magnum, .270 Winchester, 7 x 57 Mauser, .280 Remington (7mm Express Remington), 7mm Remington Magnum, .30-06 Springfield, or the .300 Winchester Magnum, to a clip style rifle. Indeed, the only long-action 700s that are not convertible are the 300 H&H Magnum, 8mm Remington Magnum, .375 H&H Magnum and the .458 Winchester Magnum.

To begin the conversion, you will need a Kwik Klip

After removing the original Remington 700 hinged floorplate, position the Kwik Klip trigger guard and clip housing into the stock.

magazine conversion for the 700LA as made by Trexler Industries Inc. and sold by Brownell's. This unit consists of a one-piece trigger guard and clip holder and is factory fitted with a push lever clip release. Also included is a magazine suitable for any of the cartridges just mentioned and some often-essential spacer washers.

Remove the two action retaining screws on BDL or Classic models. (The 700 ADL can be fitted with the Kwik Klip but requires special inletting which will be discussed a bit later.) Remove the complete factory hinged floor plate, trigger guard, and magazine—setting them aside. Keep the two action screws. Set the barrelled action aside where it will not become damaged. If the original magazine box stayed in the stock, make sure to slip it out and set it aside.

With the clip removed from the replacement trigger guard

group, attempt to slip the trigger guard into place in the stock. Occasionally, it does not slip into position. If so, you will need to remove wood from the inside stock area which surrounds the clip housing of the trigger guard unit. Usually only the sides of the front half of the magazine mortise will require wood removal. This can be done with a wood rasp. Be sure not to hit the stock edges, top or bottom, when working with the rasp. An experienced person may prefer to use chisels to remove the excess wood. Be sure to remove only enough wood to allow easy entry of the replacement trigger guard.

When the trigger guard unit is properly fitted, place it in in the stock, holding it in position with one hand. Then insert the clip and insure that it goes in easily and snaps into position. If it does not, the housing is being distorted by pressure from the stock and more wood may need to be removed.

After the trigger guard unit is fitted properly, remove it and give any raw wood a coat or two of stock finish. When the finish has completely dried you can continue the job.

Place the barrelled action into the stock and put the Kwik Klip trigger guard unit into place. Check the action's bolt release to be sure it is properly working. Some rifles may require a bit of filing to get the bolt release to clear the replacement trigger guard. It's best to file the release because it is made of steel (and can be easily touch-up blued). The Kwik Klip trigger guard is aluminum and cannot be easily touched up if it is filed.

Now replace the guard screws snugly. Insert the clip. If it does not easily latch into the locked position you will need to add one or more washers between the rear trigger guard and stock. These washers are pre-drilled for ample action screw clearance. Do not add any more washers than necessary to have the clip lock smoothly into position.

Now manipulate the bolt carefully. If it binds or rubs against the clip you will need to add one or more washers between the front end of the trigger guard group and the stock. Like in the rear, those washers are positioned so that the action screw passes through them. It is unlikely that any installation should require more than a total of three washers. Most require only one.

The complete alteration should be checked for clearance behind the rear of the trigger guard. If the trigger guard binds tightly to the stock, repeated firing may cause the stock to split. There should be a few thousandths of an inch clearance between the wood and the rear of the trigger guard. If wood needs to be removed at this point, do so carefully with a suitable wood chisel. Don't forget to add stock finish over any exposed raw wood.

Customizing a 700LA with a detachable clip will enhance the gun's usefulness and add value. The new clip will hold four rounds, except with magnum calibers which hold three rounds.

The clip should always be loaded from the front end and the cartridges pushed to the rear under the clip ears. Do not attempt to snap cartridges down past the ears.

Because the Kwik Klip feeds each cartridge from a central position under the bolt (rather than feeding first from the right and then the left side), smooth feeding is assured. Indeed, a Kwik Klip could well solve some feeding problems

It may be necessary to use one or two special washers between the Kwik Klip trigger guard and clip housing, If the original trigger guard had a washer(s) under it, replace it with the washer supplied with the Kwik Klip.

encountered with varying length handloads.

The Kwik Klip will shorten up the length of a loaded round that can be used in the 700. Naturally, all factory ammo will fit, but handloads will need to be kept to a maximum overall length of approximately 3.240-inch.

Because the 700ADL model has no factory cut in the bottom of its stock (using instead a blind magazine) it will be necessary to carefully alter the stock. First, using a punch, drive out the washer that serves as a stop for the front action screw. Insert the punch through the top of the stock and, using repeated light blows of a mallet, carefully work the punch

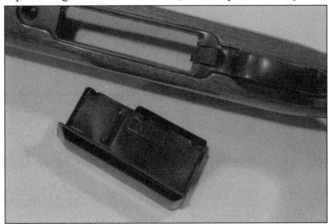

Make sure that the clip slips in and out of its housing easily before trying to reassemble the rifle. If it does not, it may be necessary to remove some wood, as described in the text.

Completely installed, the detachable clip adds a nice custom touch to any Remington 700 long-action rifle.

around the edge of the washer to drive it straight out.

Caution: If the washer is driven out at an angle or if unnecessary force is used, the stock could be split. Next, position the replacement trigger guard over the stock and trace its outline with a soft pencil. It will require great care, with the appropriate chisels, to inlet the stock to accept the new trigger guard. This is a job best undertaken by someone with some stock-making experience. Go slow and remove only a tiny bit of wood at a time. Be careful not to cause any spits or to cause the chisel to curl away too much wood. Stay well within your penciled outline until you have cut completely through the stock into the magazine mortise. By going slowly you will prevent unsightly gaps between the wood and the replacement trigger guard.

By carefully locating a number of holes and drilling through the stock into the magazine mortise, the job can be made easier. But this operation must be done very carefully.

Actually, the installation of a detachable clip into a 700 ADL stock makes a fine beginner's stock-making project. But such an effort is not without risk as less than careful work could result in a ruined stock.

JOB 10
INSTALLING APERTURE SIGHTS

Most shooters prefer a scope of low or medium power, or perhaps a variable power model, for shooting. However,

a scope is not always the best solution.

When it is known beforehand that the rifle (or shotgun) will see extensive abuse in the form of hard knocks and general banging around, and when it is known that the firearm will be used only at very short to modest ranges, an aperture (peep) sight may well prove the ideal choice. A good peep sight, will prove more rugged and will, in general, be a better sight than a cheaply made scope. And it will be less expensive.

A peep sight might prove far preferable to a scope on a rimfire rifle to be used on running rabbits or similar applications. Thus, the installation of peep sights will be a task performed by many serious individuals interested in gunsmithing.

There are a number of different mounting styles available with peep sights, depending to some extent, upon the model firearm. Some are as simple as slip-on dovetails and others require drilling and tapping two holes in the receiver.

Generally speaking, most older model firearms are pre-drilled for peep sights. This includes almost all rifles built prior to the early 1970s. Because most of today's shooters use scopes, the factory drilling and tapping of peep sight holes is done less often. Still some, such as the Marlin Model 336 carbines, are universally drilled and tapped. Also all current Marlin Model 39A and Winchester Model 94s are drilled and tapped as are many other rifle models.

The installation of a peep sight often means that the front sight on the rifle may have to be changed to a higher one. This

For a rifle that will see plenty of rough use, or will be limited to short range hunting, a good peep can prove to be the best possible sight selection. (Copyright 2003 Brownells)

can be checked before installation begins by simply taping the receiver sight to the firearm and attempting to adjust it to align with the open front and rear sights. If the peep will not adjust far enough downward then you know a higher front sight will be required. This can be accomplished with a higher bead or blade, a higher ramp, the addition of a riser between ramp and sight, or the addition of a ramp to a gun not so previously equipped.

For .22 rimfire rifles equipped with a dovetail designed to accept a scope mount, several dovetail aperture sights are available. Among these are the Williams Guide style sight and the Williams FP. The Guide sight incorporates a simple dovetail base which has another dovetail on top. Elevation adjustment is obtained by sliding the aperture housing up or down along this dovetail. A simple set screw locks the adjustment. Another set screw, when loosened, allows for windage adjustment. The FP model has 1/4-inch (at one hundred yards) click adjustment which can be positively locked once sighted in. Either of these sights are secured to the rifle by simply sliding them onto the dovetail of the rifle's receiver and locking a set screw. As with all aperture sights the most rearward position (on the receiver dovetail) is correct.

Invariably the use of a peep mounted via a .22's receiver dovetail will require a higher than normal front sight. Front sight replacement was discussed earlier in this chapter.

When installing a peep sight using factory drilled holes, such as on a Marlin .336 or a Winchester 94, remove the two factory filler screws from the peep sight mounting holes. Then carefully degrease the mounting screw holes and the mounting screws using a commercial pressurized solvent such as Rig #3. Next, install one of the peep sights and one of its mounting screws snugly. Insure that the screw does not protrude into the receiver or that, in the case of a blind hole, that it is not too long to prevent complete tightening of the aperture sight's base. Remove the one screw and repeat the procedure with the second screw. Shorten any screw that protrudes into the receiver (or bottoms in a blind hole) until it is flush with the receiver. This can be done with a small file. Be careful not to damage the screw's threads.

Place one drop of a screw locking compound on each screw and securely mount the base to the side of the gun. After the screws have been hand tightened, set each one by giving the screwdriver, while still positioned in the screw head, a light, sharp rap with a small hammer. This should enable you to gain another 1/8-inch turn or so on each screw. Then assemble the sight's staff to its base.

This Trijicon rifle sight is a self-luminous replacement sight. (Copyright 2003 Brownells)

12

BEDDING AN ACTION OR BARREL

edding, or the rebedding, of an action and/or barrel with one of the epoxy compounds (frequently called glass bedding) is a worthwhile undertaking for any rifle that, due to poor or faulty bedding, is not shooting as accurately as it could. The epoxy compound will not add some magic quality to the stock. It will, however, enable the average gunsmith to obtain a perfect fitting stock with only several hours of work, as opposed to perhaps forty to fifty hours of work by a highly skilled stockmaker. Thus, bedding a rifle in epoxy is a quick, highly accurate, and easy method to obtain a stock fit that otherwise would result in many hours of costly labor by a very skilled person. This perfect stock fit will, in turn, add a great deal of accuracy, if the stock originally did not fit well.

Obviously, epoxy bedding then puts a perfectly fitting stock within reach of almost every serious firearm owner. But before beginning the process of bedding, an understanding of the various styles of bedding systems is in order.

Universally, or nearly so, a firearm's action is bedded in epoxy to completely support the recoil lug and bottom area of

Brownells Glasbed provides and easy and almost "goof-proof" way to bed a rifle. (Copyright 2003 Brownells)

the front end of the receiver in a skin-tight sheath. This is to maintain a positive and uniform position of the action in the stock before, during, and after recoil, for as many shots as will be fired through the rifle.

Many firearm owners choose to bed the entire action in epoxy. This may add some strength to the stock and surely will help waterproof the inside of the entire receiver mortise. Also, this will prevent any possible action twisting or bending as action screws are tightened up.

The bedding of the barrel is sometimes done simultaneously with the action, depending upon the type of barrel support desired. Any simultaneous bedding will result in a full-bedded barrel with complete and total contact with the fore-end. However, this is perhaps the least desirable method with respect to accuracy.

Stockmakers have waded through a myriad of barrel bedding methods with respect to fore-end contact. Today, there are primarily three generally accepted methods. One is to apply some fore-end pressure. This is the system used by most commercial manufacturers. A small pad of wood, an inch or two from the fore-end, is left in the stock's barrel channel to supply upward pressure against the barrel. This is an effective bedding system but is subject to varying pressure by the

Epoxy bedding compounds are offered in rather simple kits, but care must be taken when using them to insure the desired results and to avoid ruining a stock. (Copyright 2003 Brownells)

fore-end against the barrel as the stock warps against, or away from, the barrel. Such warping is inevitable as the stock gains or loses moisture through months of storage, or even through a week of hunting in abnormally hot and dry weather, or perhaps three or four days of heavy rain. Thus, this method is seldom used by those who custom bed a barrelled action. These folks usually opt for one of two other methods that will provide a more uniform point of impact, season to season, year after year, let alone in heavy rain or hot dry spells.

One of the preferred methods is to bed the receiver and the first one or two inches of the chamber end of the barrel, leaving the remaining barrel free of any fore-end contact. This is effective, provides the desired stability for point of impact, and generally affords superior accuracy compared to pressure point bedding.

The third method is a variation of the second. In this procedure only the receiver is bedded, leaving the entire barrel free floating. Some shooters contend that this provides the best accuracy; others say there is no difference from the second method. A full coat of epoxy in the barrel channel, but not touching the barrel, is often used with this method to ensure fore-end stability, though some feel this step is unnecessary. Either of the last two methods should be selected when bedding in epoxy.

Generally speaking, epoxy bedding compounds require exact mixing. You cannot usually slow down or speed up the hardening process by using less or more of the catalyst (hardening compound). In fact, if the materials are not mixed exactly, hardening may not occur at all. Be very, very precise and follow the packaging instructions of the bedding material of your choice.

There are two basic consistencies for properly mixed bedding materials. One type has an oozing consistency that allows it to flow freely into recesses with excessive amounts bleeding out of stock/barrelled action junctions. This is an effective mixture, but a messy one. Excessive material must be cleaned up before the compound hardens or it will later take a great deal of effort to be cleaned up. The material can also ooze into places and crevices it was not intended to occupy. Basically, this type of compound represents, in my opinion, the early style of a satisfactory bedding material. One such compound is the excellent Acraglas sold by Brownells.

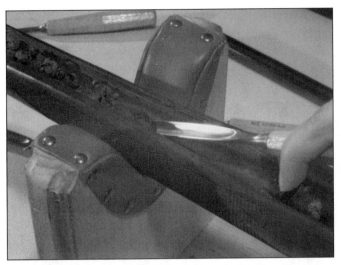

Stock inletting should be carefully don, with chisels and gouges. Do not be concerned with some inexactness as the bedding will fill in uneven areas.

Liberal use of a release agent is extremely important to prevent stock and barrelled action from being permanently glued together.

The non-running, non-dripping, gel-like materials, offer an easier-to-work-with material, with a great deal less mess, and often the avoidance of bedding compound flowing where it is not wanted. Because this style is easier to work with and as effective as those with a more liquid viscosity it is the type compound chosen for our discussion. Specifically, this text deals with the use of Acraglas-Gel, sold by Brownells.

INLETTING

Whether the stock is a new one being custom built or a factory stock being refitted, the inletting is important. You need not be precise nor exacting with the fit of the wood to metal. Nonetheless, a barrel channel that is irregular or grossly oversized will still be visible in the finished effort—regardless of how close you match the epoxy to the wood color. It pays to take great care. If the barrelled action and trigger guard do not screw together with some resemblance of a near proper fit, it will be difficult to get the action to seat to the right depth.

Inlet the stock so that you have approximately 1/16-inch space at all the wood-to-metal surfaces. A space of 1/32-inch where there are visible wood-to-metal seams is ideal around the action, barrel, and trigger guard edge. This will give a professional look to the finished job. There is no reason to be concerned with smooth internal wood surfaces as the bedding will fill in all uneven areas.

BEDDING THE BARREL

It will be necessary to first bed the barrel as a separate operation if free-floating is desired. Adequately cover the barrel and nearby action parts with several coats of release agent. Get plenty of release agent into the front action screw hole and on the screw itself. Allow ample drying time between coats. An extra coating of Simonize automobile wax on screw threads and in screw holes is a good safeguard. Just wipe on the wax, do not buff it.

Next, cover all outside stock areas with masking tape. Later, when the bedding material oozes out of the barrel channel, this tape will prevent it from ruining the stock and finish.

Then apply a liberal amount of properly mixed bedding compound (follow the manufacturer's instructions carefully) into the barrel channel. Screw the barrelled action, stock, and floor plate together and set aside to harden—approximately eighteen hours.

Caution: Do not use too much bedding material so as to cause it to squeeze excessively into the action mortise of the stock. Keep in mind that if an inadequate amount of the release agent is used on metal parts, the epoxy will glue the stock and barrel together in a manner that will prevent separating them unless you are willing to destroy the stock with an ax.

Before the bedding material sets in approximately five hours, remove the excess bedding material that has oozed out along the barrel channel. It can be peeled away with a sharp

All outside areas of the stock should be carefully masked to keep any oozing epoxy from the finished wood surface.

Apply a liberal, but not excessive, amount of epoxy to the surface areas to be bedded.

Allow ample drying time.

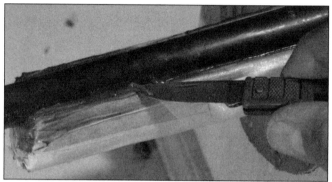

After five or six hours, remove excess bedding material with a sharp, wet knife blade.

knife. A wetted blade will help. Be extremely careful not to mar the barrel finish during this operation. Do not attempt to get a smooth, even fit at the top of the barrel channel at this time. Simply remove the major excess. You will sand the stock channel edges to a perfect fit later, when you remove the barrelled action.

After eighteen hours, remove the barrelled action from the stock and sand the edges of the barrel channel. Do this carefully and no refinishing of the wood will be necessary. Then remove the masking tape from the outside stock areas on the fore-end.

You should now have a perfectly bedded barrel channel. If there are minor voids in the epoxy, they can be ignored or filled. Major voids should, of course, be filled. This can be done by simply mixing a small bit of bedding material and placing only enough epoxy into the voids to precisely fit them without any run-over. Do not forget to get at least two coats of release agent on all metal and re-tape the stock if touch-ups are necessary. It's far better to get the job done perfectly the first time without having to make touch-ups.

After the barrel has been bedded, you need to bed the action while raising the barrel perhaps 1/32-inch to 1/16-inch off of the fore-end bedding to obtain the free-floating feature. This is the time to be certain that you have removed 1/32-inch to 1/16-inch of wood all around the recoil lug area of the stock mortise. It is important that the stock mortise has full bedding coverage in the recoil lug area.

At this point you are ready to begin bedding the action. Remove the trigger, bolt stop, and other action parts that might accidentally be glued into the stock mortise. All hollows, holes, recesses, and any other action area that might provide a river of flow for the bedding compound should be filled with putty or other inert material. It's not enough to simply put release compound in such areas because any pegs, claws or protrusions, formed by the bedding compound in any action recess or orifice, will permanently affix the action in place in the stock. Be sure any plugs are covered with suitable tape and that the tape is adequately covered with release compound. Sometimes tape and release compound can be used in place of undesirable disassembly.

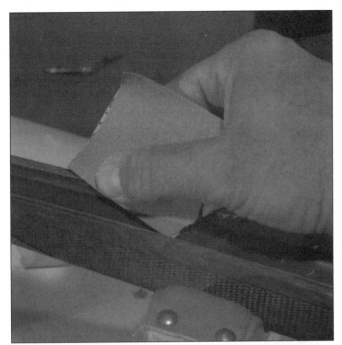

Carefully sand the edge of the epoxy to match all stock lines.

Carefully give all metal surfaces a double coat of release compound. Auto wax applied liberally on top of the release agent, is good for all screw holes and screws.

Before applying the epoxy it will be necessary to ensure that, when the barrelled action is in position, the barrel will be held at least 1/32-inch off of the bedding in the barrel channel. One way to do this is to apply several layers of heavy tape to the barrel, which will give a 1/32-inch or more thickness. The tape will need to be trimmed exactly at the receiver and then several coats of release compound should be applied to the tape. Or, shims can be placed in the bottom of the receiver mortise.

Be sure that all outside surfaces of the stock are protected with masking tape. Replace the tape previously removed at the rear of the barrel channel.

Next, apply the bedding compound to the action mortise. Use enough to fill all voids but not so much to cause displacement into the magazine, trigger, and safety or bolt release areas of the mortise. Any bedding that flows into these areas will need to be removed later. Be especially careful at the receiver/barrel joint area. Because of the 1/32-inch or more space created by the tape on the barrel, some bedding material may find its way into this area. When the job is complete you will need to clean up any such "flash."

Be certain—and this cannot be over emphasized—that you have adequately filled all action recesses with putty and adequately covered all metal parts and any tape with two coats of release compound.

Caution: Allow adequate time for the release compound to dry between coats and after the final covering.

Assemble the barrelled action, turning up the front action screw, but not enough to cause any bending of the action or barrel. A firm, one-handed hold on the screwdriver will provide adequate tension. The rear action screw should not be as tight.

After about five hours, remove any excessive bedding material from outside areas in the magazine well or on action parts. Then let the bedding harden for eighteen hours.

After disassembling the barrelled action, clean away all surplus material, trim and sand the action edges. Finally, remove all tape from the stock and the barrel.

Now assemble any removed parts such as the trigger, safety, magazine, bolt release, and so on. Check that all moving parts work properly. It may be necessary to remove bedding material around moving parts if any interference is detectable. This can be done with wood chisels or rasps and sand paper. The properly bedded stock will afford a skin-tight fit to the action, with the barrel free-floating.

If, for some reason, the free-floated barrel will not group as well as when it was pressure-bedded in the wood stock, you can add a small pad of glass bedding material to the barrel channel (perhaps a one-inch long pad approximately one to two inches behind the tip of the fore-end or fore-end cap/stock junction). A height of about 1/8-inch height will be right. Allow this pad to completely harden without the barrelled action in place. Then, using a trial and error method, you can sand down the glass pad a bit and try for accuracy until you are satisfied.

Caution: While the bedding material will appear quite hard after eighteen hours or so, it is recommended that the rifle not be used for sixty hours to ensure that full hardness has been obtained.

Special Note: For added strength, some folks like to add powdered aluminum or steel to the action bedding compound. This should only be done in exact accordance with the bedding manufacturer's instructions.

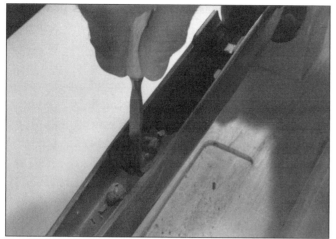

To bed the action, remove sufficient wood from the recoil lug mortise to ensure full coverage of bedding compound. This is important for accuracy.

When bedding the action, tape the barrel to a thickness of 1/32-inch to get the desired free-floating barrel channel. Then apply release compound to the tape.

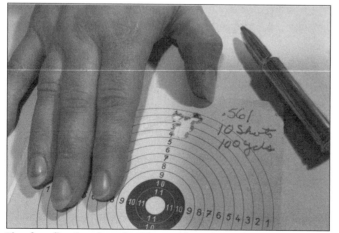

The free-floating barrel will provide enhanced accuracy and a non-shifting point of impact.

Good bedding material will provide an acid-proof, waterproof, solvent-proof surface that is not only durable but also very stable. It's not damaged easily and will provide the maximum accuracy potential with respect to proper bedding. Thus, epoxy bedding is extremely desirable. However, it cannot correct a bad barrel, poor ammunition, faulty sighting equipment or a lack of marksmanship.

If you are building a custom stock, chances are that glass bedding will enable you to get a perfect fit of wood and metal on your first attempt. That's something only a true expert can get after years of stock-making experience. All in all, learning to bed rifles in epoxy is a very worthwhile undertaking.

FITTING AND BEDDING SYNTHETIC STOCKS

After-market synthetic stocks are popular with shooters. Sometimes these are not the easy bolt-on additions we are lead to believe. But adding any of these stocks is an undertaking easily accomplished by anyone who is capable of bedding a barrelled action using one of the epoxy compounds.

The synthetic stocks can be installed rapidly. Simply sand or chisel away any tight spots to obtain a drop-in fit. Then, if the receiver recoil lug area does not appear to be snug, glass bed that portion of the new stock following procedures outlined in this chapter. I have installed "Six" stocks on Remington 700s without any difficulty other than relieving a bit of stock material around the magazine housing.

A Six Enterprises synthetic stock was installed on an extremely accurate Model 70 Winchester. To ensure that maximum accuracy potential was realized, the action area was fully glass bedded. When completed, the job resulted in a reduction of the rifle's weight and a slight gain in its accuracy which had been quite good to start. The Six Enterprises stock also added a good deal of usefulness to the rifle as it has a fold-away (and disappearing) bipod built into the forend. This restocking proved very worthwhile indeed.

13

SCOPE INSTALLATION

When the manufacturer has drilled and tapped a rifle for the mounting of a scope base, installation of a scope is a snap, right? Well, not necessarily. There are quite a few gremlins that can creep into what should be an easy task. Knowing beforehand all the factors that can cause the job to go wrong, may keep your work rolling as intended.

REMOVING PLUG SCREWS

Starting with removing the plug screws presents no potential problems, except if the factory cross threaded one. This is not a common occurrence.

But the screws used for mounting the scope base can be potential sources of trouble. It is essential to ensure that each is not unnecessarily long. A screw that is too long may bottom in a blind hole (one that does not go completely through the receiver) and lose any fastening power. Additionally, screw lengths must not be too long to protrude from through-holes. Screws protruding into the receiver can interfere with the bolt or other moving parts.

To determine if screws are too long for blind holes, install them one at a time with the mount base in position, and be sure

Be sure mounting screws are not overly long. Check each screw one at a time as described in the text.

that the base can be tightened securely with only the one screw. Then remove the screw and repeat the procedure with the next screw and blind hole. Shorten screws as required. Screws for through-holes should be checked for protrusion. Trim these screws, as required, so that they will be flush with the receiver.

As screws are checked, set them aside carefully so that,

later, they may be installed into the same screw hole in which they were checked. Excessively short screws should be replaced. It's best to ensure that the screw is long enough to supply at least four full turns in the hole's threads. Fewer turns can result in insufficient holding power or may cause screw threads to strip when the screw is securely tightened.

LEVELING THE MOUNT

Next, if a two-piece mount is used, ensure that the front and rear bases are level with one another. Check by first leveling the gun, then one of the temporarily installed bases. Then place the level across both temporarily-installed bases. If they are not level, it may be difficult or even impossible to sight in the rifle. Worse, you may damage the scope tube when everything is finally tightened up.

If the mounting base is not level, place a properly shaped and drilled piece of shim stock under it.

If a one-piece base is used it must not be bent as it is tightened. First, tighten the two front screws securely. Then look for space under the rear end of the base. Repeat the process with the front screws removed and the rear screw tightened, looking for space between the bottom of the front end of the base and the receiver.

If the mounting bases are not level, or if a one-piece base cannot be tightened without bending it, you will need to replace the base(s) or shim the offending base or base end, or alter the base(s)

as required. Do not proceed with the job until the bases fit perfectly.

To shim a base or base end, do so with a single thickness of shim stock rather than a build-up of multiple thinner shims. This will ensure the best-looking job and help eliminate any potential for it to loosen later on.

The best quality mounting job is attained by using a scope base that fits properly. However, due to variations in factory receiver dimensions, this is not always possible. But do not be too quick to blame the firearm manufacturer. I have encountered more faulty bases than I have faulty receivers.

When base(s), and shims if necessary, have been verified with respect to proper fit, remove all screws and bases from the firearm. It is now necessary to properly clean and degrease each screw and screw hole. After this has been done, place a half-drop of a commercial screw lock on each screw. The Loc-Tite compound, available from Uncle Mike's as Gun-Tite, is ideal for this purpose.

INSTALLING BASES AND RINGS

Assemble each base using the pre-tested screws in the appropriate holes. Tighten all screws with a well-fitting screwdriver. Then place the screwdriver securely into each screw slot and lightly "set" the screws with a single light hammer blow to the screwdriver. Setting the screws should allow you to get an additional one-eighth to one-quarter turn on the screw.

Next, install the scope rings according to the manufacturer's instructions. Do not take any short cuts. For example, if a Redfield Jr. style mount is used, the front ring must be secured to a short length of appropriate diameter pipe, tubing, or steel stock. The ring then needs to be turned in and out of its dovetail in the base several times. Never use the scope to accomplish this task. At worst you could severely damage the scope; at best, you may cut some ugly scars into the scope tube.

Make certain that the front and rear rings are properly aligned. Use a short piece of pipe or steel stock to verify this alignment. Then remove the top half of the rings and lay the scope in place.

Keep in mind that the scope is just lying there and that it can easily be dropped or jarred loose. For this reason, it is a good idea to have securely clamped the rifle in an appropriate work station.

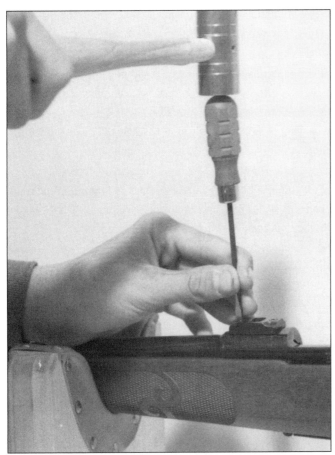

Setting base screws will give them that extra bit of tightness which will prevent them from becoming loose under recoil.

With the scope lying in position, determine that the scope's objective bell does not make contact with any part of the receiver, barrel, or open rear sights. Then make sure that the eye piece of the scope does not make contact with the bolt handle when it is manipulated, nor with any other part (such as the safety or rear receiver bridge). If contact is made between the scope and any part of the rifle, it will be necessary to replace the scope rings with higher ones.

Always mount the scope as low as possible. This enables quick alignment of eye and scope with appropriate stock support for the cheek. Higher rings mean less cheek support and this often leads to lost opportunities when a fast shot is needed.

Some dealers seem to have adopted a policy of not keeping low rings in inventory. The exclusive use of medium and high rings reduces inventory requirements and the frequency of a customer returning a too-low set of rings for higher ones.

EYE RELIEF

After scope clearance is assured, position the scope for correct eye relief. To do so, install the ring tops but do not tighten them. The most unprofessional aspect of scope installation is mounting the scope too far forward. Regrettably, due to many current scope designs, this seems to be an unsettling trend.

Keep in mind that when you're in shirt sleeves, a scope that is mounted comfortably, with respect to fore and aft position-

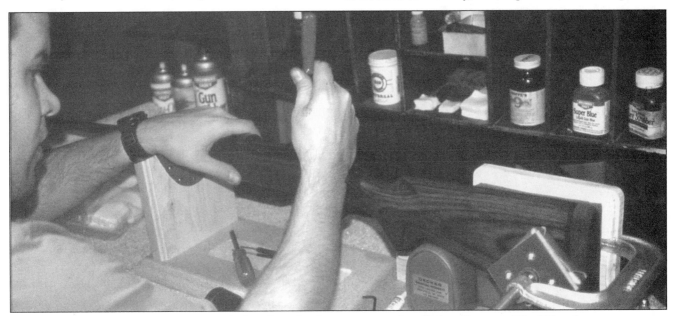

A Decker vise makes the ideal work station for scope-mount installation. (Courtesy: Mike Ahlman)

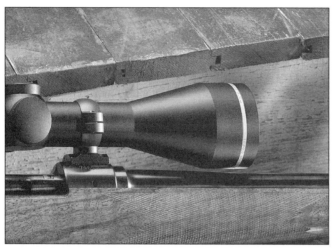

Proper scope installation demands adequate clearance between barrel and objective lens housing. (Courtesy: Leupold & Stevens, Inc.)

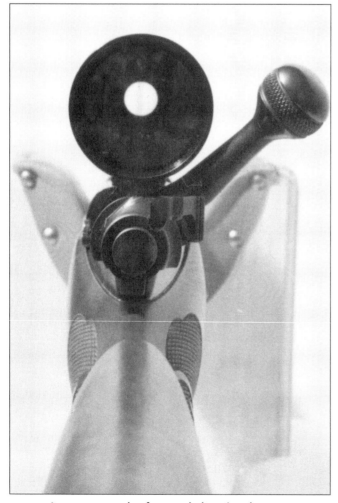

A proper example of proper bolt-action clearance.

ing, will be too far forward when you're in heavy clothing. Long underwear, a heavy wool shirt, an insulated vest, and a wool jacket can easily add a half-inch to three-quarter-inch in the effective eye-to-scope distance. If the gun is to be used with heavy clothes, mount the scope 5/8-inch farther to the rear then the ideal position in shirt sleeves. This mounting position will need to be tested by the user when fully dressed for the field.

Caution: When attempts to slide them fore and aft are made, scope tubes are easily scratched and marred if the rings are even modestly snug, do not properly align or have burrs. Be certain that the rings are loose, properly aligned, and burr-free. Make no attempt to slide or turn any scope in any ring if even the slightest resistance can be felt.

Scope, mount, and rifle combinations occasionally do not allow for sufficient rearward movement of the scope in the mount rings. If this occurs, use rings that extend the scope position. Extension front and/or rear rings are available in many brands and styles. Unfortunately, some brands of rings are available in only medium or high heights. But a slightly too-high scope is a lesser evil than one that is mounted too far forward.

ALIGNING CROSSHAIRS

Satisfied that proper eye relief (distance from eye to scope) has been obtained for the amount of clothing to be worn by the shooter, double check that the scope is still clear of all contact with the firearm. Then, turn up the ring screws using only light, two-finger pressure. At this point, the scope's horizontal cross hair must be made level with the true horizon when the gun is properly held (level) in a shooting position. This is often a trial and error undertaking. But there is a better way to get the job done.

First ensure that the firearm is level in the holding fixture. Then place a small level on top of the scope turret. Tighten the scope ring screws carefully to maintain the level position of the scope. But cross hairs and scope turret tops are not always perfectly aligned and, therefore, even this approach may not give the desired results.

Another way is to remove the bolt and insert a B-Square scope leveling jig into the recevier. Then carefully align the scope's vertical reticle with the jig's vertical scribe mark. Be

A well-mounted scope being as low as possible and having the proper eye relief positioning will handle effortlessly in the field. (Courtesy: Fiduccia Enterprises)

sure to hold the jig firmly against the bottom receiver rails as this adjustment is made. The use of the B-Square jig requires level receiver rails. It also requires some practice in being able to see its vertical scribe mark and the vertical cross hair simultaneously. But it is a talent quickly learned. This approach to scope levelling will eliminate any chances of a later determination that the scope's reticle is canted.

Scope ring screws should never be coated with any form of thread locking compound; some day it may prove necessary to change eye relief, scope, or rings. And if the ring screws are locked into place, it will not be possible to do so without severely damaging the scope.

Rings that have clamping screws on each side generally will not cause the scope to turn as they are tightened. Yet it's best to tighten screws evenly and progressively. Take up a slight amount on one screw at a time. When you have snugged up all the ring screws, verify that the scope is still level. When properly installed, the ring halves will have an identical gap between them on each side of the scope.

It is important that all screws and fasteners prevent base, ring, or scope movement which might otherwise occur under recoil or normal field-banging around. Always consider the future need to disassemble the scope rings and mount from the gun. You may decide that the scope was the wrong choice, that

Make sure the scope does not contact any open sights. (Courtesy: Leupold & Stevens, Inc.)

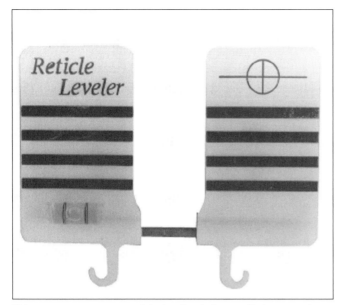

This easy-to-use scope reticle leveler, indexes off the scope base to help eliminate sight-in problems (Copyright 2003 Brownells)

the scope needs repairs, that the rings and/or base are unsatisfactory for one or a myriad of reasons, or that the firearm needs rebluing.

Screw locking compounds used on base screws are acceptable as there are ways of horsing these screws free. Several "setting" blows to the screws are often all that is needed to back them out of a receiver. And if the worst does come to pass, such screws can be drilled out if the rifle is held securely in a good drill aligning fixture, such as a Forster Universal Drill Jig.

Ring screws cannot be subject to such handling without a real risk of scope damage. Therefore, use only hand pressure with the appropriate screwdriver or Allen wrench when turning up any of these screws.

Hex head base screws, installed with a locking compound, frequently round out their wrench mating surfaces on the first attempt to remove them—that is if the wrench does not first round out its edges. I have serviced more than one receiver with a hopelessly stuck base. Oftentimes the owner gets one or two hex screws loose and the remaining ones defy extraction. On a few occasions, I've seen receivers that were totally ruined by frustrated owners who attempted to drill out a stubborn screw without a satisfactory drill aligning jig.

It's not any better with ring hex screws. Oftentimes the

hex size of these ring screws are small and the screw is too soft. Some wrenches are also sloppy with respect to dimensional tolerances and, sometimes, too soft. All this can lead to a rounded-out hex hole or wrench, and a screw that cannot be removed without drilling.

Hex screws can be satisfactory if they are of sufficient size to allow for an ample sized hex, and if they are hard enough to resist deformation, and made to very close tolerances. Even then the wrench used must be an exacting fit and of proper hardness. Yet, this all may still result in a rounded hex hole if it is not deep enough to allow for sufficient hex wrench purchase.

Properly made hex head screws and wrenches are rarer than a herd of stampeding elephants cutting through my back yard in their attempt to avoid my neighbor's tiny dog. For this reason I go very far out of my way to replace hex head screws with slotted ones.

If you are going to need to remove the scope and mount someday, or merely need to change eye relief, be very careful about the hex wrench style screws. Time spent replacing such screws can prevent a lot of grief later on.

Weaver style rings, or any that have ring tightening screws on only one side, will always result in the scope twisting (to the side of the rings on which the screws are located) as the screws are tightened. To compensate for this, deliberately cant the horizontal reticle low on the side away from the ring screws. The proper amount to cant the scope can be learned only by experience. Even then, it usually takes multiple tries to get the cross hair level. Do not overtighten this style ring as its less than one hundred percent circumferential purchase on the tube can cause some very unsightly dents in the scope tube when screws are stressed a bit too much.

Scope rings do not always supply a satisfactory fit to the ring bases. Carefully check, before scope mounting, that each ring is adequately tightened to the base. This problem occurs most often when rings and base are from different manufacturers.

Caution: Safe eye distance from the scope varies with the brand and style of scope. A scope of one brand may provide sufficient eye relief when the shooter has on heavy clothes and when the shooter wears only shirt sleeves. However, some scope designs will result in insufficient eye-to-scope distance when the shooter goes from heavy to light clothing. A slip-on recoil pad, used when shooting in light clothing, can provide the necessary increase in eye-to-scope distance to prevent potential serious injury. A scope's objective lens driven into the forehead, nose, or eye, under recoil, is no laughing matter. Be sure eye relief is correct beforehand. Make necessary adjustments as required before actually firing the rifle.

BORE-SIGHTING

The final step in scope installation is bore-sighting. This procedure aligns the cross hair with the bore so that they optically intersect on a distant target. This procedure ensures that the first shots fired will strike on, or near, the target at one hundred yards or so. It also ensures that there is no misalignment between bore and scope so it becomes impossible to sight in. Because such misalignment may mean it will be necessary to dismantle the rings and base from the firearm, it is essential to complete the bore-sighting task before any screw-locking compound sets up on base mounting screws.

Bore sighting can be accomplished by visually aligning the bore on a distant target and then adjusting the cross hairs to also align on the target. To accomplish this task it must be possible to look through the bore from the rear. Ideally, this means that the gun must have a conveniently removable bolt and open visual access from the rear of the gun through the bore. A bore-scope mirror can be used to look down the bore on firearms from which bolt removal is not practical. When aligned on the target, the gun must be held motionless while the scope is adjusted to place the reticle on the center of the target, as seen through the bore. All of this is possible, even

The use of a collimator is the best way to bore sight a rifle (or handgun) after scope installation. This compact, lightweight model by Leupold requires no metal spuds or batteries (Courtesy: Fiduccia Enterprises)

practical. But it is far easier and more concise to use a collimator to align the bore and scope.

A collimator is quick and easy to use. Lightly oil a collimator spud and insert it into the bore. Then attach the collimator to the spud. Next, while looking through the scope, square up the collimator's reticle with the scope reticle. Then adjust the scope reticle so that it coincides exactly with the collimator reticle. It's a fast, simple and very accurate way to bore sight a rifle. In most instances, a rifle bore-sighted with a collimator will put its first shots (at one hundred yards) within four inches or less of the aiming point. That can save the shooter from needless preliminary shooting at twenty-five and fifty yards, and a lot of ammunition to boot.

No rifle or handgun will perform accurately with an improperly installed scope and mount. Doing the job right takes only minutes longer than doing it sloppily.

PART 3

DISASSEMBLY, REPAIR, AND REASSEMBLY OF POPULAR FIREARMS

Firearms don't become popular unless they are well designed and manufactured. Some of the best remain in production for generations. A good many date back thirty, forty, fifty, or even almost one hundred years. The Winchester 94 and the Marlin 336, for example, trace their heritage back to the 1890s. The Browning A-5 semiautomatic has roots in the first half of this century.

In addition, there are more recent firearms whose excellence of design and manufacture have caused them to sell in the million of units. Examples are the Remington 870 pump shotgun, the Remington 1100 semiautomatic shotgun, and the Remington bolt-action high-powered rifles.

Because there are so many millions of these and other fine guns in use, some breakdowns will occur. After extensive use, even the finest firearms will require disassembly, if for no other reason than the need for a thorough cleaning.

The firearms selected for inclusion here are durable firearms which have become extremely popular. If you follow the advice and procedures given for each model, you will encounter no undue difficulty in disassembly, listed repairs, or reassembly.

Keep in mind that safety demands assuring yourself that any firearm you work on is unloaded. Safety also demands observance of every caution contained in the following pages. Whenever a doubt exists about safe procedure, it is best to consign the repair to a trained gunsmith.

In a single volume on home gunsmithing, obviously it's impossible to cover disassembly, common repairs, and reassembly of all the popular American sporting arms, let alone foreign arms, military rifles, and so on. I've chosen representative examples of popular American firearms on the basis of several criteria. In addition to popularity, practicality was a major element; some models would require far too many pages for adequate coverage and might involve procedures beyond the scope of the average home gunsmith. Still another criterion was similarity of mechanism. Additionally, so much as been written about some firearms that it would be superfluous to repeat it here. An example is the Winchester Model 70, which has been dissected, worked over, and microscopically examined in so many books and journals. I therefore chose the enormously popular but somewhat younger Remington 700 and Savage 110, rifles about which less has been written over the years.

Keep in mind that successful disassembly, repair, and reassembly requires that you proceed in a thoughtful manner, never infringing upon the safety aspects of a gun's design. And it is always advisable to read through the complete section about a specific firearm before beginning disassembly.

Every effort has been made to cover model variations, but manufacturers occasionally change specifications, designs, or parts. In some instances, changes may be very short-lived, and the passage of time will destroy any records of such temporary changes. So, if you encounter a slight variation, think the job through extra carefully. If doubt persists, consult an experienced gunsmith or the factory service department.

Parts nomenclature can be confusing. An "action-spring tube nut" may simply be a nut for the action-spring tube or some esoteric tubular-shaped nut. Whenever such doubt occurs, refer to the parts list and schematic drawing for clarification. Usually, however, any confusion will be eliminated by following the step-by-step procedures, with the gun in front of you, along with the accompanying drawings and photos.

14

REMINGTON 700 BOLT-ACTION RIFLE

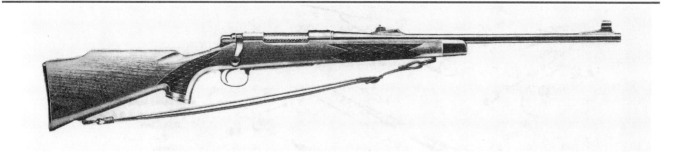

The Remington 700 series of centerfire bolt-action rifles is extremely popular and has an enviable reputation for fine accuracy and extreme durability. Shooters especially like the fine trigger. Often, 700 actions are used as the basis for building extremely accurate benchrest rifles.

The following information, while dealing specifically with the 700, can sometimes be applicable to earlier Remington rifles such as the 721, 722 or 725 models. While the Remington Model Seven is built along much smaller and lighter lines, it is also quite similar to the 700 with respect to disassembly, maintenance, and reassembly.

CYCLE OF OPERATION

The operation of the 700 is, of course, similar to many other bolt-action centerfire rifles. Pulling the bolt handle up and rearward until it stops, extracts, and ejects a fired case and cocks the firing pin. Pushing the bolt forward and down strips a round from the magazine, feeds it into the chamber and locks the action, once again readying the gun for firing.

As the bolt handle is raised, the locking lugs rotate in the receiver to a position that allows the bolt to be drawn rearward. The cocking of the firing mechanism is accomplished as the bolt handle is lifted. A cam at the rear of the bolt forces the firing pin assembly rearward, compressing the mainspring.

114

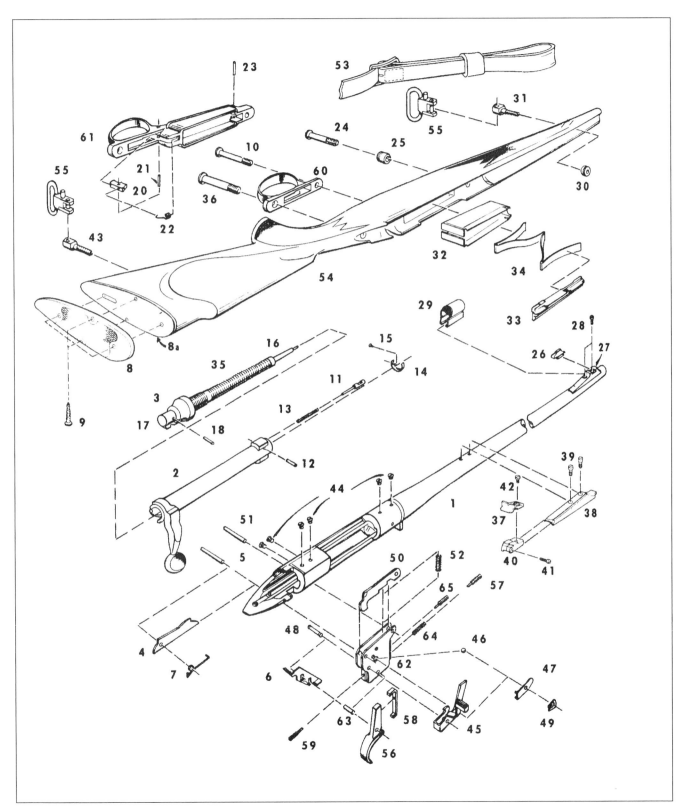

EXPLODED VIEW OF REMINGTON 700

REMINGTON 700

View No.	Part No.	Name of Part	View No.	Part No.	Name of Part	View No.	Part No.	Name of Part
1		barrel assembly	29	15363	front sight hood, BDL	52	17047	sear spring (R)
2		bolt assembly	30	15357	front swivel nut, BDL	53	30855	sling strap assembly, BDL
3	17012	bolt plug	31	15358	front swivel screw, BDL		26990	sling strap assembly and mountings complete
4	17013	bolt stop (R)		90957	grip cap, BDL (not shown)			
5	24475	bolt stop pin (R)		25380	grip cap screw	54	33366	stock assembly, ADL
6	15478	bolt stop release (R)		90958	grip cap spacer, BDL (not shown)		33371	stock assembly, BDL
7	15224	bolt stop spring (R)	32	15284	magazine, ADL		18186	stock reinforcing screw (not shown)
8	90953	buttplate		16430	magazine, BDL (not shown)			
8a	90954	buttplate spacer, BDL	33	90952	magazine follower		16970	stock refinishing screw dowel (not shown)
9	25380	buttplate screw		91017	magazine follower, BDL			
10	15287	center guard screw, ADL		15940	magazine tab screw, ADL	55	26555	swivel assembly, BD (Q.D.)
11	17017	ejector	34	17028	magazine spring	56	15280	trigger (R)
12	17676	ejector pin		15677	magazine spring, BDL	57	17053	trigger adjusting screw (R)
13	17019	ejector spring	35	17029	mainspring		26345	trigger assembly (R)
14	91816	extractor	36	26355	rear guard screw	58	19461	trigger connector (R)
15	15376	fastener, sling strap	37	32510	rear sight aperture	59	91128	trigger engagement screw (R)
16	22020	firing pin	38	91595	rear sight base	60	15281	trigger guard
17	22040	firing pin assembly	39	28505	rear sight base screw (2)	61	26376	trigger guard, BDL
18	17022	firing pin cross pin	40	90905	rear sight slide		26371	trigger guard assembly, BDL
20	15291	floor plate latch, BDL	41	90906	elevation screw	62	26655	trigger housing assembly (R)
21	16451	floor plate latch pin, BDL	42	90904	windage screw	63	24477	trigger pin (R)
22	16452	floor plate latch spring, BDL	43	15358	rear swivel screw, BDL	64	15400	trigger spring (R)
23	16453	floor plate pivot pin, BDL	44	17034	receiver plug screw	65	15481	trigger stop screw (R)
24	22035	front guard screw	45	26585	safety switch assembly (R)			
25	15161	front guard screw bushing, ADL	46	23222	safety switch detent ball (R)			
26	15373	front sight	47	15368	safety switch detent spring (R)			
	15719	front sight (low)	48	17043	safety switch pivot pin (R)			
27	28510	front sight ramp	49	17044	safety switch snap washer (R)			
	15635	front sight ramp, BDL	50	15666	sear safety cam (R)			
28	28505	front sight ramp screw	51	24476	sear pin (R)			

(R) = Restricted parts available only for factory installation.

NOTE: Basic .30-06 part numbers are listed. For other calibers, obtain the correct part number from the owner's manual.

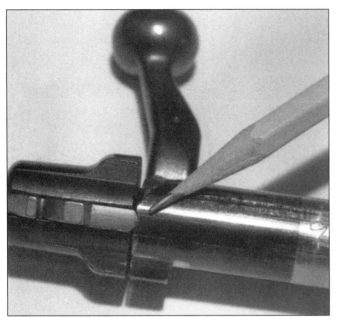

Fig. 14-1. The notch engagement holds the 700 bolt assembly in the cocked position while the bolt handle is in the upward position.

The assembly is held in the cocked position by a notch (see Fig. 14-1) on the rear of the bolt body. This engagement is held until the bolt handle is lowered on the closing of the action. Then the firing pin is held in its cocked position by the sear. Should the rifle's action be opened prior to firing, the sear's engagement will, upon the lifting of the bolt handle, be transferred to the bolt notch.

With the action closed and the safety lever in the forward (fire) position, the rifle is fired by pressing the trigger rearward. This, in turn, causes the trigger connector to move forward, leaving the sear unsupported against the cocked firing pin mechanism. The sear is then cammed downward by the pressure of the firing pin spring forcing the firing pin forward. As it nears the end of its downward travel the firing pin causes ignition of the cartridge.

The bolt handle is then raised, cocking the firing pin assembly. As the bolt handle is turned upward, primary extraction begins. The bolt's extractor, which has a firm purchase on the cartridge rim, is moved slightly rearward with the bolt as it cams from its locking surfaces. The secondary extraction takes places as the bolt moves rearward, the extractors purchase on the case causing the case to be withdrawn from the chamber.

The primary extraction occurs during the upward lift of the bolt handle which results in a rearward movement of the bolt assembly for a distance of about 1/8-inch. The mechanical advantage of this initial extraction is about eight to one.

A spring-loaded ejector, in the bolt face, maintains forward and outward pressure on the fired case as it is withdrawn from the chamber. This causes the right front edge of the cartridge to bear against the inside of the receiver as the bolt is drawn rearward. As the forward edge of the fired case clears the receiver and enters the ejection port area, the continuing pressure of the ejector causes the fired case to rotate to the right, free it from the extractor's grip and cause it to be ejected smartly in a general upward and outward direction. The rearward motion of the bolt is arrested by the bolt stop.

As the bolt is closed, the top edge of the rim of the uppermost cartridge in the magazine is engaged by the bottom front edge of the bolt. As the bolt is pushed forward, the cartridge in turn is pushed forward. At a given point in its forward movement the cartridge will free itself from the magazine (when it no longer is engaged by the ears of the magazine). It is then free to be pushed into the chamber by the bolt. The bolt is locked with its rear lug surfaces bearing on mating receiver surfaces when the bolt handle is closed.

On the Remington 700, and all similar Remington models, the head of the cartridge is completely enclosed by the bolt head when a cartridge is chambered, offering great strength in the support of the cartridge.

As the bolt handle is turned down, the cartridge's forward motion is arrested by mating surfaces in the chamber. This then causes the ejector to be compressed into the bolt face. Simultaneously, as the bolt is closed, the extractor snaps over the rim of the cartridge obtaining a very firm purchase on it.

Because the extractor does not grasp the cartridge until the bolt is locked into its final position, it is necessary to turn the bolt fully downward whenever working cartridges through the action, as when unloading ADL models or when checking feeding. If the bolt is drawn rearward before it is turned fully downward, the cartridge fed into the chamber will remain there even though the bolt is pulled rearward.

The safety switch is located at the right rear of the receiver. It is operated by rotating it rearward to engage the on-safe position. Rotating the safety fully forward places the rifle in the firing position. The safety can only be engaged when the

Fig. 14-2. Pressing in on the bolt stop release (located in the trigger guard) will allow the bolt to be withdrawn from the receiver.

action is cocked. The bolt handle can be opened when the rifle is on "safe", thereby adding to safety when manipulating the bolt of a loaded rifle.

However, the bolt handle can be inadvertently unlocked when hunting. If the bolt handle is in a partially lifted position when the trigger is pulled, the bolt will be forcefully rotated into the closed position. This may prevent the gun from firing when it is not properly locked. However, the gun may or may not fire the cartridge depending upon how much of the mainspring's stored energy is consumed in turning the bolt closed. This will be determined by the distance the bolt must rotate to properly lock the action.

The engagement of the safety when rotating rearward brings a cam into position beneath the sear safety cam. This locks the cam against the firing pin and prevents normal firing.

On earlier model Remingtons, an arm was moved into a slot to prevent the bolt from being opened, when the safety was applied.

BOLT-GROUP REMOVAL

With the safety switch in the forward fire position, lift the bolt handle up and draw the bolt rearward until it engages the bolt stop. Then press upward on the bolt stop release which is located in the trigger guard directly in front of the trigger (see Fig. 14-2). Holding the bolt stop release in a depressed position, withdraw the bolt from the rifle's receiver.

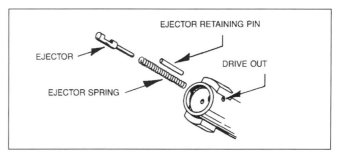

Fig. 14-3. Ejector, ejector spring, and ejector pin removal (caution - see text).

DISASSEMBLY OF EJECTOR GROUP FROM BOLT

If required, the ejector assembly is easily dismantled. The ejector and ejector spring are retained in the bolt face by a pin. Driving out the pin located in the bolt body (see Fig. 14-3) will free the ejector and its spring. *Caution:* The ejector and spring are heavily compressed, so carefully prevent their forceful exit from the bolt as the flying parts could cause injury or get lost. The ejection hole should be free from debris or burrs. The ejector should be clean and burr-free and must move freely in the bolt body for proper case ejection.

Reassembly is accomplished by placing the spring and ejector into the bolt and aligning the groove in the ejector with the pin hole. The ejector will need to be compressed into the bolt. Then drive in the retaining pin.

EXTRACTOR REMOVAL AND REPLACEMENT

The ejector pin, ejector spring, and ejector must be removed prior to any attempts to remove the extractor. Then drive the extractor rivet from the bolt using an appropriate size punch (see Fig. 14-4). Dislodge and remove the loosened extractor from the bolt rim. A small screwdriver is convenient for this operation.

The extractor rivet will probably be damaged when

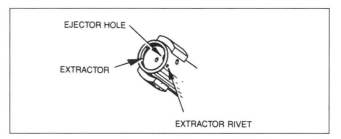

Fig. 14-4. Extractor and extractor rivet removal (caution - see text).

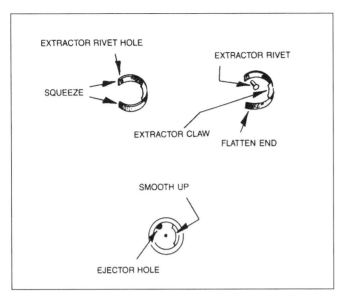

Fig. 14-5. Extractor and extractor rivet.

being removed. Therefore replace it with a new one when assembling the bolt.

Important: It is not normally required to remove any ejector or extractor parts unless these units are not functioning as intended. Normal cleaning can be accomplished with a tooth brush and solvent while these parts are assembled to the bolt body.

To reassemble the extractor, readjust the replacement extractor for proper tension before assembly. To do this, squeeze the ends of the extractor together slightly (see Fig. 14-5). Straighten the tail (flattened end) of the extractor. Place the extractor inside the rim of the bolt face. Be sure that the sloping area of the extractor claw is on the outside while the flattened side of the claw is on the inside. Align the hole in the extractor with the rivet hole in the bolt. Insert the extractor rivet.

Note: If the original extractor is replaced, squeezing the ends and straightening its tail (for proper tension) will probably be unnecessary.

Place support against the inside of the bolt rim and the head of the rivet. Then peen over the protruding end of the rivet. This will draw down the head on the rivet, tightening the extractor in the bolt. Smooth up the peening to eliminate interference as the outside surface of the bolt head contacts the receiver. The outside surface of the rivet should blend with the bolt body (see Fig. 14-5).

Check the extractor for proper tension with a fired case.

The extractor must grip the case firmly and hold the case in position when the bolt is held face downward. If the case is gripped too tightly (case snaps free with difficulty), tap the extractor back under the bolt rim, just a very small amount. Use a soft punch for this operation. Repeat this adjustment, if necessary, until the grip of the extractor is satisfactory.

If a fired case is gripped too lightly (falls away from extractor when bolt is held face downward), the extractor claw must be pulled from under the bolt rim to increase tension on the case. Disassembly and correcting the tension of the extractor may be required. After tension is correct, smooth up the face of the claw, using a suitable stone, to match the bolt rim (see Fig. 14-5). Then reassemble the ejector group to the bolt.

Note: An early-design caliber .222 Remington extractor used a snap-in unit requiring no rivet. These may be disassembled and reassembled by simply inserting a pointed tweezer into the holes provided in the ends of the extractor. When the tweezer is positioned in the holes, compress its ends together and lift the extractor out or into place.

FIRING-PIN GROUP REMOVAL

With the bolt cocked and firmly held in a padded vise, pull the firing pin head (see Fig. 14-6) rearward until a coin or washer can be inserted into the slot near the back edge of the firing pin head. This is somewhat difficult due to the need to compress the mainspring.

An alternate method is to grip the sear-engaging area of the firing pin head using a vise with hard, smooth jaws. Care must be taken not to cause damage. Then pull forward on the bolt body and slip a coin or washer into the groove as it is exposed.

The entire firing pin group can then be unscrewed from the bolt, but take care not to dislodge the coin (washer).

FIRING PIN GROUP DISASSEMBLY

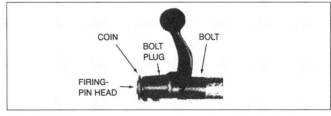

Fig. 14-6. Firing pin group removal from the bolt body *(caution - see text).*

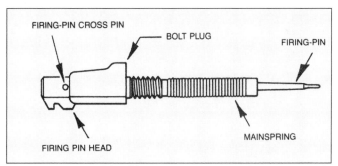

Fig. 14-7. Disassembly of firing pin components *(caution - see text)*.

Since the mainspring is under heavy compression, disassembly of this unit is, therefore, not recommended unless it is essential for the replacement of damaged parts. Suitable means must be employed to prevent the firing pin and/or firing pin head from causing personal or property injury due to sudden release.

Compress the mainspring by pushing forward on the bolt plug while the front end of the firing pin is held securely against a stop. The coin (washer) placed into position earlier will fall free and, with ample compression, the firing pin cross pin will be exposed. Another set of hands will be required to drive out the cross pin as you maintain pressure on the bolt plug. When the cross pin has been driven free, remove the punch and slowly release the compression of the mainspring by allowing the bolt plug to move gradually rearward. (See Fig. 14-7 for the relationship of the discussed parts).

Note: Complete firing pin assemblies are fully interchangeable (firing pin, mainspring, bolt plug, firing pin head and firing pin cross pin). However, the replacement of the firing-pin requires drilling a hole with a #42 drill (.093-inch).

To do this, assemble the shank of the replacement firing pin into the firing pin head. Be certain that the recess in the firing pin head is free of any debris or obstructions. Seat the shank of the replacement firing pin firmly into the firing pin head. While maintaining positive contact between the two parts, drill through the firing pin, entering and aligning the drill through the firing pin head hole. This must be done exactingly. The drill should not remove any material from the hole on either side of the firing pin head. If you have doubts, have an experienced professional do this part of the job.

Reassembly of the firing pin group and the bolt is accomplished in reverse order. Be careful with the parts as

mainspring tension is applied to drive in the firing pin cross pin. It will also be required to place a coin or washer for disassembly, in order to screw the firing pin assembly into the bolt body.

REMOVAL OF REAR SIGHT ASSEMBLY

Remove the windage and elevation screws and slide the rear sight aperture and slide from the rear sight base. Remove the two screws from the base and the base will fall free of the barrel. Reassemble in reverse order.

REMOVAL OF FRONT-SIGHT ASSEMBLY

Pry apart the bottom ears of the hood, slightly, until the hood can be slid forward from the sight base. Take care not to damage the metal finish.

REMOVAL OF BARRELED ACTION FROM STOCK

On BDL models, unscrew the trigger guard's front and rear screws. Then open the floor plate and unscrew the third action screw. For ADL models, remove forward-action screw and two trigger-guard screws. Remove trigger-guard or trigger-guard assembly. Lift away the stock.

On ADL models, the magazine spring and follower will be loose in the stock. On BDL models, they will be attached to the hinged floor plate and may be removed by sliding the spring away from its retaining grooves in the hinged floor plate. The magazine box on BDL models may remain in place (a friction fit) or may fall free from the action as the stock is removed. On ADL models, the magazine will be secured to the action with one small screw.

Because the trigger-guard assembly (BDL and Classic models) is made of aluminum, it is suggested that no attempt be made to remove the floorplate assembly. The pivot pin is very tight and if the trigger guard is not supported exactly the guard can be damaged when the pin is driven out of place.

TRIGGER ASSEMBLY WARNING

Note: Remington warns against any attempts to work on the trigger. All trigger parts are available only with factory installation.

COMMON PROBLEMS—PROBABLE CAUSES AND CORRECTIONS

Bolt Overrides Cartridges in Magazine

1. Magazine follower binds. *Adjust side angle on magazine box.*
2. Damaged follower spring. *Replace follower spring.*
3. Magazine spring caught under trigger guard. *Reposition spring.*
4. Tabs (ears) on follower bent. *Straighten tabs or replace follower.*

Cartridge Stems Chamber

1. Sharp or rough receiver rails. *Polish or file rails.*
2. Sharp edge, rear end of chamber. *Edge needs smoothing.*
3. Rough ramp in receiver. *Polish ramp.*
4. Magazine loose in receiver. *Adjust magazine box.*

Bolt Closes Hard Over Shells

1. Bolt interferes with shell rim. *Remove interference on bolt.*
2. Extractor interferes with shell rim. *Fit new extractor (grind relief in new extractor behind claw).*
3. Ejector binds or fails to retract far enough. *Free up or replace ejector.*
4. Burr at ejector hole on bolt. *Deburr hole.*
5. Sharp corners on bolt lugs. *File radius on lug corners.*
6. Extractor rivet loose. *Tighten or replace extractor rivet.*

Cartridge Fails to Extract

1. Tight or rough chamber. *Return to factory.*
2. Extractor broken or damaged. *Replace extractor.*
3. Not enough hook space on extractor. *Replace extractor.*
4. Height of claw not correct. *Replace extractor.*
5. Extractor stuck back in bolt recess. *Replace extractor.*

Cartridge Fails to Eject

1. Burr at ejector hole in bolt. *Deburr hole.*
2. Ejector binds or fails to retract far enough. *Free up or replace ejector.*
3. Extractor rivet loose. *Re-stake or replace rivet.*
4. Extractor drops shells. *Replace extractor.*

Gun Misfires

1. Short (damaged) firing-pin. *Replace firing-pin.*
2. Firing pin binds. *Free up or replace firing-pin.*
3. Short firing-pin protrusion. *Change firing-pin.*
4. Firing control out of adjustment. *Return the firearm to the factory.*
5. Faulty ammunition. *Test with a different lot of ammunition.*

Firing Pin Follows Down (Does Not Stay Cocked)

1. Trigger out of adjustment. *Return firearm to the factory.*
2. Improper vertical engagement of sear and connector. *Return firearm to the factory.*
3. Trigger does not retract. *Return firearm to the factory.*
4. Corners on sear or connector rounded. *Return firearm to the factory.*
5. Trigger binds on trigger guard. *File trigger guard.*
6. Not enough tension on weight screw (light pull). *Return firearm to the factory.*

Bolt Opens Hard
See section on "Cartridge Fails to Extract"

1. Upset extraction cam on bolt handle. *Smooth up cam surface.*
2. Burr at ejector hole in bolt. *Deburr hole.*
3. Blown or set back primer on shell. *Return firearm to factory.*

Bolt Pulls Out of Action When Manipulated

1. Bolt stop or bolt release binds or is broken. *Return firearm to the factory.*

Safety Switch Works Too Hard or Too Freely

1. Safety switch binds (works hard) or safety switch snap washer is stretched out (safety switch works too freely). *Return firearm to the factory.*

Bulges or Blown Cases

1. Oversize chamber. *Change barrel or barrel and receiver assembly (factory job).*
2. Maximum headspace (ammunition may be at fault). *Fit new bolt (factory job).*

Bolt Binds

1. Guard screws protrude into bolt track. *File ends of screws.*
2. Scope screws protrude into bolt track. *File ends of screws.*
3. Bolt-handle interference on stock. *Alter or replace stock.*
4. Step at rear of bolt lugs. *File to blend.*

Rifle Does Not Group Well

1. Crown of barrel damaged. *Recrown barrel.*
2. Fouling in bore. *Remove fouling.*
3. Oversize bore. *Change barrel (factory job).*
4. Improper bedding of barrel in stock. *Correct bedding or replace stock.*
5. Loose sight. *Tighten or replace sights.*

Note: For the correction of all other problems except those of a minor nature, the rifle should be returned to the manufacturer's service department.

15

REMINGTON 1100 SEMIAUTOMATIC SHOTGUN

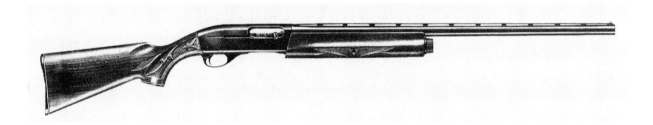

The Remington Model 1100 semiautomatic shotgun is without a doubt the most popular autoloading shotgun ever produced. There are many millions in use and these give superb service when properly maintained. The 1100 action is operated by exhausting a tiny amount of powder gases downward through two holes located in the barrel near the front of the fore-end. (Only one hole is used for 3-inch Magnum guns.) These tapped gases then cause a series of part movements which cycle the firearm's action.

The 1100 has been made available in 12, 16, 20, 28 and .410 gauges. In 12-gauge and 20-gauge models chambered for 2³/₄-inch shells, any shell of that length, from light target loads to short magnums, may be used without adjustment to the shotgun. The 3-inch Magnum barrels (12- and 20-gauge) will allow the shotgun to function properly with any 3-inch shell or with 2³/₄-inch Magnum loads. The 28-gauge model accepts all 2³/₄-inch ammunition, while the .410 model accepts both 2¹/₂-inch and 3-inch ammunition.

There is a difference in parts, including barrels, between older model 20-gauge guns (built on 12-gauge size frames) and the new 20-gauge Lightweight (LW) models. And 3-inch Magnum parts are sometimes different from 2¾-inch shell models.

CYCLE OF OPERATION

The 1100 is operated by the energy from a small amount of the propellant gases metered from one or two mid-bore orifices. The barrel does not move during cycling and, thus, the 1100 does not have a barrel that recoils first rearward and then forward. The gas from the barrel enters into the gas cylinder and accelerates a piston device within the fore-end. Excess gases, not needed to operate the piston, are automatically vented. The pressure of the gases imparts a rearward thrust to the piston which in turn pushes upon the action-bar sleeve, causing the action-bar assembly to move the breech block rearward. The rearward movement of the action parts stores energy into the return spring (located in the buttstock) by causing it to be compressed. The release of this energy is what forces the bolt forward to feed a cartridge and close the action, ready for firing.

The actual series of functions and manipulations that operate the 1100 begin with the loading procedure. Withdraw the bolt until it is locked in its rearward position. Place the safety button into the "on-safe" position. A shell is then simply dropped into the ejection port and the carrier release button, located just ahead of the trigger guard, is pressed. This causes the bolt to start forward and for the cartridge in the ejection port to be raised up into the loading position by the shell carrier. The cartridge is pushed forward, chambered, and the bolt is locked into battery position.

As many as four shells may then be loaded into the magazine by pushing them into place through the loading port in front of the trigger guard. Proper manipulation is to compress the carrier-release button with the nose of the shell. This will allow the cartridge carrier to be pressed upward into the action, allowing room for the shell to enter the receiver (see Fig. 17-1) and then to be pushed into the magazine tube. Be sure the shell is pushed well into the magazine so that the cartridge stop can snap into place behind it and secure it properly.

Pressing the cartridge latch with the shell nose, pushing the shell carrier up into the receiver and the continuing motion of pushing the shell into the magazine, should be one fluid

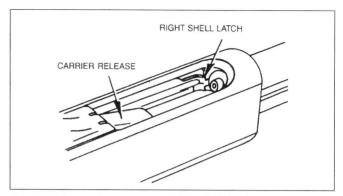

Fig. 17-1. The carrier release and right shell latch locations in the bottom receiver opening.

motion. The 1100 loads easily and any fumbling of the loading process is a sure sign that the shooter is not familiar with proper manipulation of it.

The 1100 is now ready to fire, once the safety button is pushed to the "fire" position (from right to left). The gun is fired, naturally, by pulling the trigger. When the trigger is pressed rearward, the top section of the trigger rotates forward carrying the connector, in its ready position, forward against the sear. This movement pivots the sear out of engagement with the hammer. The hammer is then free to rotate forward under compression of its spring and plunger. As the hammer rapidly moves forward it strikes the firing pin. The firing pin in turn moves forward to ignite the cartridge. The firing pin spring is compressed as the pin moves forward. After the cartridge ignites, the spring's stored energy is used to return the firing pin to its retracted mode.

Just before the firing pin reaches the primer, the upward motion of the hammer plunger engages the disconnector. This engagement causes the disconnector to rotate so that its forward end is lowered from position at the rear of the left action bar and cams the left shell latch to release the next shell in the magazine. The rear section of the disconnector rises with the sear. Now the gun cannot be fired again until the breech block cycles fully and the trigger is released. Once the trigger is released, the disconnector seats behind the left action bar and the connector to again make contact with the sear.

The two-way performance of the disconnector is an important safety feature which demands that the breech bolt be fully locked and the trigger released before the sear can be released again for succeeding shots to be fired.

As the bolt moves rearward after firing, unlocking, extraction, ejection, and cocking cycles are accomplished. Described in detail, these occur as follows:

Unlocking occurs with the initial rearward movement of the action-bar sleeve causing the slide block to move to the rear of the bolt. As the slide block moves to the rear of the bolt it cams the locking block away from the mating shoulder of the barrel extension. This unlocks the action and cams the firing pin fully rearward preventing the firing pin from protruding from the bolt face.

Extraction occurs when further movement of the action bar moves the bolt rearward. The extractor's purchase on the shell rim holds the shell against the bolt face thus causing it to be extracted from the chamber.

As the bolt moves rearward, it forces the hammer to rotate downward, compressing its coiling mainspring and causing its mating notch surface to engage the sear. Pressure of the sear spring locks the sear in this position.

When the shell impacts against the ejector located on the left rear side of the barrel, the shell pivots free off the extractor, escaping out the ejection port.

The rearward motion of the action-bar assembly and sleeve carries the breech bolt and locking lug until the motion is terminated with full compression of the action spring. The action bar assembly then begins its forward movement carrying with it the breech bolt and locking block. The entire unit moves forward only a small distance when it is intercepted and stopped by the carrier dog, which is attached to the rear of the carrier. The carrier dog engages a notch on the bottom of the action bar.

The shell that was released from the magazine under spring pressure, moves swiftly rearward while the interceptor latch prevents another shell from escaping the magazine. The shell carrier remains in its bottom (normal) position, held by the carrier latch, until the head of the shell, moving rearward, impacts the carrier latch causing it to pivot out of engagement and to release the carrier.

The released carrier is then forced upward by the carrier dog which simultaneously frees the action bar assembly, action bar sleeve, bolt, and locking lug to move forward under pressure of the compressed mainspring.

As the action closes, the upraised carrier holds the shell in position so that the advancing bolt face contacts the rear of the shell rim, pushing the shell forward into the chamber. The carrier dog is released from pressure by the passing action bar assembly and is forced upward by the carrier dog follower and spring. This movement pivots the carrier downward into its normal depressed position. The disconnector, relieved from pressure by the left action bar, releases the depressed interceptor latch, enabling it to rotate. This allows the shell it was retaining in the magazine to move rearward until the shell's rim contacts the feeding latch, arresting the shell's motion. This shell is then held in place until the next feeding cycle.

As the bolt completes its forward travel and stops, the travel of the slide block beneath the bolt continues—camming the locking block into the recoil shoulder of the barrel. The locking block, when fully engaged by the recoil shoulder, locks the bolt face securely against the chambered shell, and it is held in this position by the slide block as it reaches its forward-most position.

When the locking block is fully rotated into position, a passageway through the bolt aligns to allow for proper protrusion of the firing pin (when struck by the hammer) to ignite the chambered shell. All forward motion is curtailed when the slide block comes to rest within and against the front section of the bolt.

When the action is so fully locked, the disconnector clears the end of the left action bar. The spring-actuated connector is then released and drops into position to connect the notch on the sear. When this is completed, the action bar sleeve pushes the piston and piston seal into a forward position against the barrel seal in the gas cylinder. The shotgun is now ready to begin its operating cycle anew, when the trigger is once again pulled rearward. But, before this can occur, the trigger must be released from its rearward position (from the last firing). When the trigger is released, it moves forward rotating its top half rearward. The gun is now ready to fire.

After the last shell has been fed from the magazine and fired, the cycle of operation differs and retains the bolt in its rearward, open action position. This occurs because when a shell is not fed from the magazine to in-turn impact the carrier latch, the carrier latch cannot be actuated with the carrier. Therefore, locked in its down position, the carrier dog remains engaged with the action-barrel assembly, thus locking the gun in the open position.

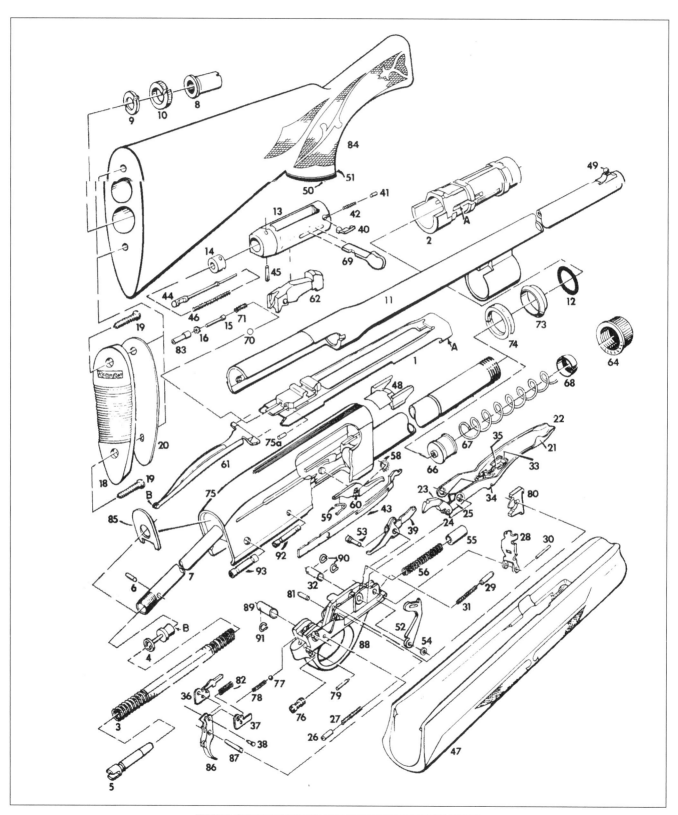

EXPLODED VIEW OF REMINGTON 1100

The exploded view drawing and the following parts list are for 12-gauge field model 1100s.
For other gauges or models, refer to the owner's manual or contact Remington.

View No.	Part No.	Name of Part	View No.	Part No.	Name of Part	View No.	Part No.	Name of Part
1	33950	action bar assembly	36	17419	connector, left (R)	68	91657	magazine spring retainer
2	15241	action bar sleeve	37	17551	connector, right (R)	69	91197	operating handle
3	15252	action spring	38	17420	connector pin (R)	70	23222	operating handle detent ball
4	15171	action spring follower	39	92060	disconnector	71	91200	operating handle detent spring
5	15440	action spring plug	40	16176	extractor	73	15384	piston
6	15441	action spring plug pin	41	17432	extractor plunger	74	15385	piston seal
7	15443	action spring tube	42	17433	extractor spring	75	26080	receiver assembly (R)
8	15442	action spring tube nut	43	26630	feed latch	75a	17676	return plunger retaining pin
9	15498	action spring tube nut washer	44	17436	firing pin	76	25115	safety switch
10	15499	action spring tube nut lock washer	45	18623	firing pin retaining pin	77	23223	safety switch detent ball
11		barrel assembly	46	15702	firing pin retractor spring	78	17514	safety switch spring
	Note:	Please list choke needed.	47	26870	fore-end assembly, 12-gauge	79	17515	safety switch spring retaining pin
12	15899	barrel seal	48	91658	fore-end support	80	18750	sear
13	15738	breech bolt	49	27730	front sight—for vent rib use	81	17463	sear pin
	26865	breech bolt assembly			No. 18796	82	17518	sear pin
14	15172	breech bolt buffer		27725	front sight base, 12-gauge	83	91198	slide block buffer
15	91199	breech bolt return plunger	50	15388	grip cap	84	34770	stock assembly
16	5711	breech bolt return plunger		15390	grip cap inlay	85	19993	stock bearing plate
		retaining pin		15757	grip cap screw	86	25370	trigger (R)
18	20616	butt plate	51	15389	grip cap spacer		20610	trigger assembly (R)
19	25410	butt plate screw	52	15249	hammer	87	17533	trigger pin
20	15387	butt plate spacer	53	16600	hammer pin	88	26235	trigger plate, R.H.
21	15628	carrier	54	15809	hammer pin washer		26236	trigger plate, L.H. (for R.H. gun)
22	26875	carrier assembly, 12-gauge	55	17465	hammer plunger		27300	trigger plate assembly, R.H.
23	15480	carrier dog	56	19014	hammer spring		27301	trigger plate assembly,
24	18781	carrier dog pin	58	15398	interceptor latch retainer			L.H. (for R.H. gun)
25	18760	carrier dog washer	59	15383	interceptor latch spring	89	17541	trigger plate pin bushing
26	17416	carrier dog follower	60	26635	interceptor latch	90	17539	trigger plate pin detent
27	17415	carrier dog follower spring	61	26075	link			spring, front (need 2)
28	15257	carrier latch	62	26640	locking block assembly	91	17540	trigger plate pin detent
29	15703	carrier latch follower		15855	locking block retainer			spring, rear
30	16345	carrier latch pin	64	15239	magazine cap	92	20601	trigger plate pin, front
31	16966	carrier latch spring		91078	magazine cap detent	93	20606	trigger plate pin, rear
32	90295	carrier pivot tube		15892	magazine cap detent spring			
33	16347	carrier release (action release)	66	2225	magazine follower			
34	16983	carrier release pin		18097	magazine plug (3-shot)			
35	16327	carrier release spring	67	15382	magazine spring			

R=Restricted part, available only for
factory installation.

If the gun is not once again loaded, the action can be closed by depressing the carrier release.

To unload the shotgun without firing a shell, start by placing the safety in the "on" position. Pull the operating handle fully rearward and the chambered shell will be extracted and ejected. The bolt will then lock in the rearward position. Depressing the carrier release will feed another shell and close the bolt. Continue repeating the process until the last shell has been ejected.

REMOVING THE FORE-END ASSEMBLY AND BARREL

Unscrew the magazine cap and simply slide the fore-end assembly forward. No further disassembly of the fore-end unit is suggested. If one or more parts needs replacement, replace the entire unit.

With the action closed, grab the barrel above the gas cylinder and pull forward to remove the barrel and free it from the magazine tube. *Caution:* Do not allow the action to slam closed while the barrel is removed. Doing so can damage the shotgun.

No attempt should be make to remove the ejector or front sight base from the barrel. These are factory assembled and brazed or silver soldered to the barrel. Factory replacement of these parts is urged.

REMOVING THE BARREL SEAL AND PISTON

With the action opened, grasp the barrel seal, piston, and piston seal (as a unit) and slide these three components forward off of the magazine. Use a quick but smooth motion.

REMOVING THE OPERATING HANDLE

Gently close the action, easing the bolt forward. Then grip the operating handle and, applying adequate pressure, pull it outward from the bolt. The operating handle is held in place with a detent and plunger arrangement. The operating handle will resist movement until sufficient pressure is applied to "snap" it free.

Fig. 17-2. Removal of the fore-end assembly: Simply pull the fore-end forward after removing magazine cap.

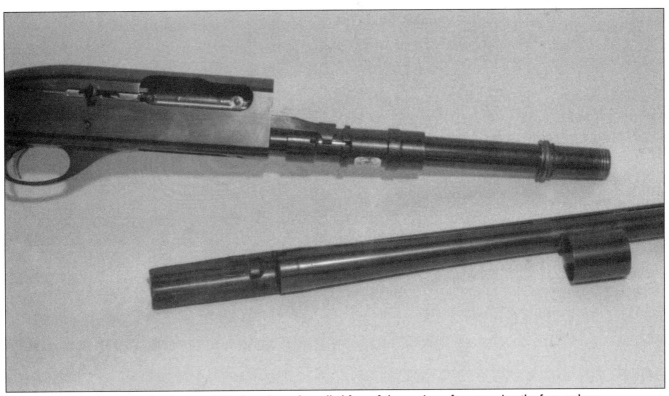

Fig. 17-3. Removing the barrel. The barrel may be pulled free of the receiver after removing the fore-end cap.

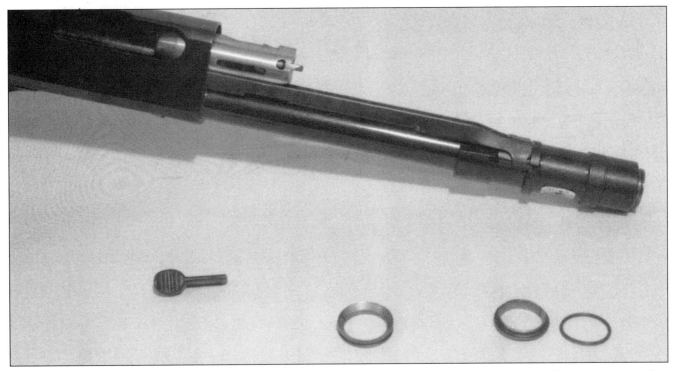

Fig. 17-4. To remove the bolt assembly, action bar, and action sleeve unit, first remove the operating handle, by pulling the entire unit forward and off the magazine tube.

REMOVING THE ACTION BAR ASSEMBLY, BOLT ASSEMBLY, AND ACTION SLEEVE

Depress the carrier release and push the carrier up into the receiver. This will allow access to the right shell latch (see Fig. 17-1). Press the right shell latch until the action bar moves forward with an audible click. Grasp the action-bar sleeve and slide the entire unit forward off of the magazine tube. Remove the breech bolt from the action-bar by simply lifting it upward.

ACTION-BAR SLEEVE DISASSEMBLY

Caution: It is not usually required to disassemble this unit. The action bar can be bent during disassembly or reassembly. Therefore, it is prudent not to disassemble this unit unless necessary.

To disassemble (see Fig. 17-5) insert a screwdriver behind the action bar in the slot (either side) on the sleeve. Gently pry the action bar from the slot.

ACTION-BAR UNIT DISASSEMBLY

The slide block is brazed to the action bar and no disassembly should be attempted. Ditto for the brazed-on link-retaining block.

The operating handle plunger can be removed if necessary. Depress the plunger and hold it downward. Slide the unit sideways out of the slot in the slide-block. Take care not to lose the plunger or its spring.

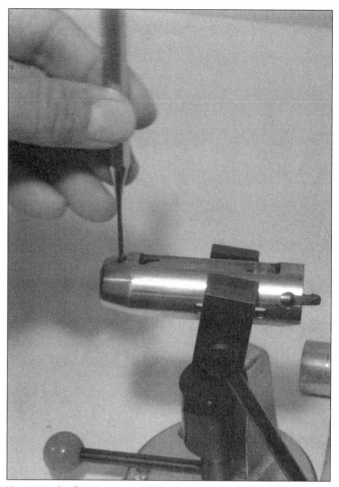

Fig. 17-6. The firing-pin retaining pin is removed by driving it from top to bottom.

SLIDE-BLOCK BUFFER SYSTEM AND RELATED PARTS

These parts are designed to absorb stress within the breech bolt when the action is opened after firing. These parts should not be disassembled except to replace worn or damaged parts.

To disassemble, drive out the return-plunger retaining pin from right to left. Grasp the plunger tightly and pull it from the slide block. Examine it carefully to determine if any damage was caused by disassembly.

Note: There is a newer style of operating handle detent and slide block buffer system. With these style parts, proceed as previously described until the plunger has been pulled free of the slide block. Then tip the rear of the action-bars down to allow the detent spring and ball to slide from the rear of the

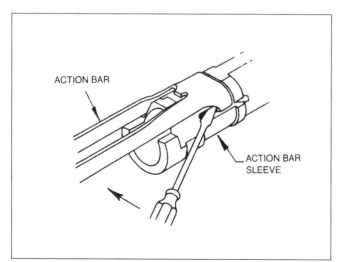

Fig. 17-5. The action-bar sleeve can be removed by using a screwdriver to pry the bar from the slot *(caution - see text).*

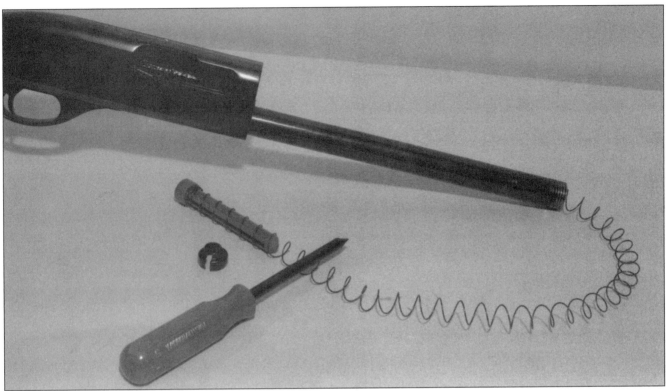

Fig. 17-7. Removal of magazine spring retainer, spring, and follower should be done carefully to prevent the spring and retainer from flying free.

slide block. *Caution:* Do not disassemble the new style units unless absolutely necessary for the installation of replacement parts.

BREECH BOLT DISASSEMBLY

Drive out the firing pin retaining pin located at the rear of the bolt (see Fig.17-6). Drive it from top to bottom. Pull the breech bolt buffer, firing-pin, and retractor spring from the bolt. Remove the locking block assembly.

The extractor can be removed by forcing the extractor plunger rearward in the bolt until the claw of the extractor can be pivoted inwards towards the front face of the bolt. The rear of the extractor can then be forced upward past the plunger and removed from the bolt. Slowly release tension on the plunger. *Caution:* Don't allow the plunger or its spring to escape under pressure. Remove the extractor plunger and spring.

DISASSEMBLY OF MAGAZINE COMPONENTS AND TRIGGER PLATE UNIT

Pry out the retainer from the end of the magazine. Use caution to prevent it from flying free as it is removed. Ditto for

the magazine plug (if any). Then slide out the magazine spring and follower. A retainer or magazine plug that is allowed to escape can cause personal injury (see Fig. 17-7).

The trigger-plate group (and all of its many parts) is easily removed. Simply push out the front and rear retaining pins and withdraw the plate assembly from the receiver (see Fig. 17-8 and Fig. 17-9).

Important: Do not allow the hammer to snap forward on the disassembled trigger-plate unit. Hold the hammer with thumb pressure and gently allow it to move forward. This will prevent damage to the forward components of the assembly.

All of the fire control components are removed from the gun, as a unit, when the trigger-plate group is taken from the shotgun.

No further disassembly of this group is required for routine maintenance. Pressurized solvents and degreasers can be used to adequately clean this assembly. Thus, further take-down is not suggested unless it is needed to repair or replace worn or damaged parts.

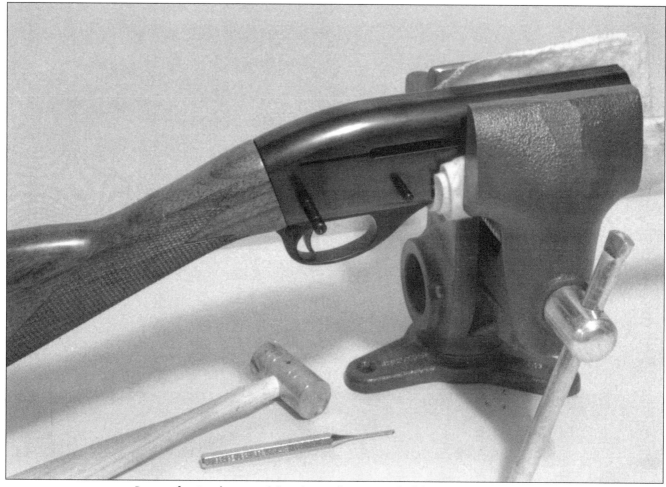

Remove front and rear retaining pins to allow removal of the trigger plate group.

DISASSEMBLY OF CARRIER GROUP

Slip a trigger plate pin detent spring (either one) from the end of the carrier pivot tube. Hold the carrier-dog follower down to prevent it from popping free of the plate (see Fig. 17.10). Push out the carrier pivot tube. Pull the carrier latch rearward and disassemble it from the trigger plate.

Drive the carrier-dog pin to the inside of the carrier, and out of place, and disassemble the carrier-dog and washer parts (seeFig. 17.12).

To remove the carrier spring, disengage the bent front end of the spring from the carrier and push the front end of the spring rearward (see Fig. 17-12).

The carrier release is disassembled by driving out the carrier release pin (see Fig. 17-13). The carrier release pin is swaged at both ends to tighten it to the carrier. Therefore, it will

be necessary to use a replacement pin when reassembling the gun.

To disassemble the carrier latch, press the carrier latch follower down and hold it in place to prevent it from popping loose. Push out the carrier latch pin and slowly release the carrier latch from the trigger plate. Pull the carrier latch and spring from the trigger plate.

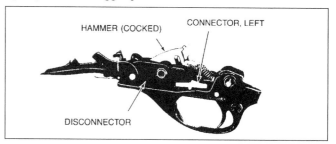

Fig. 17-9. Trigger plate group.

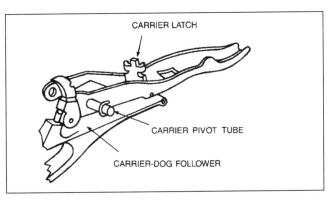

Fig. 17-10. Carrier disassembly and parts location.

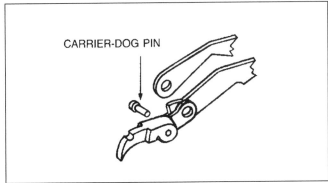

Fig. 17-11. Carrier dog and pin removal.

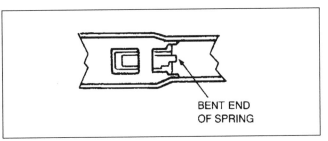

Fig. 17-12. Carrier spring location.

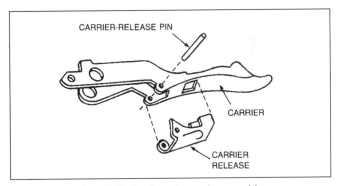

Fig. 17-13. Carrier release disassembly.

HAMMER, PLUNGER, HAMMER SPRING, SEAR, AND TRIGGER ASSEMBLY

Do not disassemble these parts at home. Doing so requires that the staked end of the hammer pin be ground down to the surface of the hammer-pin washer. Reassembling them requires extreme caution to ensure that a malfunction will not occur. Refer any need to disassemble these parts to an experienced person or the factory. All the trigger group parts are available only for factory installation.

SAFETY SWITCH DISASSEMBLY

Remove the retaining pin by pushing it from left to right (see Fig. 17-14). Notice that the pin is tapered and remember to properly orient it during assembly. *Caution:* Hold your forefinger over the spring hole in the top of the trigger-plate, as the pin is withdrawn. This prevents the safety switch spring from popping free. Remove the spring and detent ball from the trigger-plate. Then push out the safety switch.

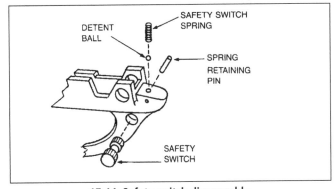

17-14. Safety switch disassembly.

BUTTSTOCK REMOVAL

Unscrew the buttplate (or recoil pad) screws and remove the buttplate and spacer. Insert a long, heavy screwdriver into the rear of the stock and unscrew the action-spring tube nut. Remove the nut and washers. Disassemble the stock from the action by pulling it rearward.

ACTION SPRING COMPONENTS DISASSEMBLY

Push in on the action spring plug by inserting a suitable tool, such as a narrow punch or Phillips screwdriver, to relieve the tension on the action spring plug pin. Push out the pin and then slowly relieve the tension on the action spring and plunger. Do this carefully as they are both under considerable tension.

To disassemble the link from the action spring follower, use a pair of long-nosed pliers and squeeze the tails of the link together directly in front of the follower which retains them. With the link tails compressed, pull the link forward and out of the receiver with a lifting and twisting motion. The follower can then be removed from the action spring housing by letting it fall free.

INTERCEPTOR LATCH SPRING

This component is staked into the receiver and should not be removed. If the spring is faulty, have an experienced professional replace it unless you are sure of your ability to perform this task.

Note: The action spring tube, magazine tube assembly, barrel lock and interceptor latch stud are all brazed or welded to the receiver. No attempt at disassembly should be made. If any need replacing, return the shotgun Remington.

INTERCEPTOR LATCH AND SHELL LATCH

The interceptor latch is mounted on a stud in the lower left wall of the receiver. To remove it, spread the tabs on the interceptor latch retainer, lift, and remove it from the stud. Disengage the interceptor latch spring from the groove in the interceptor latch and disassemble the latch from the receiver (see 17-15).

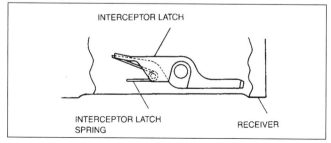

Fig. 17-15. Interceptor latch disassembly. Caution—no attempt should be made to remove the interceptor latch spring—see text.

Because the shell latch is staked into position, it is suggested that this component not be disassembled unless necessary for replacement. Then, because staking will be required, it may be best to let a professional handle this job, unless you feel confident about your ability to do it.

It should be noted that the shell latch occasionally works loose and will slide forward or rearward when the shotgun is disassembled. If the trigger plate pin hole in the receiver does not align with the hole in the shell latch (see Fig. 17-16) the shell latch should be properly aligned and positively restaked in position.

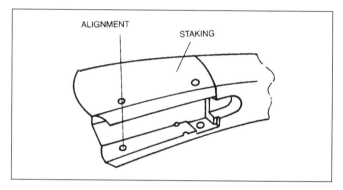

Fig. 17-16. Shell latch alignment and restaking.

FORE-END SUPPORT ASSEMBLY

The fore-end support assembly may, if required, be removed from the action-bar assembly. Proceed by wedging a screwdriver blade between the fore-end support assembly and the left (wide) action bar. Pry the support outward and down, away from the bar until it can be lifted free.

For the most part, reassembly of the Remington 1100 is accomplished in reverse order of the disassembly procedures. However, some special cautions and procedures do need to be followed. These are covered in the following text. Where no specific mention of reassembly procedures is made, simply reverse disassembly methods.

FORE-END SUPPORT GROUP ASSEMBLY

Before reassembly, check the sides of the fore-end support to ensure they are straight and not spread apart. If necessary, squeeze inward to straighten them. With the pointed ends facing forward and the block facing up, hook the right side of the support over the right (narrow) action bar. Squeeze the bars inward and press upward on the support until the support snaps over the bars (see Fig. 17-17).

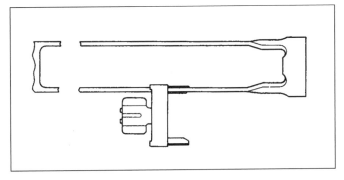

17-17. Fore-end support assembly.

INTERCEPTOR LATCH INSTALLATION

Place the interceptor latch over the mounting stud so that the recess on the latch faces up and the hook is forward. Depress the top of the latch spring and fit it into the groove in the bottom rear of the latch. Push the latch down against the wall of the receiver. Be sure that the small letters on the tab of the interceptor latch retainer are facing upward. Then spread the tabs and place the retainer over the stud and into the recess in the latch. The retainer should snap into the groove in the stud.

LINK ASSEMBLY

Hold the long tails of the link with a needle-nosed plier so that the curved tails face toward the bottom of the receiver. Insert the tails into the conical recess in the action-spring follower and release the grip on the tails.

BUTTSTOCK ASSEMBLY

Be certain that the flat steel stock-bearing plate is positioned against the receiver. After slipping the buttstock into place and lightly tightening the buttstock nut (action-opening tube nut), align the edges of the stock with the edges of the receiver. Then carefully tighten the stock nut. Don't forget to place the nut washer and nut lock washer on the action spring tube before placing the nut onto the tube. The lock washer goes onto the tube between the nut and flat washer.

CARRIER GROUP ASSEMBLY

To reassemble the carrier dog and carrier dog washer assembly, it is necessary to restake the small end of the carrier dog pin to tighten the pin to the carrier.

Be sure to position the carrier dog over the follower making sure that the prong on the carrier enters the hole in the carrier latch. Then align the carrier, carrier dog washer, and trigger-plate holes. After inserting the trigger pin bushing, insert the detent spring.

TRIGGER PLATE GROUP ASSEMBLY TO RECEIVER

Dip the carrier into the receiver while guiding the disconnector past the receiver rail. Then lift the carrier slightly and settle the rear of the trigger plate into the receiver. Slide the entire unit rearward in the receiver until the retaining pin holes of the trigger plate align with the corresponding holes in the receiver.

MAGAZINE TUBE ASSEMBLY

Do not forget to install the magazine-capacity reducing plug if needed. This plug reduces the 1100's total shell capacity to adhere with federal and state hunting regulations limiting shell capacity to three rounds.

BREECH BOLT GROUP ASSEMBLY

Make certain that the extractor reseats properly on the shoulder of the extractor. The claw of a replaced extractor should be tightened on the rim of a dummy cartridge to ensure a proper purchase. Make this adjustment by removing metal from the pad at the mid-section of the extractor.

Be careful to ensure that the firing pin retaining pin is tapped flush with the bottom of the bolt. If the tightening ridges on the retaining pin are worn, replace the pin.

Whenever a replacement buffer is required, it will need to be drilled. Do this by placing the buffer completely into the bolt and, while holding it in position, drill through the bolt and buffer it with a #24 drill. Take care not to remove any material from the bolt.

OPERATING HANDLE DETENT AND SLIDE BLOCK BUFFER SYSTEM ASSEMBLY

Ensure that the return plunger retaining pin is driven in from left to right. When in place, the pin must be flush with the left side of the slide block. Check the breech bolt return plunger to ensure that it works freely.

Note: When a replacement slide buffer is used, it must be drilled through with a .078-inch drill. Use the slide block as a drill jig.

ACTION BAR GROUP AND BOLT GROUP ASSEMBLY

Insert one side of the action-bar into the sleeve (see Fig. 17-5). Tap other side downward until action-bar slips into its groove. *Caution:* Do not bend or twist the action bars.

Place the breech bolt unit over the slide block at the rear of the action bar. Slide the entire unit over the magazine tube. Move it rearward into the receiver until the action bars contact the right shell latch. At this point the unit will be one-inch or so into the receiver. While holding the gun in a vertical position, depress the carrier release which will allow access to depress the right shell latch (see Fig. 17-1) until the entire bolt and action bar unit can be moved rearward into the receiver.

If the carrier raises up and interferes, reach through the ejection port and push it down. Before the barrel is inserted, the entire bolt group needs to be locked in the rearward position (open action).

PISTON SEAL, PISTON, AND BARREL SEAL

The piston seal is slipped over the magazine tube first, followed by the piston. The barrel seal O-ring is put onto the magazine tube next. Do not damage the O-ring when installing it. Slide all three pieces rearward on the tube until the O-ring drops into the channel cut for it around the magazine tube.

COMMON PROBLEMS—PROBABLE CAUSES AND CORRECTIONS

Gun Fails to be Loaded

1. Magazine follower, spring, or tube defective; prevents cartridge from leaving magazine with sufficient velocity. *Replace follower or spring. Have factory replace magazine tube, if required.*
2. Carrier release fails to release carrier latch. *Replace or adjust prong contacting latch.*
3. Carrier latch jams carrier release. *Replace carrier latch and/or its spring.*

Gun Fails to Feed Shell from Magazine

1. Shell latch does not slip off shell properly. *Adjust shell latch or replace it.*
2. Shell latch stop surface rough or damaged. *Smooth up notch or replace.*
3. Carrier sits too high, holding shells in the magazine. *Adjust or replace carrier. Check carrier latch and carrier dog follower spring.*
4. Magazine spring damaged. *Replace magazine spring.*
5. Magazine double feeds—shell latch failing. *Replace shell latch or adjust.*
6. Broken interceptor latch spring. *Replace interceptor latch spring.*
7. Broken or worn interceptor. *Replace interceptor.*

Gun Fails to Feed a Shell up on Carrier

1. Carrier latch defective, jamming carrier release. *Replace carrier latch spring.*
2. Carrier release defective, jamming carrier movement. *Replace carrier release or adjust carrier prong to contact carrier latch.*
3. Carrier jams, shell latch binding carrier. *Adjust latch to free carrier.*
4. Carrier action defective, or sluggish. *Replace carrier. Check carrier is pivot-tube and slide-to-carrier-dog contact.*
5. Extractor too tight—shell feeds under claw too hard. *Replace extractor, or relieve claw tension, or smooth up inside radius of claw.*

Action Fails to Close

1. Action bar bent, jamming action. *Replace or straighten action bar.*
2. Carrier movement impeded and jamming. *Replace carrier (see Gun Fails to Feed a Shell up on Carrier).*
3. Action spring defective. *Replace action spring.*
4. Piston assembly dirty, defective. *Clean piston—check movement.*

Gun Fails to Lock When Closed

1. Too little headspace. *Return firearm to factory.*
2. Locking block binds (or missing). *Check assembly, free up locking block.*
3. Defective or mutilated shell rim. *Remove shell.*
4. Action binds. *Free up—check slide movement, action bar.*
5. Chamber is rough. *Have the factory polish the chamber or replace the barrel.*
6. Extractor or extractor slot in barrel is damaged. *Replace extractor or repair slot in barrel.*

Gun Fails to Fire

1. Firing pin damaged, too short, or bent. A light firing pin blow is indicative of these problems. *Caution: Do not open the action immediately after a misfire. Wait approximately two minutes. Replace firing pin or free up movement. Pin should protrude from bolt face a minimum of 0.030-inch to a maximum of 0.060-inch.*

2. Right connector not seated against sear. *Clean assembly or have factory replace sear and/or connector.*

3. Disconnector binds connector, cannot slide down. *Free up disconnector or replace.*

4. Disconnector (bent tail) assembled above connector. *Reassemble properly (below connector).*

5. Hammer fails to cock. *Check engagement of hammer and sear notch; check spring or replace.*

6. Trigger binds. *Free up trigger or have factory replace it.*

Gun Fails to Extract

1. Extractor damaged. *Replace extractor.*

2. Extractor claw loose on shell rim. *File mid-section on extractor.*

3. Extractor slot in barrel damaged. *File slot for proper fitting.*

4. Extractor spring and/or plunger defective. *Replace spring and/or plunger.*

5. Chamber of barrel rough. *Replace barrel or have factory polish chamber.*

Action Fails to Open

1. Action binds. *Free up action bars (see Action Fails to Close).*

2. Piston assembly defective. *Clean or replace defective piston and/or O-ring.*

3. Gas holes in barrel-guide ring are mutilated. *Check for proper size opening (see table of Gas Orifice Size at the end of this chapter).*

4. Gun fails to open when using light loads. *Replace piston with split-piston design.*

Gun Fails to Eject

1. Ejector defective or damaged. *Return to factory for replacement.*

2. Action binds, slow timing. *Free up action (see Action Fails to Open).*

3. Extractor loose on shell or defective. *Tighten extractor by filing middle pad. Check extractor and spring. Replace extractor if damaged.*

4. Carrier feeds up too fast and interferes with ejecting shell. *Adjust shell latch—replace carrier or latch.*

5. Rough chamber. *Replace barrel or have factory polish chamber.*

6. Gun fails to open on light loads. *Replace split-design piston.*

Gun Fails to Lock Open

1. Carrier latch or spring defective. *Replace carrier latch and/or spring.*

2. Action binds. *Free up action (see Action Fails to Open).*

3. Carrier-dog-to-slide engagement, is faulty. *Adjust engagement replacing either part if necessary.*

BARREL GAS CYLINDER DAMAGE

Any damage to the gas cylinder producing an "out of round" condition, may cause gas piston parts to be inoperable. The gas cylinder is brazed to the underside of the mid-section of the barrel. Within it are positioned the piston, piston seal, and barrel seal. To operate properly, these parts must slide freely upon the end of the magazine tube. Therefore, it is necessary to make certain that any barrel-holding devices do not damage the gas cylinder.

MODEL 1100 VARIATIONS

In 1975, various components of the Remington Model 1100 shotgun were redesigned to improve function and/or durability. These improvements can be added to most 1100s with the following instructions.

FORE-END TUBE GROUP

These redesigned parts are made of heavier materials and the series of tabs used to hold the fore-end tube in position have been replaced by a single tab. To install the newer style tube made sure that the hole in the front of the fore-end is large enough to accept the new tube. If necessary, the hole diameter should be increased to 1.093-inch +/-0.005-inch. Then, with the small tab facing upward, insert the fore-end tube group into the fore-end. Bend the tab upward (see Fig. 17-18) and flush against the fore-end wall.

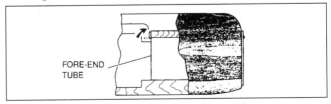

Fig. 17-18. Fore-end tube assembly.

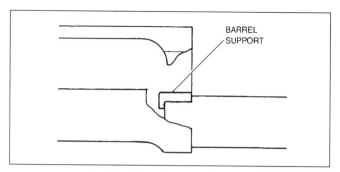

Fig. 17-19. Barrel support location.

GAS-ORIFICE SIZES FOR REMINGTON MODEL 1100 SHOTGUNS

Gauge & Barrel Length	Number of Orifices	Orifice Diameter & Drill Size
12 ga. 2¾"; 34" Full Trap	2	.079"/No.47
12 ga. 2¾"; 30", 28", 26", 22"	2	.079"/No.47
12 ga. 2¾"; Skeet	2	.086"/No.44
12 ga. 2¾"; Skeet w/compensator	2	.086"/No.44
12 ga. 3"; 30" (Magnum)	1	.073"/No.49
12 ga. 3"; 34" (duck & goose)	1	.073"/No.49
16 ga. 2¾"; 28", 26"	2	.076"/No.48
20 ga. 2¾"; 28", 26", 22"	2	.076"/No.48
20 ga. 3"; 28" (Magnum)	1	.076"/No.48
20 ga. 2¾"; 26" w/compensator	2	.086"/No.44
20 ga. 2¾"; 28", 26" (light weight)	2	.067"/No.51
20 ga. 3"; 28" (LW Magnum)	1	.064"/No.52
28 ga. 2¾"; Reg & Skeet	2	.067"/No.51
.410 ga. 3"; Reg	1	.067"/No.51
.410 ga. 2¾"; Skeet	2	.060"/No.53
20 ga. 3"; (Magnum LT20)	1	.064"/No.52
20 ga. 2¾"; (LT20s)	2	.064"/No.52
20 ga. 2¾"; (LT Skeet)	2	.067"/No.51

FORE-END SUPPORT GROUP

Remove the action bar assembly. Then remove the fore-end support as noted earlier. With the pointed ends facing forward and the inside of the radius facing upward, place the new fore-end support assembly over the center of the right (narrow) action bar (see Fig. 17-17). Rotate the fore-end support assembly clockwise 180 degrees, press inward on the left (wide) action bar and snap the support over the bar. Replace the action bar assembly and the barrel.

If the barrel assembles tightly or the vent rib does not align with the receiver mating, remove a very small amount of material from the top of the barrel support to align the barrel and achieve a snug fit (see Fig. 17-19).

To fit extra barrels that assemble excessively tight, remove a very small amount of material from the bottom of the breech end of the barrel to achieve a snug fit.

INTERCEPTOR LATCH

The new latch has had a skirt added to shroud the loop on the interceptor latch spring. Remove the old style parts. The loop of the spring should fit between the inside wall of the receiver and the skirt on the interceptor latch. Place the latch over the stud with the recess side facing upward and the hook facing forward. Depress the top of the spring and fit it into the groove in the bottom rear of the latch. Press the latch downward against the receiver wall. Make sure that the small letters on the tab of the interceptor latch retainer are facing upward. Then spread the tabs and place the retainer over the stud and into the recess in the latch. The retainer should snap into the groove in the stud (see Fig 17-15).

16

REMINGTON MODEL 870 PUMP SHOTGUN

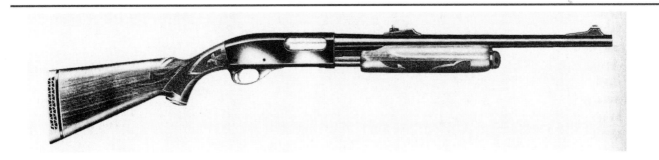

The Remington 870 Pump shotgun has out-sold every other model shotgun. Many millions of satisfied owners speak highly of its reliability and durability. Indeed, during the thirty-five years that I have used 870s, not one has ever failed in any manner while in the field. This Remington has been made available in 12, 16, 20, 28 and .410 gauges. And it has been offered in both standard and magnum length chambers, as well as in right and left hand models.

CYCLE OF OPERATION

With the shotgun's action cocked and open, place the safety switch in the "safe" position by pushing in on its left end. Then drop a shell into the ejection port and push the operating slide fully forward. This will chamber the cartridge and lock the shotgun in the battery position. The magazine may then be loaded by pushing up on the shell carrier, through the bottom receiver opening, and moving the shell forward into the magazine until it is positively latched into place. Repeat this manipulation until the magazine is fully loaded.

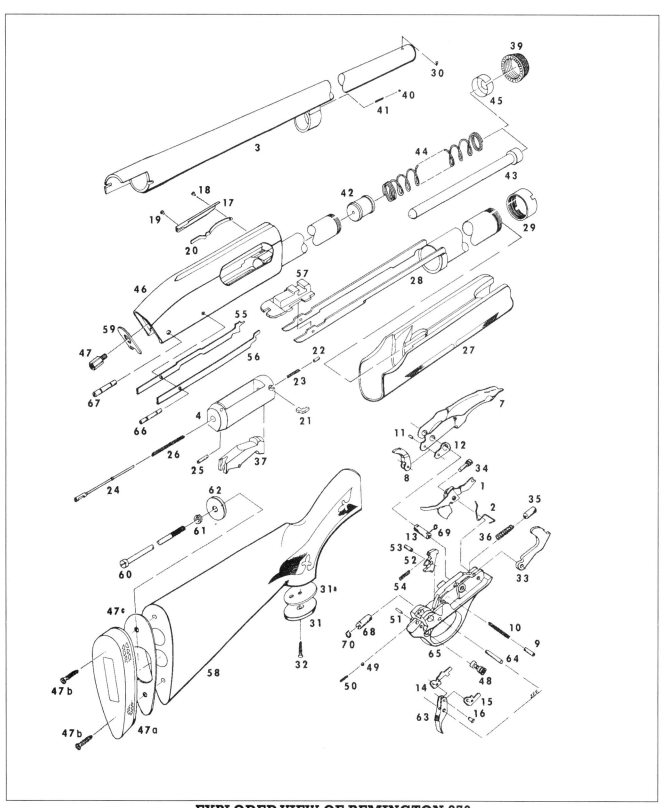

EXPLODED VIEW OF REMINGTON 870

View No.	Part No.	Name of Part	View No.	Part No.	Name of Part	View No.	Part No.	Name of Part
1	18849	Action Bar Lock		20089	Fore-end (wood only) 16-20 ga.	50	17514	Safety Switch Spring
2	19622	Action Bar Lock Spring				51	17515	Safety Switch Spring Retaining Pin
	Note:	All barrels (same gauge)	27	34785	Fore-end Assembly, 12-ga	52	18750	Sear
		interchangeable without adjustment.		34786	Fore-end Assembly, 16-20 ga.	53	17463	Sear Pin
		Also give choke needed.	28	20065	Fore-end Tube Assembly	54	17518	Sear Spring
3		Barrel Assembly	29	18634	Fore-end Tube Nut	55	20040	Shell Latch, Left, 12-ga.
4	18545	Breech Bolt, 12-ga.	30	18673	Front Sight (plain barrel)		20041	Shell Latch, Left, 16-ga.
	20015	Breech Bolt, 16-ga.	31	18015	Grip Cap		20042	Shell Latch, Left, 20-ga.
	20016	Breech Bolt, 20-ga.		14943	Grip Cap Spacer	56	20048	Shell Latch, Right, 12-ga.
	22860	Breech Bolt Assembly, Complete, 12-ga.	32	91634	Grip Cap Screw		20046	Shell Latch, Right, 16-ga.
	22861	Breech Bolt Assembly, Complete, 16-ga.	33	18749	Hammer		20047	Shell Latch, Right, 20-ga.
	22862	Breech Bolt Assembly, Complete, 20-ga.	34	16600	Hammer Pin	57	14543	Slide
7	18584	Carrier		15809	Hammer Pin Washer	58	34800	Stock Assembly
	20060	Carrier Assembly	35	17465	Hammer Plunger	59	19993	Stock Bearing Plate
8	15480	Carrier Dog	36	19014	Hammer Spring	60	18571	Stock Bolt
9	17416	Carrier Dog Follower	37	22325	Locking Block Assembly	61	18572	Stock Bolt Lock Washer
10	17415	Carrier Dog Follower Spring		24075	Locking Block Assembly, (oversize)	62	18573	Stock Bolt Washer
11	18781	Carrier Dog Pin	39	25375	Magazine Cap	63	25370	Trigger (R)
12	18760	Carrier Dog Washer	40	17451	Magazine Cap Detent		20610	Trigger Assembly (R)
13	17417	Carrier Pivot Tube	41	16791	Magazine Cap Detent Spring	64	17533	Trigger Pin
14	17419	Connector, Left (R)	42	32350	Magazine Follower	65	25035	Trigger Plate, R.H. (right hand safety)
15	17551	Connector, Right (R)	43	18097	Magazine Plug, 3-shot, wood		25036	Trigger Plate, L.H. (for R.H. Gun)
16	17420	Connector Pin (R)	44	19479	Magazine Spring		22985	Trigger Plate Assembly, R.H.
17	25431	Ejector, 12-ga.	45	91657	Magazine Spring Retainer		22986	Trigger Plate Assembly, (L.H. Safe), for R.H. Gun
	24446	Ejector, 16-ga.	46	20030	Receiver Assembly, 12-ga. (R)	66	20601	Trigger Plate Pin, Front
	24447	Ejector, 20-ga.		20031	Receiver Assembly, 16-ga. (R)	67	20606	Trigger Plate Pin, Rear
18	18646	Ejector Rivet, Front		20032	Receiver Assembly, 20-ga. (R)	68	17541	Trigger Plate Pin Bushing
19	18647	Ejector Rivet, Rear	47	18551	Receiver Stud	69	17539	Trigger Plate Pin Detent Spring, Front
20	18648	Ejector Spring	47a	14705	Recoil Pad	70	17540	Trigger Plate Pin Detent Spring, Rear
21	16176	Extractor	47b	25410	Recoil Pad Screw			
22	17432	Extractor Plunger		14944	Recoil Pad Spacer			
23	17433	Extractor Spring	48	25115	Safety Switch			
24	17436	Firing Pin	49	23223	Safety Switch Detent Ball			
25	18623	Firing Pin Retaining Pin						
26	17437	Firing Pin Retractor Spring						
	20088	Fore-end (Wood only) 12-ga.						

(R) = Restricted Part, available only for a factory instalation.

With the cross bolt safety pushed from right to left to the "off" position, the gun is fired by pulling the trigger rearward. This allows the top portion of the trigger to rotate forward carrying the connector, in its ready position, forward against the sear. This movement pivots the sear out of engagement with the hammer. The released hammer, under compression of the hammer spring, pivots forward and strikes the firing pin. The firing pin then moves forward compressing its retractor spring and ignites the primer of the shotshell in the chamber. The firing pin is then pushed to the rear by the firing pin retractor spring.

Just before the firing pin is struck by the hammer, the hammer plunger, in its upward movement, engages the action bar lock. Movement of the front of the action bar lock in a downward direction is restrained if the fore-end is being held tightly rearward until pressure against it is briefly released. This happens involuntarily as the shotgun recoils rearward. When the action bar is freed, the forward end of the action bar lock is lowered from its position at the rear of the left action bar and the rear section rises and lifts the connector from contact with the sear.

The two-fold guardian performance of the action bar lock is a safety feature that disconnects the trigger assembly and sear until a shell is fully seated in the chamber and the breech is fully locked.

After the gun is fired, pulling the slide handle rearward will unlock the action, extract and eject the fired case, cock the hammer, and start the feeding cycle. The details of these are as follows.

The initial rearward movement of the fore-end carries the slide to the rear of the breech block. As it travels to the rear of the bolt, the slide cams the locking block from the recoil shoulder of the barrel, freeing the bolt for rearward movement. As this is done, the firing pin is cammed rearward and locked into this position.

As the bolt moves rearward, the fired case is extracted from the chamber. The extractor, powered by its springs, is pivoted so as to hold the fired case firmly against the bolt face. Ejection occurs as the rim of the fired case impacts the ejector spring shoulder causing the case to pivot so that it is ejected through the receiver port.

Just before ejection is completed, the rearward motion of the bolt moves the hammer downward compressing its coil spring and it engages the sear. Pressure of the sear spring locks the sear in a notched position against the cocked hammer.

The final motion forces the entire slide and breech block group to the most rearward position in the receiver. At this point, the left action bar is free to cam the left shell latch, releasing the next shell from the magazine. The shell is ejected from the magazine with sufficient force to carry it far enough to the rear so it comes to rest on the carrier. As the shell is ejected from the magazine onto the carrier, the right shell latch is cammed into position by the right action bar and retains the next shell in the magazine.

When forward motion of the bolt is started by the closing stroke ("pump"), the carrier dog attached to the rear of the carrier is engaged by the returning slide. This causes the carrier to pivot upward placing the new shell in front of the bolt. The advancing bolt depresses the ejector spring into its channel while simultaneously forcing the loaded cartridge forward into the chamber.

The carrier dog, released from the pressure of the passing slide, is forced upward by the carrier dog follower and its compressed spring and the carrier pivots downward. The right shell latch is released and the left shell latch, no longer being cammed out of the way, intercepts the shell in the magazine—preventing its escape. The shell is held in this position until the next feeding cycle begins.

As a shell is loaded into the chamber and the action closes the bolt against the shell, the travel of the slide within the bolt continues and cams the locking block into position in the recoil shoulder of the barrel. In turn, the locking block secures the breech bolt firmly against the chambered shell. When the locking block is fully positioned, the passageway through the bolt then is opened to allow the firing pin the necessary freedom of movement to travel forward to impact the primer.

The fore-end return motion is stopped as the slide comes to rest against the front section of the bolt. The fully locked position enables the action bar lock to clear the end of the left action bar. The suspended connector will then be released by spring pressure and dropped to a ready position to begin the firing cycle again.

DISASSEMBLY

The Remington Model 870 is basically an easy firearm to disassemble, repair, and reassemble. But like any firearm, certain part fits are critical to safe operation. Remington, therefore, restricts certain parts availability. These parts include the left and right connectors and their mounting pin, the receiver, trigger, and trigger assembly. Before beginning to disassemble the shotgun, check to make certain that both the chamber and magazine are unloaded.

BARREL REMOVAL

Move the fore-end half-way back along its travel path. If the shotgun is cocked it will be necessary to press in the action bar lock (see Fig. 16-1) before the fore-end can be moved rearward. With the fore-end correctly positioned, unscrew the magazine cap and then slide the barrel forward out of the receiver. *Caution:* Do not slam the action forward after the barrel has been removed as the action bar will bind on the shell latch.

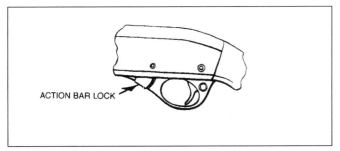

Fig. 16-1. The action bar lock is at the front of the trigger guard on the left side.

FORE-END UNIT REMOVAL

Press in the front end of the left shell latch. To do this, reach up into the receiver through the loading port. With the left shell latch compressed, pull the fore-end gently forward off of the magazine tube. *Caution:* The breech bolt assembly,

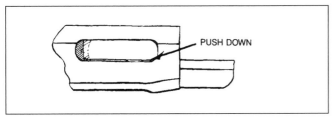

Fig. 16-2. Push down on the bolt when disassembling the shotgun if it binds on the bottom of the ejection port.

locking block, and slide will be simultaneously withdrawn from the receiver (see Fig. 16-5). As these are simply sitting in grooves on the action bar, they will fall easily away. Take care not to drop them on any surface that could cause damage to these parts.

The slide may catch on the bottom of the ejection port if the trigger-plate assembly is in the shotgun. Push the bolt assembly downward (see Fig. 16-2) to free it.

REMOVAL OF MAGAZINE SPRING, RETAINER, AND FOLLOWER

Carefully pry out the magazine spring retainer using a screwdriver. Do not damage the end of the magazine and keep a hand cupped over its end. *Caution:* The magazine spring and retainer can escape with some velocity due to the compression of the magazine spring. After the magazine spring has been removed, point the magazine tube downward and allow the magazine follower to slide out of the magazine tube.

STOCK REMOVAL

There is seldom a reason to remove the buttstock but it can be easily done. Loosen the top buttplate screw and remove the bottom buttplate screw. Swing the buttplate to the side and insert a long, heavy screwdriver into the buttstock hole, engaging the slot of the stock bolt. Remove the bolt and the stock will come away from the receiver.

TRIGGER-PLATE GROUP REMOVAL

Push out the front and rear trigger-plate pins. Lift the rear end of the trigger-plate group from the receiver, slide the assembly rearward, tilting it clockwise to clear the action bar lock from the receiver.

Normally, no further disassembly of the Model 870 is necessary. The entire trigger-plate can be adequately cleaned with pressurized solvents or by immersion in solvent. Residual solvents can be removed after cleaning by using a pressurized degreasing and solvent-removing compound.

TRIGGER-PLATE COMPONENT DISASSEMBLY

Disengage the hammer by holding it in the cocked position while the trigger is pulled. Then allow the hammer to move slowly forward. *Caution:* Do not allow the hammer to snap forward under spring tension as parts could be damaged.

Push out the carrier pivot tube from the left side, with the front trigger-plate detent spring attached. Remove the carrier assembly, carrier dog follower, and carrier dog follower spring.

The hammer plunger can then be compressed and the hammer pin driven out. Remove the hammer action bar lock, hammer plunger, and hammer spring.

Push out the trigger-plate pin bushing from the right side with the rear trigger-plate pin detent spring attached. Remove the sear spring and drive out the sear pin from the right side, and lift out the sear. Push out the safety switch spring retaining pin and remove the safety switch spring, retainer, and the safety switch.

CARRIER GROUP AND BREECH BOLT DISASSEMBLY

First file off the peened metal from the carrier dog pin and then drive it out from the peened side. Remove the carrier dog and carrier dog washer.

Using the appropriate size punch, drive out the firing pin retaining pin from the top side of the bolt. Release the firing pin slowly until all spring tension is relieved. Then remove the firing pin and its retractor spring.

Force the extractor plunger rearward in the bolt with a small-bladed screwdriver, and roll the extractor forward out of the extractor slot. Then remove the extractor plunger and spring (see Fig. 16-3).

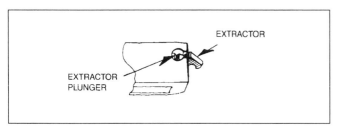

Fig. 16-3. Removal of the shell latch.

SHELL LATCHES

Both the shell latches are peened into place in the receiver. Therefore, they should not be removed unless necessary. A loose shell latch can often be re-peened without removal. Place the trigger-plate group retaining pin through the receiver and shell latch

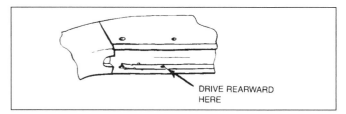

Fig. 16-4. Installation and removal of extractor.

when peening to keep the shell latch properly located (see Fig. 16.7).

To remove a shell latch, secure the action in a suitably padded vise with the bottom side up. Using a heavy drift punch inserted into the hole in the latch (but not contacting the receiver), drive the latch rearward (see Fig. 16-4). The same procedure is used for either the left or right shell latch. This wipes away the peened metal that held the latch(es) in place. Proper and adequate staking will be required when replacing the shell latch(es).

REASSEMBLY

Reassembly of the 870 is for the most part a reversal of the disassembly order. However, a few notes should be made.

BUTTSTOCK ASSEMBLY

Don't forget to place the flat steel stock-bearing plate between the stock and the receiver when replacing the buttstock. The stock washer goes on the stock bolt with its projections forward (against the stock).

MAGAZINE TUBE ASSEMBLY

If required, do not forget to install the wood or plastic plug used to reduce the 870's total shell capacity to three rounds. The magazine spring retainer is placed into the magazine with its rimmed end down. It should be tapped into place so it is flush with the front end of the tube. If the Vari-Weight steel plug is used to reduce the magazine capacity (and increase the gun's weight to reduce perceived recoil), the magazine spring retainer is not used. The magazine tube must have a hole drilled in it, appropriately sized, to accept the Vari-Weight retaining screw.

EXTRACTOR ASSEMBLY

Place the extractor spring into the hole in the rear of the extractor slot. Insert the small end of the extractor plunger into the spring. Holding the extractor by the claw, place the rear end of the extractor into the extractor seat and force the extractor rearward against the plunger and spring. *Caution:* Do not let the extractor spring and plunger escape. They are easily lost and can cause physical injury should they fly free. See Fig. 16-3 for the correct starting position to snap the extractor into place. The extractor plunger must snap over the rear shoulder of the extractor.

FIRING PIN ASSEMBLY

Assemble the firing pin with the firing pin retractor spring on the front end of the firing pin. Push the parts into the hole at the rear of the bolt and position the firing pin retractor spring in the hole in the front end of the bolt. Push the tip of the firing pin into the same hole. While maintaining compression on the firing pin retractor spring, align the clearance cut on the firing pin with the firing pin retaining pin hole (in the rear of the bolt). Drive in the retaining pin from the bottom of the bolt, until it is flush with the bottom surface of the bolt.

FORE-END UNIT, SLIDE, BOLT, AND LOCKING BLOCK

Place the bolt (with the locking block assembled to it) and the slide onto the action bars in the correct position (see Fig. 16-5). This is best accomplished after installing the fore-end unit over the magazine tube. Gently insert the action bars, slide, and bolt into the receiver until the unit contacts the right shell latch. Depress the front end of the right shell latch (to clear the action bar) and move the assembly rearward until it contacts the front end of the left shell latch. Depress the front end of the left shell latch and move the assembly rearward.

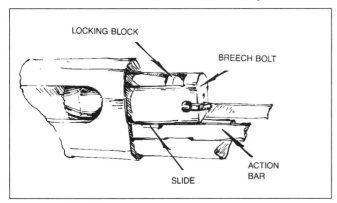

Fig. 16-5. Parts orientation when removing and installing the breech bolt group and operating bar with fore-end.

SHELL LATCHES

If the shell latches have been removed, the left shell latch can be identified by the bend in it (to clear the action bar lock). This bend is located in the middle of the latch. Be sure to assemble shell latches in the proper groove. The front ends of the latch must be positioned between the receiver and the magazine tube (see Fig. 16-6). Before staking a latch in position, use the front trigger-plate pin (placed through the receiver and shell latch), to properly align the latch. Be certain the front end of the shell latch is properly located before staking it into position (see Fig. 16-7).

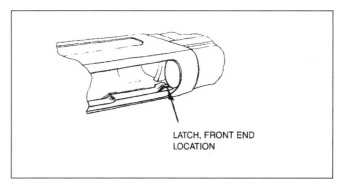

Fig. 16-6. Front ends of shell latches must be positioned between the receiver and magazine tube.

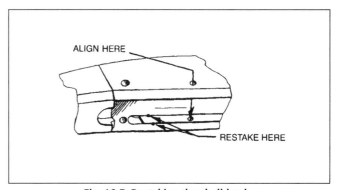

Fig. 16-7. Restaking the shell latch.

TRIGGER-PLATE COMPONENTS, CARRIER ASSEMBLY, AND BARREL

These are assembled in reverse order to takedown, but it may be necessary to restake the right side of the trigger-plate to tighten the hammer pin. The projection on the rear of the action bar lock must be assembled under the left connector (see Fig. 16-8).

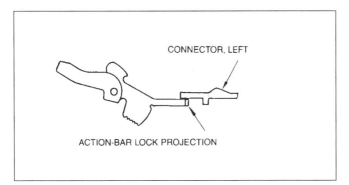

Fig. 16-8. Correct assembly of action bar lock and left connector.

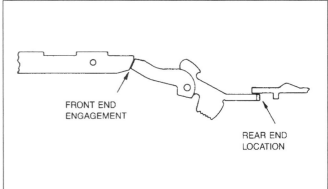

Fig. 16-9. The correct engagement of the action bar and action bar bolt when the gun is in its locked position.

For carrier reassembly, it will be necessary to restake the small outside end of the carrier dog pin to hold the pin in position.

The hammer should be cocked and the safety switch should be in the "on" position before attempting to install the trigger-plate group. Also, the slide handle should be in its rearward most position, thus placing the bolt unit fully rearward in the receiver. Insert the trigger-plate (fire control) unit into the receiver, tilting the assembly clockwise to clear the action bar lock. *Caution:* Use care when assembling the trigger-plate unit to the receiver. Any deformation of the action bar lock will prevent proper engagement with the end of the action bar. Align the pin holes properly before inserting the rear and front pins.

In addition, the action should be opened about halfway when mounting the barrel to the receiver.

FITTING NEW PARTS AND ADJUSTMENTS

ACTION BAR LOCK

Follow disassembly procedures and then assemble the new action bar lock. It is important to check that the rear end of the action bar lock is correctly positioned under the left connector. The front end of the action bar lock must have full engagement with the action bar (see Fig. 16-9) when the shotgun is in the locked position.

EJECTOR AND EJECTOR SPRING

It is not advisable to attempt to replace these parts. Once the rivets that hold these components in place have been reassembled, the receiver will need to be reblued.

FORE-END REPLACEMENT

A special spanner or screwdriver will be needed to remove the fore-end tube nut from the front of the fore-end. When replacing the fore-end tube nut be sure to locate the fore-end centrally between the action bars. Avoid splitting the fore-end when replacing the fore-end tube nut.

EXTRACTOR REPLACEMENT

If, after replacing the extractor, the shell feeds up under the extractor with difficulty, the lower corner of the extractor claw will need to be rounded (see Fig. 16-10).

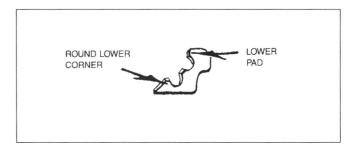

Fig. 16-10. The lower corner of a replaced extractor can be rounded if shell feeds up and under the extractor with difficulty. The extractor's lower pad may be rounded slightly to help with this problem.

TRIGGER, CONNECTORS, AND CONNECTOR PINS

All trigger related problems require factory service. The shotgun or the complete trigger-plate unit should be returned to the factory.

COMMON PROBLEMS—PROBABLE CAUSES AND CORRECTIONS

Shell Cannot be Loaded into Magazine

1. Carrier allows the shell to load too low and hits the rim of the magazine entrance. *It may be necessary to install a new carrier dog to correct this problem.*

2. Improper position of the front end of both shell latches. *Check that the front ends of both shell latches are between the magazine tube and the receiver (see Fig. 16-6).*

Gun Fails to Feed as the Forearm Moves Rearward

1. Action bar hindered. *Check that the action bar notches, which contact the shell latches, are free from deformation. Repair or return to factory.*

2. Shell latches not moving freely or engaging correctly. *Check that the front end of the latch has a maximum engagement over the shell head of approximately 1/16-inch. The shell latches should be free of deformity.*

3. Magazine spring and follower not moving freely. *Check for dents in the magazine tube which can hinder the free movement of the follower. Also, if the spring is weak, replace it.*

4. The carrier not dropping low enough (to allow the shell to pass onto it) or dropping too low (below the loading port of the receiver). *If the carrier tip is bent, repair or replace. Check for burrs on the rails and remove if required.*

Gun Fails to Lift the Shell into Position for Loading into the Chamber or Balks as the Cartridge Starts to Chamber

1. Action bar movement must be free. *See "Gun Fails to Feed as the Forearm Moves Rearward."*

2. Shell latches hindered in retaining the next shell in the magazine. *See "Gun Fails to Feed as the Forearm Moves Rearward."*

3. The carrier dog and carrier dog follower spring are not working smoothly. *Check for a secure, correct fit in the notch of the slide to prevent the shell from hanging in the bottom of the chamber. If necessary, replace the carrier dog and/or carrier dog follower spring.*

4. Extractor claw not functioning properly. If the claw has

been altered or if the sharp edge that grips the shell is worn or rounded, the extractor must be replaced. *The only recommended extractor alteration for hard feeding of the shell rim up under the extractor, is to round the lower corner of the extractor (see Fig. 16-10). If still more clearance is necessary, remove material from the lower pad of the extractor; but too much clearance will allow a shell to drop from the grip of the extractor prior to ejection.*

Gun Fails to Close Fully and Lock Up

1. Action bars not moving freely. *See "Gun Fails to Feed as the Forearm Moves Rearward."*

2. The chamber of the barrel is rough. *Look for pits, rust or other deformation to the area of the chamber where the shell rim seats. The locking block must be fully seated in its recess in the barrel extension. If the chamber is damaged, a new barrel may be needed.*

3. The extractor's passage into the corresponding slot in the barrel is hindered. *If necessary, chamfer the front lower corner of the extractor to allow free passage.*

Gun Fails to Fire

1. The firing pin is broken, short, or binding in the bolt. *Replace the firing pin.*

2. Locking block is not free and fully in position, so firing pin cannot contact the primer. *Reassemble with the locking block properly positioned.*

3. The slide is not fully forward in the breech bolt and positioned under the locking block. *The fore-end may simply need to be moved forward.*

4. The action bar lock is not free to allow full engagement with the left connector in the trigger assembly. *Check for correct installation of action bar lock and for burrs or damage. repair or replace if necessary.*

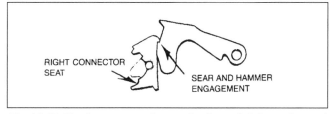

Fig. 16-11. The hammer notch must be free of deformation and capable of full engagement with the corresponding sear notch.

5. Hammer malfunctioning. *The notch on the rear of the hammer (see Fig. 16-11) must be free of deformation and capable of full engagement with the corresponding sear notch. Replace the hammer if necessary.*

6. The sear is malfunctioning. *The notch on the front of the sear must be free of deformation and capable of full engagement with the hammer notch. Replace the sear if necessary.*

7. The trigger is malfunctioning (with safety switch in "off" position). *The end of the right connector, when cocking the hammer, must be capable of seating fully into the notch on the rear of the sear. Failure to seat could be a faulty trigger-plate pin bushing. Return the trigger-plate assembly or complete shotgun to the factory.*

8. Hammer spring is weak *Replace with a new one.*

Gun Fails to Extract (Or Action Opens Hard)

1. Faulty extractor movement in bolt and in barrel slot. *The claw of the extractor must have full purchase on the shell rim. Replace the extractor if the claw is deformed or altered.*

2. The locking of the barrel extension is rough or deformed. *Check the area where the extension joins the barrel for excessive metal or recess which could possibly hinder extraction (see Fig. 16-12). Smooth up the area to correct the condition.*

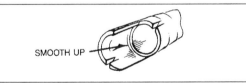

SMOOTH UP

Fig. 16-12. Smooth up any excessive metal in this area.

3. Deformation of the barrel where the shell's rim seats, in the throat or extractor slot, and/or rusting and pitting of the chamber. *It may be possible to smooth minor deformations at the breech end of the barrel or replacement of the barrel may be necessary.*

4. The action bar is not moving freely. *Check for deformation of the shell latch notches. Repair or replace.*

5. The action bar is not moving freely. *Check for sufficient clearance between it and the action bar to assist unlocking when under recoil.*

6. The firing pin retaining pin is not staked firmly flush with the bottom of the bolt to prevent it dropping into the path of the slide. *See instructions for Firing Pin Assembly.*

Gun Fails to Eject

1. The ejector is not tight on its rivets and binds the movement of the ejector spring. *Return the shotgun to the factory for the necessary replacement.*

2. Extractor is not moving freely and its claw is not gripping the rim of the fired shell. *Check for deformation of the claw. If necessary, tighten the grip of the claw by removing a very small amount of material from the middle pad of the extractor. Removal of too much material will cause the shell to feed up under the claw with difficulty.*

3. Shell latches lack full working engagement to keep the next shell in the magazine until the fired case has been ejected. *Check for proper installation of latches, and repair or replace if necessary.*

Barrel Out of Line

Magazine tube is sprung. *Bend carefully to realign the barrel.*

Safety Binds

Return the firearm to the factory.

Slide Binds on Rear of Ejection Port

Slide slightly misaligned. *This is caused by the occasional twisting motion on the action bars when shooters extract shells. Chamfer the rear corner of the slide to clear the ejection port.*

Action Jammed Forward with Barrel Removed

This condition is caused by attempting to remove the fore-end unit without depressing the right shell latch or by closing the action too harshly when the barrel is removed. *If damage has occurred to the action bars or the right shell latch, it may be necessary to replace the fore-end tube assembly and/or the right shell latch.*

17

WINCHESTER MODEL 94 LEVER-ACTION RIFLE

The Winchester Model 94 began its career in the mid-1890s and, as such, is now just about over one hundred years old. Other than cosmetic changes and slight model variations, the 94s manufactured and sold until 1963 were surprisingly alike, with a great many interchangeable parts. However, in 1964 a major revamping was undertaken, beginning with serial number 2,700,000. This brought about a number of physical part modifications as well as some dimensional changes. Because the so-called "post-'64" models were so poorly accepted, a number of changes occurred during the 1970s and 1980s that resulted in still more part and dimensional changes. Thus, it is imperative to establish exactly which era 94 you will be working on and which part numbers apply.

It is possible that some parts for older models may no longer be available from the manufacturer, such as heavy locking blocks for renewing headspace tolerances on older firearms. In many cases, the factory can supply alternate parts that can be adapted. Dealers such as Gun Parts Corp., and others, have large quantities of older parts.

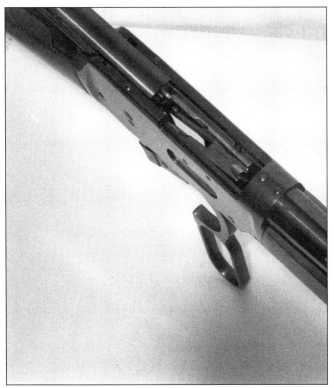

Fig. 19-1. Almost all of the 94's working mechanism can be viewed and inspected from the top of the opened action.

Basically, the 94 is a trouble-free rifle requiring only minimal repair or service and it is an easy rifle to work on. Almost all of the workings of a 94 can be viewed through the top of the receiver and, hence, difficulties are usually easy to diagnose.

The only routine repair is limited to the first post-'64 models which employed a sheet metal carrier that was easily damaged if subjected to even slightly abnormal stress. These sheet metal carriers should be routinely replaced with the later machined steel (from a casting) part. This will eliminate difficult feeding from magazine to chamber.

94 ACTION OPERATION

The 94 is the classic lever-action with a tubular magazine design. The cartridges are loaded into the right side of the receiver, through the loading gate, and pushed forward into the magazine by the nose of the following cartridge. When the lever is manipulated downward, it draws the locking lug down away from the locked position at the rear of the bolt. Once the locking lug (which contains a firing pin striker) has cleared the

bolt, the continuing lever motion forces the bolt rearward. As the bolt moves rearward, it compresses the hammer into the cocked position. As the lever nears the lowest point of its travel, a cartridge is raised on the carrier into the feeding position. When the lever is raised to the closed position, the bolt moves forward, chambering a fresh round. As the cartridge is chambered, the carrier is lowered into the bottom of the receiver. As it reaches this point, a cartridge is released from the magazine and escapes partially into the carrier. When the lever is again cycled and the bolt begins to move rearward, this cartridge can then escape fully onto the carrier and be raised up to the feeding position.

When the trigger is pressed, it causes the sear to release the hammer which, under compression of its spring, is driven forward against the firing pin striker in the locking lug. The striker then moves against the firing pin which, in turn, ignites the primer.

Extraction is achieved by a single claw mounted on the bolt and ejection is accomplished by the spring-loaded ejector which is also mounted to the bolt.

There is a protrusion on the front end of the link which serves as a cartridge stop to prevent cartridges from escaping from the magazine except when the gun is closed. At this point, only one cartridge will move partially from the magazine.

The following description of takedown deals with an earlier and one of the most popular model 94s.

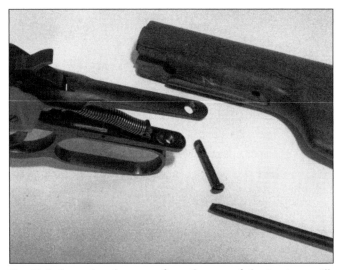

Fig. 19-2. Removing the screw from the rear of the top tang will allow the buttstock to be pulled rearward off of the receiver.

94 BUTTSTOCK REMOVAL

A single screw, located at the rear of the top tang, holds the buttstock to the rifle. After the screw is removed, slide the buttstock rearward and away from the rifle (see Fig. 19-2). If it sticks, jar the stock loose by slapping it with a cupped hand, striking rearward.

LOWER TANG GROUP REMOVAL

The lower tang group includes the mainspring, hammer, hammer retaining roll pin, trigger, sear, trigger stop, and related parts. With the buttstock removed, the entire group pivots on a single screw. This screw is removed from the lower left rear side of the receiver and the tang group is slid away from the receiver (see Fig. 19-3).

Once removed, the group may easily be disassembled into component parts. Start by cupping a hand around the tang and mainspring to capture the spring securely. Then uncock the hammer (the trigger stop will first need to be pushed inward by depressing the trigger and allowing the hammer to move slowly forward). Now, slowly pivot the hammer forward until the spring and its strut jump free. The hammer retaining pin can then be removed and, in turn, the hammer. A drift pin holds the trigger and sear in position. They can be removed after drifting out the pin.

Another pin holds the trigger stop and the combination trigger and trigger stop pin in position. Drift the pin free and then parts can be easily removed.

Reassembly is accomplished in reverse order except that the hammer (main) spring will need to be compressed on its strut and a slave pin or drift punch must be inserted (from the top side) into the hole in the strut to keep the spring compressed. After the hammer, hammer strut (see Fig. 19-4), and main-spring are in place, pull the slave pin or drift punch free.

LOCKING BLOCK REMOVAL

Lower the lever to its bottom position. Then grasp the locking block and pull it rearward, free of the link. The lever may have to be moved slightly upward before the locking block will pull free (see Fig. 19-5). Should it be necessary to remove or replace the firing pin striker, drive the retaining roll pin free from the locking block and the striker will fall free of the rear side of the locking block. Reassemble in reverse order.

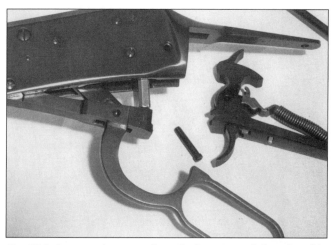

Fig. 19-3. Remove the screw from the lower rear, left action side and the tang group can be slid away from the receiver.

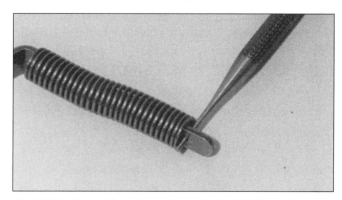

Fig. 19-4. A pin punch can be used to compress the hammer spring on its strut when reassembling the tang group.

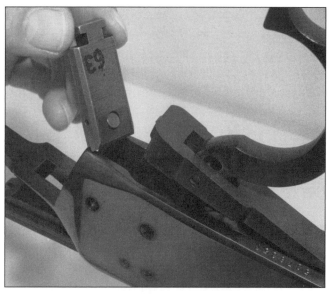

Fig. 19-5. Removing the locking block.

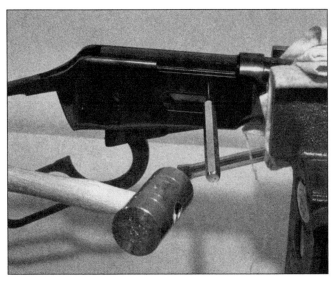

Fig. 19-6. After removing the large-headed screw from the left side of the action, a pin punch is used to drive out the link/bolt assembly pin.

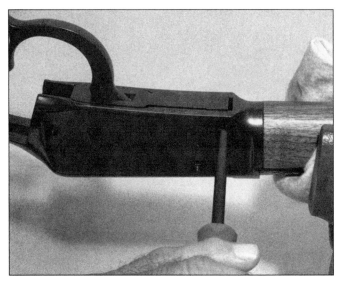

Fig. 19-7. Removing the link retaining screw will allow withdrawal of the lever and link from the receiver.

REMOVAL OF BOLT ASSEMBLY

Remove the large-headed screw that is located on the left side of the receiver at the front top edge. Then, with the lever held in the closed position, insert a pin punch in the hole located at the top forward section on the right side of the receiver (see Fig.19-6). Tap the pin punch lightly and a retaining pin will push out of the hole left open by the removal of the large-headed screw from the left side of the receiver.

Now, remove the link-retaining screw from the forward bottom edge of the left side of the receiver. Then, withdraw the lever and link from the bottom of the receiver. Pivot the cartridge carrier so that it points straight downward out of the receiver bottom. Pull the bolt free of the receiver.

Reassembly of the bolt is accomplished in reverse order. Note that the finger lever pin is started from the left side of the receiver with its bevel end entering first.

LEVER AND LINK DISASSEMBLY

It is seldom necessary to separate these parts. But to do so, drive out the retaining pin and the two will separate (see Fig. 19-7). The friction stud and spring, which lock the lever in the closed position, can be removed from the link by driving out the retaining pin. Don't lose these small parts as they will jump free when the drift punch is pulled out. Cup your hand over the parts to capture them as you pull the punch free.

Reassembly of the lever and link is accomplished in reverse order.

BOLT AND CARTRIDGE CARRIER DISASSEMBLY

At this point, the firing pin can be slid from the rear of the bolt (see Fig. 19-8). Further bolt disassembly is seldom needed. However, the ejector can be removed by driving out the roll pin that holds it in place. *Caution:* It is under heavy spring pressure and care must be taken to prevent losing parts when disassembling. Drive the roll pin out from left to right. Because this pin is riveted on the right end it will be necessary to replace it before assembly. Remember to rivet it in place. The extractor may be removed by unscrewing the retaining screw. Reassemble in reverse order. Remove the remaining large-headed screw from the left side of the receiver and withdraw the cartridge carrier (see Fig. 19-9).

LOADING GATE REMOVAL

Disassembly is not suggested as a special tool is required for assembly. If necessary, however, remove the remaining large-headed screw from the right side of the receiver to free the loading gate. Reassembly requires holding the loading gate in position and compressing it. Do this with a screwdriver (bent into an L-shape) pressed against the loading gate from inside the receiver.

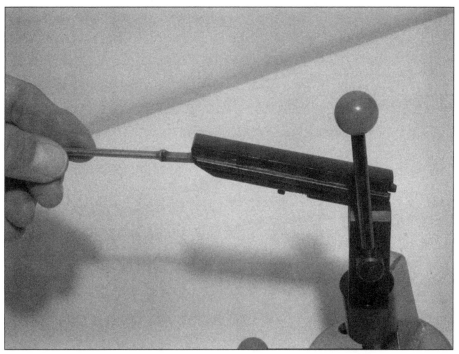

Fig. 19-8. The firing pin is withdrawn from the rear of the bolt.

CARTRIDGE GUIDES AND CARRIER SPRING REMOVAL

Disassembly is seldom required and not recommended as these parts can be bothersome to reassemble.

The cartridge guides are held in position by two small head screws (one for each guide) located on each side of the receiver. They are somewhat difficult to tighten securely and require a very exacting screwdriver fit. The cartridge carrier spring can be removed by carefully inserting a screwdriver through the loading gate opening (with gate removed). Replacing the spring requires some patience and dexterity.

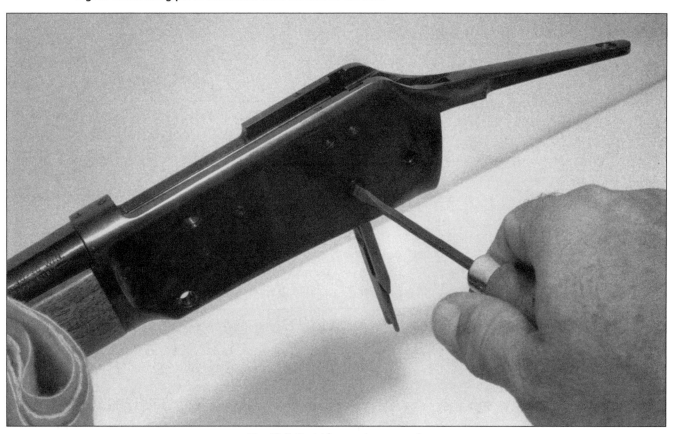

Fig. 19-9. Cartridge carrier removal.

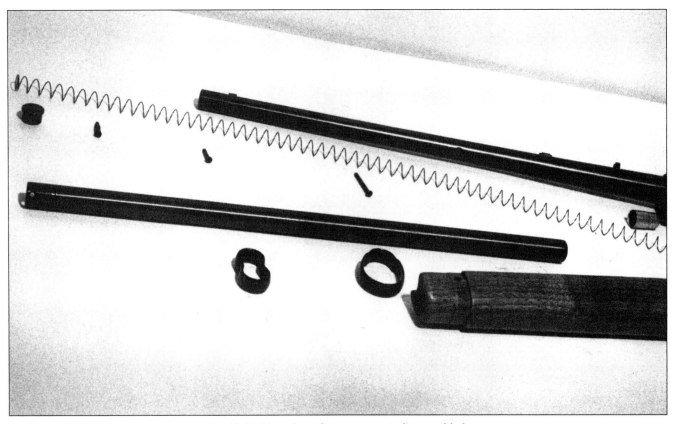

Fig. 19-10. Magazine tube components disassembled.

ACTION REASSEMBLY NOTES

When pushing the bolt into the receiver, with the firing pin in place, be sure the cut in the firing pin aligns with the pin hole in the bolt. Also, the cartridge carrier should be swung upward against the bolt when assembling the finger lever and link. Insert the link screw before attempting to insert the finger lever pin.

Use a drift punch placed into the right side of the receiver to align the pin hole in the bolt, firing pin, and finger lever before starting in the pin from the left side. The pin will start with finger pressure and go into place easily. If it does not, the parts are not properly aligned. All you'll need is a bit of patience and very little force. Some manipulation of the finger lever will be required.

DISASSEMBLY OF MAGAZINE TUBE, BARREL BANDS, AND FORE-END

Disassembly of these parts is straightforward, but reassembly

alignment of barrel bands can sometimes be quite bothersome. Therefore, disassembly is not suggested unless necessary.

Start by removing the magazine cap screw from the front bottom edge of the magazine tube. Be careful not to let the magazine cap and spring fly free as the screw is removed. Tip the muzzle down and allow the magazine follower to fall free of the magazine.

Next, remove the two barrel band screws and pull the magazine forward and free of the gun. The barrel bands may now be removed. It's a good idea to coat the barrel liberally with oil before sliding the barrel bands free. This will prevent a tight band from scratching the barrel's finish. The front band will need to be rotated 180 degrees in order to clear any front sight ramp.

Reassembly is accomplished in reverse order. The fore-end may need to be tapped into position. Use a block of soft wood placed over the end of the fore-end and tap it lightly with a small hammer. Do this carefully to not damage it. The rear barrel band may have to be driven carefully into place to align the barrel band and fore-end screw hole. Do this carefully also. Many fore-ends are damaged by a moment of carelessness when tapping the rear barrel band into place. Using a soft wood dowel and a light mallet will help prevent such damage.

Make no attempt to force the barrel band screw into place. Properly align the hole and everything will go together easily.

That's all there is to disassemble and reassemble the 94.

COMMON PROBLEM—PROBABLE CAUSES AND CORRECTIONS

Gun Balks on Loading

The loading gate may be binding on the shell head. *Replace the loading gate.*

Gun Fails to Feed

Bent magazine tube. *Replace it and/or the magazine spring as required. If the carrier does not operate unless the gun is forcefully opened, the carrier and carrier spring should be replaced.*

Gun Double Feeds or Fails to Cam Cartridge Back into Magazine

The link stop lug is upset or worn. *Replace link. Also replace the cartridge carrier if it is made of sheet metal. It is a good idea to simultaneously replace the loading gate to prevent recurrence of link damage.*

Shells Do Not Rise High Enough to Chamber

Loose, broken, or blunt carrier spring. *Replace parts as required. Loose cartridge guide screws can also be the problem. Tighten screws.*

Action Binds on Closing

Extractor does not have sufficient clearance. *Inspect cartridge rims for nicks or burrs. Also be sure extractor aligns with matching cut in the barrel. If the ejector binds in the breech bolt it can also be part of the problem. Replace or refit extractor.*

Gun Fails to Fire

Broken or binding firing pin or weak mainspring. *Replace part.*

Other Problems

Winchester 94 problems are most often self-explanatory when the firearm is examined closely. There are no difficult-to-solve problems. Those that require factory service will include any headspace or barrel problems.

EARLIER MODEL 94s

The current 94s are without doubt the easiest 94s on which to work. Early models had a number of variations that made for modifications in disassembly and reassembly procedures. It is impossible to cover all of these variations in this space. Some variations include: cartridge guide screws that mount from the inside of the receiver, a drift pin instead of a screw to hold the link in position (this variation used a set screw to keep the pin in place); flat hammer springs; hammers with stirrup; and lower tangs dovetailed to the receiver. Before working on pre-1980 94s, be sure you know what variations are present on your specific firearm.

The style of the 94s covered in this disassembly and reassembly procedure can be easily recognized in that no provision for a half-cock safety notch is provided on the hammer. Instead, the hammer has only two basic positions—fully cocked and at rest. For carrying safety, the hammer is left in the at-rest position. In this position, it is withdrawn from contact with the firing pin striker. Also the hammer cannot be moved forward unless the lever is held fully closed and the trigger is depressed.

1987 WINCHESTER 94 LEVER-ACTION STANDARD VERSION PARTS LIST
FOR 30-30 CARBINE

Note: Part numbers vary by caliber, barrel length, model, etc. Check with Winchester before ordering parts other than for standard .30-30 Carbine

Part No.	Name of Part	Part No.	Name of Part
94120005	Barrel, Carbine(.30-30 Win.), 20" Standard	4994X	Link Complete - Standard comprising:
94120020	Breech Bolt		link with friction stud, friction stud
94120025	Breech Bolt Complete, comprising bolt		spring and friction stud stop pin
	with extractor and screws, firing pin,	5094X	Locking Bolt - Standard
	ejector, ejector spring and ejector stop pin	5194X	Locking Bolt Complete - Standard
3394X	Buttstock Complete - Standard		comprising: locking bolt with firing pin
694X	Buttplate -Standard		striker and firing pin striker pin
9112	Buttplate/Pad Screws (2 required)	10494X	Lower Tang
94070035	Carrier	94121040	Lower Tang Complete comprising: (R)
1394X	Carrier Screw		lower tang with hammer, hammer bushing,
1494X	Carrier Spring		hammer spring, hammer spring guide rod,
1594X	Carrier Spring Screw		sear, trigger with hammer block assembly,
1794X	Cartridge Guide L.H. - Standard		trigger pin, trigger stop, trigger stop
1694X	Cartridge Guide R.H. - Standard		pin, trigger stop spring, and trigger spring
1894X	Cartridge Guide Screw (2 required)	5794X	Magazine Follower
94070050	Ejector	11394X	Magazine Plug - Standard
94070051	Ejector Complete comprising: ejector	11994X	Magazine Plug Screw - Standard
	with spring and ejector stop pin	11294X	Magazine Spring- Standard
2394X	Ejector Spring	13394X	Magazine Tube - Standard
94070055	Ejector Stop Pin	13894X	Magazine Tube Complete - Standard
94070060	Extractor		comprising: magazine tube with magazine
94070065	Extractor Retaining Screw (2 required)		follower, magazine plug, magazine plug
16994X	Finger Lever		screw and magazine spring
2994AX	Finger Lever Link Pin	15194X	Rear Band - Standard
3494X	Finger Lever Link Screw	15294X	Rear Band Screw
2894X	Finger Lever Pin	94120100	Receiver - Standard (R)
2994X	Finger Lever Pin Stop Screw	94120421	Sear and Hammer (R)
2594X	Firing Pin	94	Sight Assembly, Rear - Standard
4094X	Firing Pin Striker	94A	Sight Binding Screw, Rear (2 required)
4194X	Firing Pin Striker Stop Pin	94B	Sight Blade, Rear
8194X	Forearm - Standard	3281	Sight Cover, Front
6194X	Friction Stud	3C	Sight Elevator, Rear - Standard
6094X	Friction Stud Spring	103F	Sight, Front - (.360" High) -Standard
6394X	Friction Stud Stop Pin	12970C	Sight Plug Screw, Telescope (4 required)
8594X	Front Band - Standard	6994X	Spring Cover
38594USA	Front Band Screw	7094X	Spring Cover Screw
94120421	Hammer and Sear (R)	94120770	Trigger with Hammer Block Assembly
4394X	Hammer Bushing	7794AX	Trigger/Sear Pin
3494X	Hammer Screw - Standard	94120773	Trigger Spring
94120450	Hammer Spring	7594X	Trigger Stop
94120470	Hammer Spring Guide Rod	33270	Trigger Stop Pin
94070082	Hammer Spur Assembly	7494X	Trigger Stop Spring
		16494X	Upper Tang Screw

(R) = Restricted part, available only for factory installation.

18

SAVAGE 110 BOLT-ACTION RIFLE

The Savage 110 bolt-action rifle has been offered in a number of variations. The popular Model 110E is the most numerous of all these. This basic 110 rifle has also been sold under private labels using different names and model designations. These include the following:

Company	Brand Name	Model No(s).
Canadian Industries Ltd.	CIL	950, 950-D, 950-C
Colter & Company	Westpoint	410
Talo	Golden	
	West	710DL
Western Auto Supply	Revelation	250D, 250
Gamble Skogmo, Inc.	Hiawatha	510

The information contained in this chapter will generally apply to all Savage rifles in the 110 series, as well as the five brands indicated.

It should be pointed out that Savage Arms provides parts, service and repair for Savage manufactured rifles from 1995 to present. Small Arma Shop out of Inverness, FL provides parts, service and repair for Savage manufactured rifles older than 1995.

The Savage 110 receivers vary somewhat. The Models 110ED, 110D and 110C differ from older models in that the older receivers are not machined to accept the 110C-style trigger nor the later-style magazines. Also, rifle models with suffixes C or D are equipped with a newer sliding extractor and integral ejector. Newer models do not have a recessed chamber to accept the bolt head as do earlier models.

DESIGN AND CYCLE OF OPERATION

Designed by Nicholas Brewer and introduced in 1958, the original Model 110 incorporated construction features that were then new, but essentially thosse novel aspects of design were in no way a departure from the traditional Mauer-type turnbolt action using a bolt with forward dual-opposed locking lugs and a staggered-column box magazine.

Brewer's original bolt was guided only by its locking lugs, and sometimes too much play developed in the raceway–and had to be worked carefully to avoid jamming. This was corrected in 1972 by broaching a groove inside the receiver to form a guide.

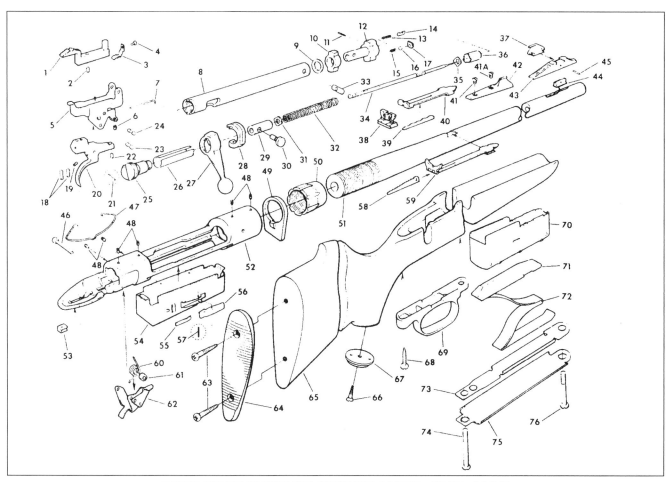

EXPLODED VIEW OF SAVAGE 110ED, 110D, 110C

View No.	Part No.	Name of Part	View No.	Part No.	Name of Part
1	113-192	Safety	21	113-563	Trigger Spring Pin
2	110-593	Trigger Pull Adjusting Screw	22	113-593	Trigger Engagement Adjusting Screw
3	113-776	Safety Detent Spring	23	110-285	Trigger Pin
4	99-444	Safety Detent Spring	24	110-590	Safety Bearing Pin
5	113-280	Trigger Bracket	25	110-583	Bolt Assembly Screw
6	113-593	Trigger Pull Adjusting Screw	26	110-587	Cocking Piece Sleeve
7	113-871	Trigger Pull Adjusting Spring	27	113-17	Bolt Handle (specify left or right)
8	113-16	Bolt body (specify caliber, left or right)	28	113-584	Rear Baffle (specify left or right)
9	110-582	Front Baffle Friction Washer	29	110-34	Cocking Piece
10	110-581	Front Baffle		110-36	Cocking Piece Pin (specify left or right)
11	113-55	Ejector Retaining Pin		110-588	Cocking Piece Lock Washer
12	113-19	Bolt Head (R)	32	110-166	Mainspring (specify caliber)
		Bolt Head Assembly Complete (R)	33	110-20	Bolt Head Retaining Pin
		(113-734)(Specify caliber, left, right hand)	34	113-77	Firing Pin (specify caliber)
13	340-56	Ejector Spring	35	110-586	Firing Pin Stop Nut Washer
14	113-53	Ejector	36	110-585	Firing Pin Stop Nut
15	110-284	Extractor Spring	37	99-218	Front Sight
16	76-178	Steel Ball	38	110P-229	Rear Sight (folding)
17	113-59	Extractor	39	110-233	Rear Sight Step
18	113-870	Trigger Travel Adjusting Screw	40	3-229	Rear Sight
19	113-869	Trigger Pin Retaining Screw	41	325-227	Front Sight Screw (short)
20	113-279	Trigger	41A	325-226	Front Sight Screw (long)

View No.	Part No.	Name of Part	View No.	Part No.	Name of Part
42	342-218	Front Sight		114M-708	Stock with Recoil Pad (Model 110D, Magnum Only)(specify caliber, right or left hand)
43	110-219	Front Sight & Base Assembly			
44	110-607	Front Sight Dovetail Black		114E-708	Stock Complete (Model 110ED) (specify caliber)
45	110-599	Front Sight Pin			
46	110-206	Sear Pin		114EM-708	Stock with Recoil Pad
47	110-154	Magazine Retainer Spring		114P-708	Stock Complete (Model 110DP-110DPE) (specify caliber, right or left hand)
48	99R-289	Dummy Screw			
49	110-176	Recoil Lug (R)			
50	110-10	Barrel Lock Nut (R)	66	99-423	Pistol Grip Screw
51	113-1	Barrel (specify caliber) (R)	67	110M-422	Pistol Grip Cap
	113M-1	Barrel (magnum) (R)	68	110-311	Trigger Guard Screw
52	113-2	Receiver (specify caliber) (R)	69	110-99	Trigger Guard
53	110-604	Trigger Pull Adjusting Screw Cover	70	110D-142	Magazine Box (specify caliber)
54	113-293	Magazine Guide (specify caliber)	71	113-143	Magazine Follower
55	113-486	Magazine Latch Spring	72	110-156	Magazine Spring
56	113-495	Magazine Latch	73	110-625	Floor Plate Insert
57	113-484	Magazine Latch Pin	74	110-85	Floor Plate Screw, Rear
58	110-233	Rear Sight Step	75	110-84	Floor Plate
59	110-229	Rear Sight Step	76	110-594	Floor Plate Screw, Front
60	113-209	Sear Spring	77	113-857	Magazine Latch Button
61	110-439	Sear Bushing	78	113-420	Escutcheon
62	113-205	Sear	79	113-708	Stock Complete (Model 110C) (specify caliber, right or left)
63	94-32	Buttplate Screw			
	110-60	Recoil Pad Screw	80	113-84	Floor Plate (specify caliber)
64	110-5	Buttplate	81	113-735	Magazine Assembly (specify caliber)
	775-5	Buttplate	82	113-99	Trigger Guard
	110-314	Recoil Pad	83	113-868	Magazine Ejector Spring
65	114MC-708	Stock Complete (specify caliber) (Model 110)(right or left hand)			

(R) = Restricted part, available only for factory installation.

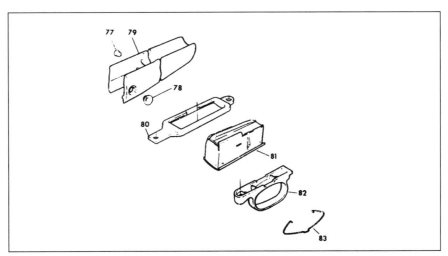

Model 110C parts that are different from other 110 parts.

system with a tongue protruding from a baffle lug.

Depsite its unique design features, the Savage 110 employs a cycle of operation that typifies bolt-actions–essentially similar to other descendants of the Mauser. The characteristic bolt-action cycle was described for the Remington Model 700 and will not be repeated here.

BOLT REMOVAL AND REASSEMBLY

Raise the bolt handle and draw the bolt fully rearward. Then, while simultaneously depressing both the bolt release (located at right rear side of the action) and the trigger, withdraw the bolt to the rear. This awkward maneuver is best accomplished by using the right thumb to depress the bolt stop and the right middle finger to pull the trigger (see Fig. 18-1). Withdraw the bolt using the left hand. To disassemble the bolt, unscrew the assembly screw from the rear of the bolt (see Fig. 18-2). The cocking piece sleeve attached to the screw will be withdrawn with the screw. Slide off the bolt handle and rear baffle. The cocking piece pin can now be withdrawn from the rear side of the bolt body. This is the large-headed pin that enters the bolt perpendicularly in front of the rear baffle. The firing pin assembly can now be withdrawn.

Fig. 18-1. The bolt release must be depressed while simultaneously pulling the trigger in order to withdraw the bolt from from the receiver.

Next, push out the bolt head retaining pin, located behind the front baffle. The bolt head, front baffle, and friction washer can now be removed from the front end of the bolt.

When reassembling the bolt, be sure the friction washer is placed in position before the front baffle. The chamfered side of the baffle is positioned toward the front of the bolt.

Disassembly of the striker and mainspring unit is not recommended unless it is necessary to replace a broken firing pin or mainspring. To disassemble, unscrew the cocking piece (the tubular piece at the back of the spring) and then remove the cocking piece lock washer (see Fig. 18-3). The mainspring might escape as the cocking piece is unscrewed, so use caution. The firing pin stop nut lock washer is then disengaged and the firing pin stop nut removed (see Fig. 18-4).

Fig. 18-2. Removing the assembly screw from the rear of the bolt.

Reassemble the bolt in reverse order. When reassembling the firing pin stop-nut to the firing pin, adjust it so that there is 0.055-inch to 0.065-inch protrusion of the firing pin through the bolt head. This distance must be carefully measured. When the adjustment is right, engage the nut with the firing pin stop-nut lock washer to secure its position. Then double check the amount of protrusion of the firing pin from the bolt head.

When the cocking piece is installed, it must be adjusted so that the hole for the cocking piece pin will have 0.005-inch to 0.015-inch clearance from the bottom of the cam cut in the bolt body to the firing pin in the forward position. This hole will have to be in line with one of the protrusions on the cocking piece lock washer.

The bolt will need to be cocked before it can be reinserted into the receiver. Do this by forcing the cocking piece pin up the cam surface until it rests in the cocked notch. Be sure the bolt is firmly held in a well-padded vise before attempting this.

Fig. 18-3. Removing the cocking piece.

The ejector and extractor should not be removed from the bolt unless absolutely necessary. The sliding extractor can be removed simply by sliding the extractor out of the slot in the bolt head. *Caution:* The steel ball and spring will snap out as the extractor is slid away. The ejector, also under heavy spring tension, is held in place by a pin. Driving out the pin and then removing the drift punch will allow the ejector and spring to escape the bolt.

Note: Various styles of ejectors have been used in Savage 110 type rifles. It is impossible to cover all the variations. However, whether bolt-mounted or located in the magazine latch, disassembly is seldom necessary. The previous description applies to rifles with serial numbers above 100,000.

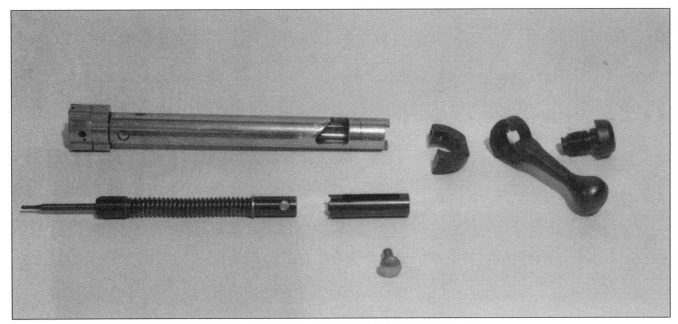

Fig. 18-4. Savage 110's disassembled bolt looks like this.

STOCK REMOVAL

Remove the front action screw and rear action screw (front trigger guard screw). The stock will then separate from the barrelled action, with the magazine spring and follower falling loose. The magazine guide is staked into position on the receiver. The magazine box should not be disassembled from the receiver. The trigger bolt release and safety parts should also not be disassembled.

TRIGGER PULL ADJUSTMENT

Be sure the rifle is unloaded and cocked. Turn in the adjustment screw (see Fig. 18-5, Key No. 1) on the front end of the trigger until the sear releases. Stop turning immediately upon its release. Then back up the screw exactly one-half turn outward to give the minimum 0.015-inch sear engagement. This step alone is often all that is necessary to get the right trigger pull.

Recock the action and move the safety to the on position by sliding it rearward. If the safety will not move, back out the screw at the rearmost part of the trigger (see Fig. 18-5, Key No. 2) until the safety will go "on". This screw should be carefully adjusted to allow the safety to slide freely, yet allow no movement of the trigger if it is pulled while the gun is "on" safety.

Slide the safety forward and pull the trigger to uncock the action. Then adjust the screw immediately behind the trigger (see Fig. 18-5, Key No. 3) so that the trigger has minimum movement when pulled. Test this by cocking the rifle and pulling the trigger. If the gun will not fire, insufficient trigger travel is present. Correct this by turning the screw outward a half-turn at a time. Then check the cocking of the rifle. If the sear binds on the trigger and the rifle will not cock, adjust by backing out the screw (see Fig. 18-5, Key No. 3) a half-turn at a time.

The weight of the pull may now be adjusted by using the screw located on the right outside trigger position. This is the screw against which the long piano wire spring is positioned. *Caution:* Savage literature suggest a four-pound minimum pull. Turning in the screw (see Fig. 18-5, Key No. 4) will increase the trigger pull weight, while backing it out will decrease the trigger pull weight. The screw must be turned to allow the spring to rest in one of the two notches provided; in other words, rotate it in half-turn increments.

After all the screws have been properly adjusted, lock each into position by placing a drop of nail polish over each screw. Allow the nail polish to dry completely before use.

When reassembling the rifle, be sure the correct end of the follower is positioned forward. The high step of the follower will be on the left side of the receiver when the follower is positioned correctly.

If the bolt does not open after reassembly the front action screw has gone too deep and is binding on the locking lug. Remove the screw and shorten it as necessary. Do not damage its threads when doing so.

Note: The bolt stop also serves as a cocking indicator. When the bolt stop is in its high position, the rifle is cocked. When the rifle is fired, the bolt stop drops to its lowest position, approximately flush with the stock.

COMMON PROBLEMS— PROBABLE CAUSES AND CORRECTIONS

As noted earlier, the design of the 110 incorporates features (new and unusual in 1958 but now more common) for ease of production and strength of the action, but this rifle operates essentially like any Mauser-type bolt-action. Common bolt-action problems, their causes and corrections, were covered in the chapter on Remington Model 700. It is unlikely that you will encounter any malfunctions or other problems peculiar to the Savage Model 110. Broken, worn, or damaged parts should be repaired or replaced as in other bolt-action rifles.

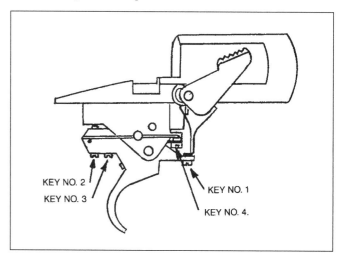

Fig. 18-5. Trigger adjusting screws.

19

MARLIN 336 LEVER-ACTION RIFLE

The Marlin 336 has been popular since the late 1890s as a woods carbine in caliber .30-30 Winchester and, to a lesser extent, in caliber .35 Remington. But this Marlin has also been offered in a number of other cartridges such as .32 Winchester Special, .45-70 Government, and .444 Marlin. The 336 has not only been offered as a carbine, but also as a rifle, a shorter than normal carbine, and even in deluxe and "plain-Jane" versions (Glenfield line). In some of these instances the 336 designation has not been applied, although the gun being sold indeed had a 336 action for its basics.

Most of the Marlin variations have been cosmetic ones, though several mechanical or parts changes have occurred in varying models. This discussion of the 336 will center on models which, in addition to the normal half-cock hammer safety, incorporate a cross-bolt, through-the-receiver safety.

336 CHARACTERISTICS

The 336 Marlin is a typical exposed-hammer, lever-action rifle. Cartridges are loaded through the loading port on the right side of the receiver with the nose of each cartridge pushing the round in front of it (lying half in the receiver and half in the magazine) fully forward into the magazine.

As the lever is lowered, the cartridge lying only partially in the magazine escapes so that it lies fully on the cartridge carrier. The remaining cartridges are locked into the magazine by the cartridge carrier.

Also, as the lever is lowered, the bolt is moved rearward cocking the hammer. Simultaneously, any shell or empty case in the chamber is withdrawn by the bolt-mounted extractor. As the bolt clears the receiver-mounted ejector, the ejector enters a cut in the bolt and is held tightly against it by the ejector

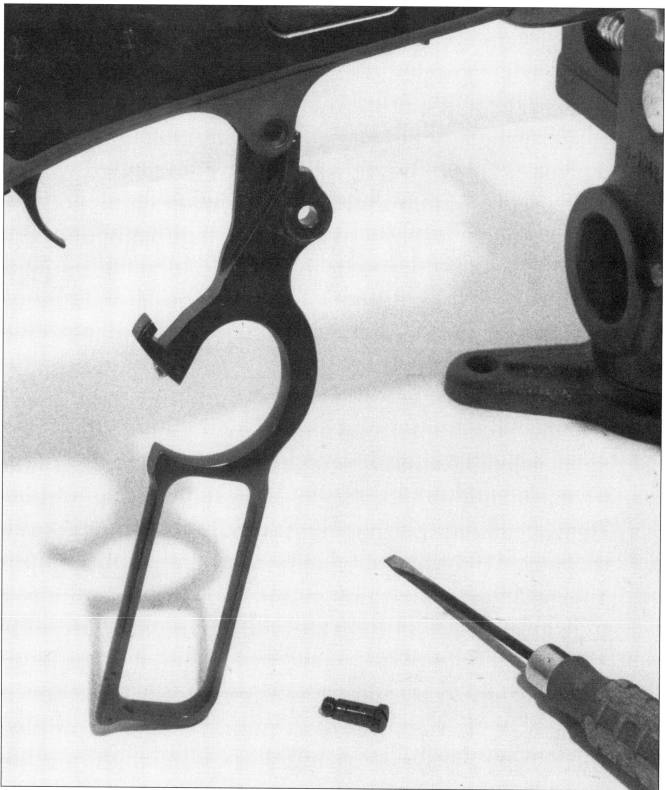

Fig. 19-1. To disassemble the 336, begin by removing the lever pivot screw, then pull the lever back and down, away from the receiver.

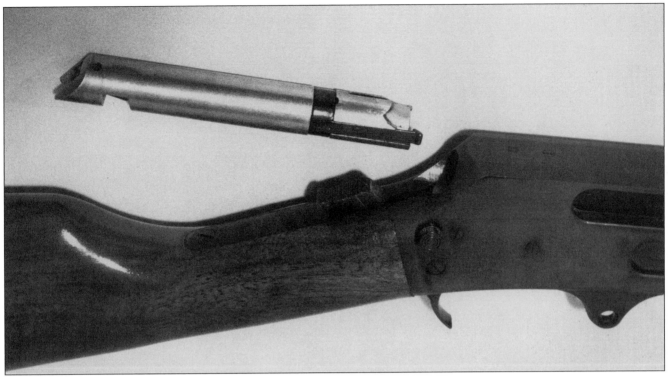

19-2. The bolt is withdrawn directly from the receiver. Keep the receiver on its left side to prevent loss of the ejector.

spring. When the cartridge impacts the ejector it is pivoted about the extractor and thrown from the right side of the receiver.

As the lever is closed, the cartridge carrier raises up and places a new cartridge in front of the bolt. As the stroke is continued, the bolt is moved forward pushing the cartridge into the chamber. During the final closing movement of the lever, the bolt is locked into place by the locking block as it cams into the bolt's lower rear half. The cartridge carrier then drops to its lowest position and another round partially escapes the magazine. Its rearward travel is stopped by the loaded gate readying the gun for the next manipulation of the lever.

FINGER LEVER, BOLT ASSEMBLY, AND EJECTOR REMOVAL

The Marlin is simplicity in design and disassembly. With the lever partially open, begin by removing the lever pivot and retaining screw located in the lower receiver tang protrusion, directly in the front end of the lever. Then pull back and down on the lever, pulling it away from the rifle (see Fig. 19-1).

With the rifle lying on its left side, withdraw the bolt assembly from the rear of the receiver. The hammer may have to be compressed slightly with your thumb to do this step. It

will be necessary to lower the lever far enough to disengage the locking block to allow for bolt withdrawal (see Fig. 19-2).

The ejector, which is lying in a recess in the right side of the receiver, can be lifted out with a needle nose plier or tweezer-type tool. Or, you can simply roll the receiver over onto its right side and shake the ejector out of the receiver after it falls from its notch (see Fig. 19-3).

Note: When replacing the ejector, the pin-like protrusion goes into the corresponding receiving hole. The pin protrusion is positioned so that it is at the rear, and the spring faces forward and is fully contained in the receiver groove. It may be necessary to hold the ejector in place until the bolt has been started past it.

BUTTSTOCK REMOVAL

Remove the large screw from the upper rear tang (located at the end of the tang). Then pull the buttstock away from the receiver. If the buttstock does not slide easily to the rear, a few slaps using a cupped hand over the stock comb, directed so as to drive the stock rearward, will accomplish the task (see Fig. 19-4).

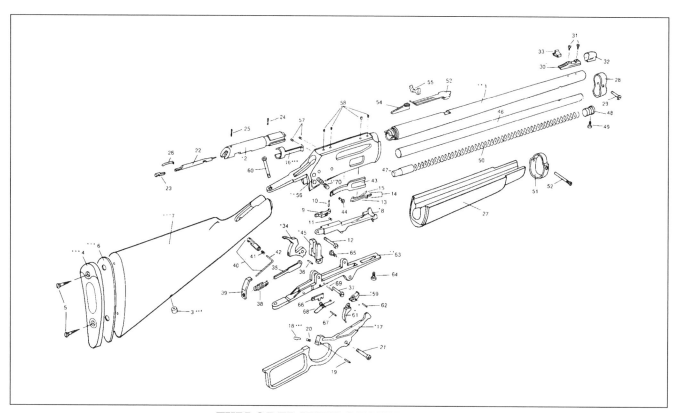

EXPLODED VIEW OF MARLIN 336

View No.	Part No.	Name of Part	View No.	Part No.	Name of Part
1	101340	Barrel (R)	18	201071	Finger Lever Plunger
2	101686	Breech Bolt, caliber .30-30	19	301197	Finger Lever
	501686	Breech Bolt Assembly			Plunger Pin
		(consisting of Parts 2, 16 and 22 through 26)	20	401196	Finger Lever Plunger Spring
		(Not shown)	21	301192	Finger Lever Screw
3	320101	Bullseye	22	401299	Firing Pin, Front
4	320202	Buttplate with Spacer	23	401199	Firing Pin, Rear
5	320590	Buttplate screw (2)	24	420299	Firing Pin Retaining Pin, Front
6	320103	Buttplate Spacer	25	420299	Firing Pin Retaining Pin, Rear
7	501016	Buttstock Complete	26	401295	Firing Pin Spring
8	101161	Carrier	27	101227	Forearm
9	201063	Carrier Rocker	28	301233	Front Band
10	401062	Carrier Rocker Pin	29	301291	Front Band Screw
11	401094	Carrier Rocker Spring	30	220539	Front Sight Base
	501161	Carrier Assembly, cal. .30-30	31	320190	Front Sight
		(consisting of above 4 parts) (Not shown)			Base Screw (2)
12	301190	Carrier Screw	32	320245	Front Sight Hood
13	201168	Ejector	33	330644	Front Sight Insert
14	501168	Ejector With Spring		520539	Front Sight Complete
15	401294	Ejector Spring			(Consisting of above 4 Parts)
16	301169	Extractor	34	101273	Hammer
17	501370	Finger Lever	35	320174	Hammer Strut

View No.	Part No.	Name of Part
36	401397	Hammer Strut Pin
37	301090	Hammer Screw
38	420294	Hammer Spring (mainspring)
39	320175	Hammer Spring Adjusting Plate
40	520377	Hammer Spur Complete
41	420193	Hammer Spur Screw
42	420204	Hammer Spur Wrench
43	101594	Loading Spring
44	301091	Loading Spring Screw
45	101081	Locking Bolt
46	201022	Magazine Tube
47	301024	Magazine Tube Follower
48	301225	Magazine Tube Plug
49	301092	Magazine Tube Plug Screw
50	401395	Magazine Tube Spring
51	201521	Rear Band
52	301590	Rear Band Screw
	501342	Rear Sight, Complete
53	520241	Rear Sight Base
54	320242	Rear Sight Elevator
55	201342	Rear Sight Folding Leaf
56	101760	Receiver (R)
57	320690	Receiver Sight Dummy Screw (2)
58	320493	Scope Mount Dummy Screw (2)
59	201051	Sear
60	320391	Tang Screw
61	201143	Trigger
62	401097	Trigger and Sear Pin
63	501258	Trigger Guard Plate (R)
64	301390	Trigger Guard Plate Screw
65	301490	Trigger Guard Plate Support Screw
66	301859	Trigger Safety Block
67	320397	Trigger Safety Block Pin
68	401095	Trigger Safety Block Spring
69	401099	Trigger Guard Plate Latch Pin
70	599183	Safety Button Assembly (R)

(R) = Restricted part, available only for factory installation.

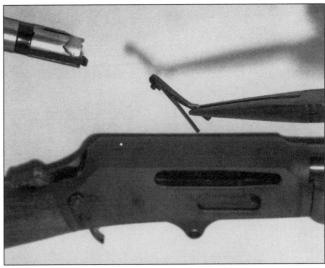

Fig. 19-3. Lift the ejector from the receiver.

HAMMER REMOVAL

Fig. 19-4. The buttstock is removed by drawing it rearward after its retaining screw has been removed.

With the buttstock removed, slide the hammer spring retainer out of the left side of the receiver. the top portion should clear the receiver first. Then slide out the bottom portion. It will be necessary to slightly compress the hammer spring while sliding out the bottom end of the retainer. To do this, grasp and manipulate the top end of the retainer forward (see Fig. 19-5).

Then remove the hammer screw (located just below the cross bolt safety on the right side of the receiver). To slip the

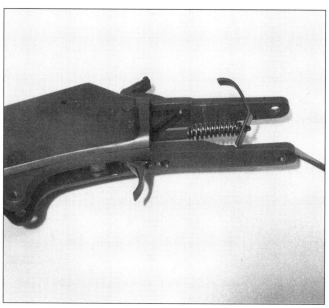

Fig. 19-5. Removing the hammer spring retainer.

hammer from the top back end of the receiver, depress the trigger allowing the hammer to pivot forward. To depress the trigger, manually push the trigger stop pin located behind the trigger, into the lower tang. When the hammer is fully pivoted forward, simply pull up on it and it will clear the receiver easily (see Fig. 19-6).

LOWER TANG, LOCKING BLOCK, AND CARRIER REMOVAL

Remove the retaining screw at the bottom front edge of the receiver. Next, remove the other retaining screw at the bottom edge of the receiver's left side. The lower tang may be removed by pulling downward on the rear end of the tang. If it is tight, hit the front edge of the finger lever retaining pin protrusion with a light leather mallet. Use a few light blows to move the tang rearward about 1/4-inch. Then pull down on the rear end of the tang and pull it away from the receiver (see Fig. 19-7).

When reassembling the rifle it may be necessary to use a leather mallet to align the lower tang with its retaining screw holes.

Now, lift the locking block from the rear end of the receiver, pulling it out of the receiver bottom (see Fig. 19-8). Its hook, which engages a corresponding hook on the finger lever, is positioned facing the rear of the rifle. The locking block must be installed in this position when reassembling the rifle.

The cartridge carrier may be withdrawn by removing the retaining screw located on the right side of the receiver directly in front of the cross bolt safety (see Fig. 19-9).

Fig. 19-6. Hammer removal.

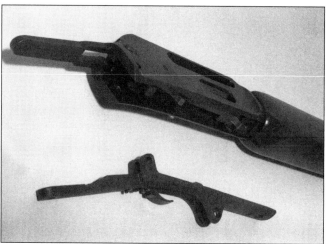

Fig. 19-7. Lower tang removal.

Fig. 19-8. Locking block removal

CROSS BOLT SAFETY

The cross bolt safety does not usually need to be removed except for repair or replacement. It is retained in the receiver by a set screw located on the left rear edge of the receiver. Do not lose the spring and detent when disassembling.

LOADING GATE REMOVAL

The loading gate is held in place by the only remaining screw on the right side of the receiver. However, the loading gate should not be removed as it can be difficult to replace. Replace the loading gate by compressing it against the inside of the receiver while its screw hole is aligned. This is done with an offset (right angle) screwdriver blade pressed firmly against the inside edge of the loading gate. The gun should be firmly held in a vise during this operation.

MAGAZINE TUBE AND FORE-END REMOVAL

As with all similar rifles, it is suggested that the magazine

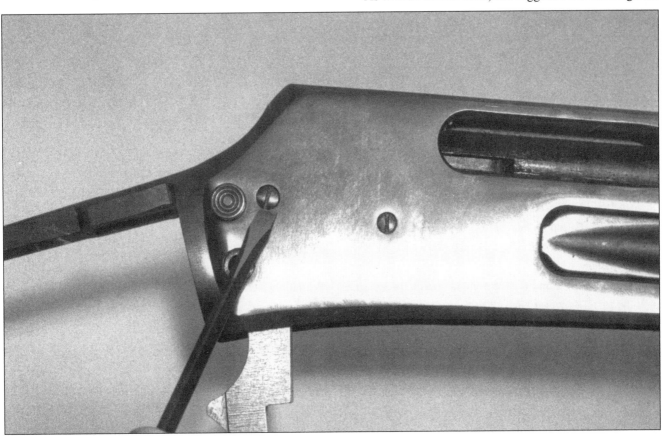

Fig. 19-9. Remove the retaining screw on the right side of the receiver to withdraw the cartridge carrier.

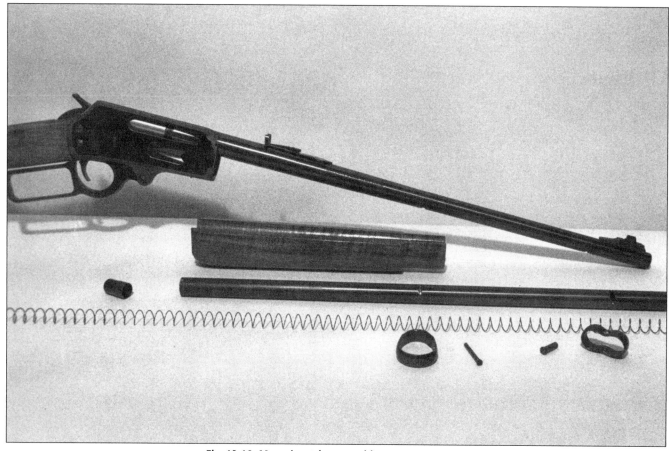

Fig. 19-10. Magazine tube assembly component parts.

tube not be removed due to the difficulty when aligning the barrel-band screw holes. However, such disassembly may be necessary from time to time. Start by removing the magazine tube cap from the forward end of the tube.

Caution: The cap is under spring pressure and will fly free as the screw is withdrawn. Cup your hand over the cap as the screw is withdrawn.

Set the cap aside and withdraw the magazine spring. Then point the barrel downward and allow the magazine follower to slide free of the magazine tube.

Now remove both barrel-band screws. Both the barrel and magazine should be liberally oiled to prevent finish damage before proceeding.

The magazine tube can now be pulled free. Rotate the front band 180 degrees to clear the front sight ramp (if required) and slide the front barrel band free of the rifle. The rear band can now be removed. It may require a few light taps

with a mallet and wood dowel to get it started.

The fore-end can now be pulled free. *Note:* The fore-end may fit the receiver tightly and care should be taken not to break it (see Fig. 19-10). When reinstalling the fore-end it may have to be tapped into place. Use a soft piece of wood placed across its front end and tap it lightly with a mallet.

The rear barrel band may also have to be tapped into place to align the screw holes. Many folks have stripped the threads of barrel bands and screws by attempting to force a screw into alignment. Avoid this by making ssure that the barrel band holes are properly aligned (check with a tight fitting punch) before attempting to install the barrel-band screw.

REASSEMBLY

Reassembly is accomplished in reverse order. No special problems will be encountered except as already noted and as follows:

When sliding the bolt into the receiver be sure the gun is

in an upright position and that the locking lug and carrier are in their down positions or they will interfere with bolt entry. Keep the ejector in place and align the corresponding bolt cut with the ejector.

The bolt must not be pushed fully into the receiver. When it is two-thirds of the way in, stop and position the finger lever in the receiver so that its tip, which goes into the bolt groove, is properly aligned. Also ensure that the finger lever screw is put into place securely. When this has been done, the action will work smoothly and is properly assembled.

Earlier models will not have the cross bolt safety and some may require minor modification of procedures.

BOLT DISASSEMBLY

It may be necessary to replace the extractor, firing pin, firing pin striker, or spring. To do so will require disassembly of the bolt.

The extractor can be pried from its groove using a screwdriver. When reassembling be sure that its collar is not bent beyond being contained in the groove. If it is, replace the extractor. Assembly is accomplished by simply pressing the collar over the corresponding bolt groove.

The firing pin striker, is removed by driving out its roll pin retainer (top to bottom). Then slide the striker rearward taking care not to lose its spring. When reinstalling the striker, the roll pin should be driven slightly below flush with the bottom of the bolt.

The firing pin is removed by driving out its retaining pin (located under the extractor collar). The pin can then be removed from the rear of the bolt. Be sure the finger lever groove and pin hole areas are properly aligned during reassembly.

TRIGGER SPRING, TRIGGER STOP, SEAR, AND TRIGGER REMOVAL FROM LOWER TANG

It is not often necessary to disassemble these parts. If need be, however, drive the stop and spring retaining pin from the tang. Be careful to not lose the spring or trigger stop. Carefully note the position of the spring before disassembly. The spring's long end must rest on the right rear top of the sear when reassembled. Also the spring lies flat on the bottom of the tang recess.

To remove the sear and trigger, drive out the retaining pin.

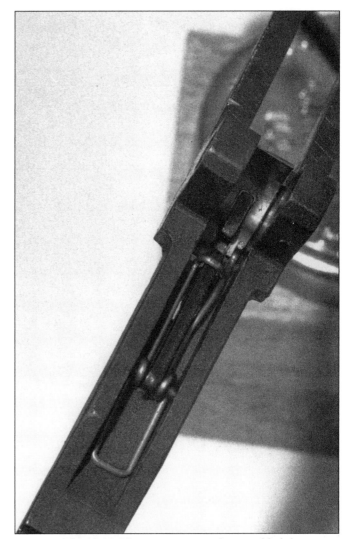

Fig. 19-11. Trigger group properly assembled.

The forward pin does not require removal. It serves only as a catch for the lever locking plunger located in the finger lever (see Fig. 19-11).

COMMON PROBLEMS— PROBABLE CAUSES AND CORRECTIONS

Marlin 336s are among the easiest firearms to repair. There is little to do in the way of actual parts repair. Most repairs, when required, are simply parts replacement.

20

MARLIN 70 SEMIAUTOMATIC RIMFIRE RIFLE

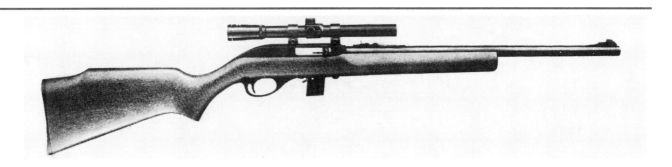

There are more semiautomatic .22 caliber rifles in use than perhaps any other style firearm. Rifles made by a number of manufacturers, rifles with clip magazines, tubular-under-the-barrel magazines and tubular-in-the-butt magazines are all popular. But the Marlin Model 70, with its clip magazine, has been among the most popular of .22s.

CHARACTERISTICS

The Marlin 70 is a non-takedown .22 caliber semiautomatic rifle designed to function with .22 LR ammunition, both high speed and standard velocity types. Its clip allows seven shots to feed smoothly. The action has a hold-open feature on the bolt (pull the operating handle full rearward and press it in). The bolt does not automatically stay open on the last shot.

Most Model 70s provide a very high level of accuracy and require only minimum maintenance. The action parts should be cleaned every 250 rounds or so. Actual cleaning frequency can vary depending upon the brand and type of ammunition used.

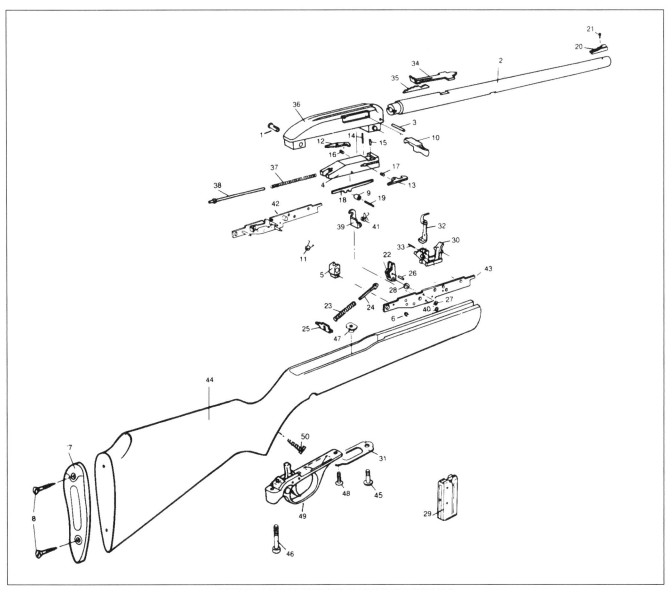

EXPLODED VIEW OF MARLIN 70

View No.	Part No.	Name of Part	View No.	Part No.	Name of Part
1	407997	Assembly Post	9	307188	Cartridge Lifter Roller
2	107420	Barrel (R)	10	207050	Charging Handle
3	307897	Barrel Retaining Pin	11	407196	Disconnector Spring
	507086	Breech Bolt Complete (not shown)	12	320269	Extractor, Left Hand
4	107086	Breech Bolt	13	320369	Extractor, Right Hand
5	407082	Buffer	14	420798	Extractor Pin, Left Hand
6	407178	Buffer Pin Ring	15	407097	Extractor Pin, Right Hand
7	320102	Buttplate	16	407895	Extractor Spring, Left Hand
8	320590	Buttplate screw (2)	17	407895	Extractor Spring, Right Hand

View No.	Part No.	Name of Part
18	407299	Firing Pin
19	407198	Firing Pin Retaining Pin
20	330144	Front Sight
21	420593	Front Sight Screw
22	207173	Hammer
23	407094	Hammer Spring
24	407179	Hammer Strut
25	307075	Hammer Strut Bridge
26	407199	Hammer Strut Pin
	507173	Hammer Complete
		(consisting of above 5 parts)
27	407178	Hammer Pin Ring
28	420176	Hammer Space
29	407346	Magazine Complete (7-shot)
30	207349	Magazine Guide
31	307347	Magazine Guard Plate
32	307348	Magazine Latch & Ejector
33	320797	Magazine Latch Pin
	520641	Rear Sight Complete (includes 34 & 35)
34	220641	Rear Sight Base
35	320942	Rear Sight Elevator
36	507160	Receiver (R)
37	307496	Recoil Spring
38	307071	Recoil Spring Guide
39	407051	Sear
40	407178	Sear Pin Ring
41	407795	Sear Spring
42	207164	Sideplate, Left Hand
43	307563	Sideplate, Right Hand
	507363	Sideplate Assembly Complete (not shown)
44	507514	Stock
45	307192	Takedown Screw, Front
46	307392	Takedown Screw, Rear
47	307391	Trigger Guard Nut, Front
48	307690	Trigger Guard Screw, Front
49	507258	Trigger Guard Complete (not shown)
50	320791	Stock Reinforcement Screw

(R) = Restricted part, only available for factory installation.

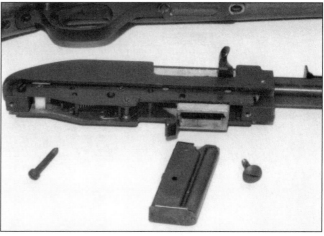

Fig. 20-1. Begin disassembly by separating the barrel and receiver from the stock and trigger group. This is done by removing the two action screws.

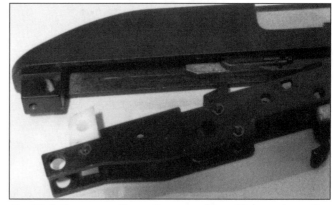

Fig. 20-2. To remove the action assembly, withdraw the action assembly post and then lift the rear end of the action assembly away from the receiver.

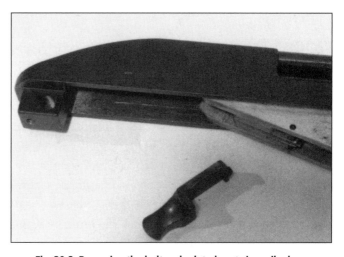

Fig. 20-3. Removing the bolt and related parts is easily done.

Fig. 20-4. Removal of trigger group.

STOCK REMOVAL

Be sure the firearm is unloaded and remove the magazine. Turn out the front action screw. This is the large-headed screw in front of the magazine opening at the bottom of the stock. Then take out the rear action screw which is located in the back end of the trigger guard (see Fig. 20-1). Do not remove the X-slot head screw that goes into the wooden pistol grip (located behind the rear action screw). This is a non-functional part of the Model 70 and never needs removal. Separate the stock and trigger group from the barrelled action. It may be necessary to "snap past" the magazine release lever by pulling upward and forward on the barrel as the unit is also pivoted to the rear.

ACTION ASSEMBLY REMOVAL

With the barrelled action held upside-down, press in on the assembly post by pushing the slotted end into the action assembly and withdrawing it from the other side. Now grasp the rear end of the action assembly, lifting it up and away from the receiver (see Fig. 20-2). Further disassembly of this unit is not advised. Marlin strongly suggests that repairs to the action assembly be undertaken only by qualified gunsmiths.

BOLT, BOLT HANDLE, RECOIL SPRING, AND SPRING GUIDE REMOVAL

With the bottom of the receiver in an upward position and

the barrel held in padded vise jaws, pull the operating handle about a half-inch rearward. While holding the handle in this position, lift the front end of the bolt upward to bring it out of the receiver's bottom. As you do this, the bolt handle will free itself of the bolt. Pull it out of the receiver. By slightly compressing the action spring with the bolt, you will be able to lift the bolt free of the rifle, removing it and the action spring (see Fig. 20-3).

TRIGGER GUARD AND TRIGGER REMOVAL

Remove the screw in front of the trigger guard and you can separate the entire trigger unit from the rifle. Do not lose the small metal escutcheon to which the screw secures (see Fig. 20-4).

No further disassembly should be made. The Marlin 70 can now receive the necessary thorough cleaning which is required of all semi-auto rifles to ensure reliability. Use pressurized solvents and cleaning fluids as well as an old toothbrush to rid all parts of firing by-products and other residue or foreign material.

REASSEMBLY

Reassembly is accomplished in reverse order. Be sure the small escutcheon used in conjunction with the trigger group retaining screw is positioned so that its protrusion enters into the screw hole. Also be sure that it does not infringe upon the magazine opening mortise.

Place the recoil spring into the corresponding hole in the bolt. Then install the long end of the spring guide into the spring. Do not bend this spring during assembly. Use one hand to start the spring guide into the hole in the receiver. Then carefully compress the spring by pushing the bolt rearward over it while guiding the spring into the bolt. When properly compressed, rotate the bolt into the receiver so that it is held in position by the front end of the receiver. Swing the bolt in only far enough for the operating handle cut to be fully visible through the side opening of the receiver. Place the bolt handle in the notch and, using a screwdriver, press the bolt rearward allowing it to enter the receiver fully. Maintain the bolt handle's position in the bolt while performing this maneuver. Operate the bolt back and forth once or twice to ensure it has been properly reinstalled.

When installing the action screws, start both screws loosely to ensure correct alignment. Then tighten the front action screw and snug up the rear screw—but not too tightly.

COMMON PROBLEMS–PROBABLE CAUSES AND CORRECTIONS

The Model 70 is, of course, subject to broken parts, or to failure due to burrs or normal wear Most problems will be related to weak firing pin blows.These can be caused by a short firing pin or a weak hammer psring. Replacement of the bad part usually corrects the problem

Keep in mind that bent clip lips can cause problems with feeding and ejection. Replace any clip which shows signs of bent or worn material at the cartridge-retaining lips.

Frequent cleaning and proper lubircation will keep most Model 70s in good shape for a long useful life.

PART 4

ADVANCED TECHNIQUES

21

INSTALLING INTERCHANGEABLE CHOKE TUBES

SAAMI Choke Diameter Specifications

Choke[1]	10 ga.	12 ga.	16 ga.	20 ga.
Cylinder[2]	.775" - .780"	.725" - .730"	.670" - .675"	.615" - .620"
Improved				
Cylinder	N.A.	.724" - .726"	.664" - .666"	.609" - .611"
Full	.740" - .745"	.694" - .699"	.640" - .645"	.590" - .595"

[1]Chokes not listed are interpreted by the individual manufacturer.
[2]Cylinder is equal to bore diameter–no constriction.

Pattern percentages and choke constrictions are not absolute numbers. One shotgun manufacturer may elect different degrees of constriction or different pattern percentages than another, for a choke of the same nomenclature. But further complications arise due to variations with the ammunition used to test pattern density.

A change in ammunition can cause a notable change in choke performance. For example: Lead shot hardness plays an important role in pattern density. Harder shot (shot with a higher antimony content) will pattern more densely than softer shot. Hard shot may have a 3% or higher antimony content, while soft shot often has 0.5% or less antimony. The reason for the difference in pattern density is that the harder shot is less deformed in its passage through forcing cone, bore and choke. Thus, it emerges from the muzzle rounder than soft shot. It is, therefore, less likely to veer from its original course compared to deformed soft pellets. Air resistance on the irregular surface of deformed pellets causes random and exaggerated dispersion. The velocity of the shot also plays an important role in pattern density. The faster shot is accelerated through the bore, the greater the individual pellet deformation. Thus, lower velocity means denser patterns, while higher velocity means less pattern density. Other aerodynamic factors also contribute to this characteristic, to a minor degree.

Shot size also plays a role. Usually, smaller pellets pattern more densely than larger sized pellets. Pattern density can also be affected by the use of plated shot versus unplated shot. Plated pellets (usually copper or nickel) have increased surface tension factors. Because of this, they are less deformed during acceleration to the muzzle and will pattern more densely than unplated shot. Another variable is the use of a granulated polyethelene buffering mixed in with the shot. Buffered pellets are better protected from deformation during acceleration and, therefore, will pattern more densely than unbuffered shot charges.

Before evaluating a specific choke's performance it is necessary to establish a performance reference to a specific type of ammunition. Many shooters have decided that the extra hard shot and lower velocity levels encountered in light target loads (2¾-dram equivalent) are ideal for pattern testing. Shot size #7½ seems to be favored in these target loads as there are fewer pellet holes to count compared to 8, 8½ or 9 size shot. And, at least in 12- and 20-gauges, the charge weight of shot used (1⅛ and 7/8-ounce respectively) seems to provide ideal pattern density. Heavier shot charge weights seldom pattern with as high a density. This is all satisfactory except, for the waterfowler, who simply never uses shot sizes smaller than #4, and always uses very heavy shot charges and has to learn the pellet sizes and characteristics of steel shot rather than lead.

It is, therefore, important to analyze choke performance with the type of ammunition normally used. Except for testing with steel-shot waterfowl loads, select ammunition that has high antimony content (hard) pellets, and that uses the smaller size shot, plated and buffered if applicable.

HOW TO PATTERN A GUN AND LOAD

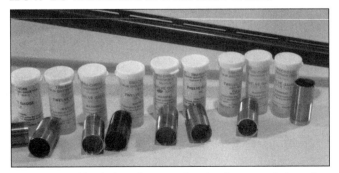

Interchangeable choke tubes can give the shooter a choice of up to ten different borings to customize patterns to specific shooting requirements.

A minimum of ten patterns is needed to obtain a meaningful average. Gross errors in choke performance can be made if the target pellet count is figured as a percentage of an assumed total pellet count taken from a table based upon various assumptions. It is vital to weigh the shot charges from ten rounds of the ammunition to be used for pattern testing. From these ten rounds a useful average shot charge weight can be determined. Then weigh ten pellets, simultaneously, to determine the average pellet weight. Dividing the actual average pellet weight into the actual average shot charge weight will provide you with the actual average total pellet count. This count can easily be pattern density by as much as plus or minus five percent. But a ten percent up or down error can sometimes result.

Because aiming errors are possible at forty yards, and with a shotgun they can be substantial, always draw the thirty-inch pattern circle after the shot has been fired, and draw it to include the maximum number of pellets. Only when this is done is a true evaluation of a choke's performance be possible.

With a fixed-choke gun, pattern density can be decreased by carefully polishing the choke's diameter over its full length. This is a difficult task and requires exacting equipment to maintain choke concentricity and uniformity. And when the job is done, if an ammunition change is introduced, pattern results can be notably different than expected.

The density of a pattern can be increased by altering forcing cone dimensions, to reduce velocity, or by increasing the bore diameter immediately before the choke. Again, this is a difficult task. When the job is done, it will be right only for the same ammo used for the testing during adjustment.

Because of the great variations caused by different ammunition, the most practical solution to the problem is to be able to vary the amount of choke present in the barrel. In the past, this was accomplished by installing appendages on the end of the barrel that contained collets that could be increased or decreased in diameter. In some instances, fixed choke tubes could be removed and replaced with others of different dimensions. Such choking devices never proved popular. They were heavy, often ugly, and changed the gun's balance. They caused the shotgun's point of impact to be substantially altered because they invariably placed the front sight considerably higher than normal due to their large diameters.

The 10-Choke Interchangeable Tube System
(as adopted by Tru-Choke)

Choke Nomenclature	Traditional Nomenclature	10-ga.	12-ga.	20-ga.	Approx. Pattern Density[1]
cylinder	cylinder (all)[2]	.775"	.730"	.620"	40
skeet I	12-ga. improved cylinder[2] .	770"	.725"	.615"	45
improved cylinder	20-ga. improved cylinder[2] .	765"	.720"	.610"	50
skeet II		.760"	.715"	.605"	55
modified		.755"	.710"	.600"	60
improved modified		.750"	.705"	.595"	65
full	20-ga. full[2]	.745"	.700"	.590"	70
trap	12-ga. full[2]	N.A.	.695"	N.A.	75[3]
extra full	10-ga. full[2]	.740"	.690"	.585"	80[3]
super full		.730"	.685"	.575"	85[3]

[1]Actual pattern density can vary substantially depending upon specific ammunition used. See text for details.

[2]A tolerance of +0.005" applies to traditional choking based on SAAMI specifications.

[3]Pattern density with these very tight percentages can prove erratic, especially with pellet sizes of #3 or larger.

CONSTRICTIONS AVAILABLE WITH SCREW-IN CHOKES

Fortunately, choking systems have evolved to the point where interchangeable choke tubes are simply screwed directly into the barrel. The tubes are quite thin and do not require any excessive thickness of the barrel, either at the muzzle or over its entire length. A shotgun fitted with such tubes can be adjusted to fire pattern densities of any desired degree if tube selections include sufficient ranges of constriction change. The shooter or gunsmith can choose a tube system with as many as ten potential changes.

The practical maximum amount of choking, from the bore diameter, has proven to be 0.045-inch. More constriction causes patterns to become erratic and can even be potentially dangerous, especially with steel shot loads. This amount of total choking allows for a total of ten steps in a practical and proven 0.005-inch increments. A nearby table shows the names given to each of these choke constrictions.

Choke changes of less than 0.005-inch do not, in practice, cause a measurable amount of change in pattern density. Thus, the table of chokes shows all of the choke variations that are

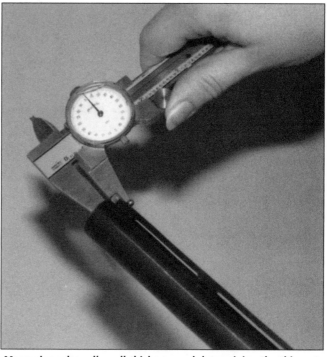

Measuring a barrel's wall thickness and determining the thinnest wall is an important part of deciding if a barrel is suitable for a screw-in choke alteration.

Any barrel to be converted to screw-in chokes must be straight at least over its last fifteen inches of length.

possible from a practical standpoint. The accompanying table also lists the traditional choke nomenclature on the line corresponding to the appropriate choke diameter. In some instances it may be necessary to increase or decrease choking by two "chokes" (.010-inch) to note any meaningful pattern differences.

Altering most fixed choke shotgun barrels to accept screw-in chokes is not difficult and does not require any special machinery. It is something that most at-home gunsmiths can accomplish. Only a few bore pilots, a reamer, a tap, a brace, a long screwdriver, a vernier, and a vise are required as tools.

BARRELS SUITABLE FOR CHOKE TUBE CONVERSION

Some preliminary barrel wall thickness measurements will need to be made in order to ensure the safety and practicality of altering the barrel to accept screw-in choke tubes. Because of the wide range of tubes available, and the ease of purchasing the necessary pilots, reamer and tap from the manufacturer (the Trulock Tool Company), the Tru-choke system was chosen for our instructions. Other choke tube systems are installed in a similar manner.

Not every barrel is suitable for alteration to accept screw-in chokes. Fortunately, however, most are. Barrels with internal bore diameters that are outside of normal tolerances should not be adapted to a screw-in choke. Oversized bore diameters will result in a step up occurring at the junction of the choke tube and bore. This can be damaging to the barrel and choke.

No attempt should be made to install a screw-in choke into any shotgun whose bore diameter exceeds the following: 0.785-inch for 10-gauge, 0.735-inch for 12-gauge, 0.680-inch for 16-gauge and 0.625-inch for 20-gauge. *Never!*

For the finest possible results, shooters and gunsmiths should limit themselves to barrels measuring 0.005-inch less than just stated. You will also need to determine that a minimum barrel wall thickness, after reaming, will always be maintained. The absolute minimum for all gauges is a wall thickness of 0.010-inch at the thinnest portion of the barrel. This will ensure ample strength when combined with an appropriate choke tube and proper installation. Under no circumstances should barrels with less than the following outside diameters (at the muzzle) be considered for adapting the screw-in chokes: 0.900-inch for 10-gauge, 0.825-inch for 12-gauge, 0.770-inch for 16-gauge, and 0.700-inch for 20-gauge.

It is suggested that double barrelled guns not be altered

for screw-in chokes as even a tiny amount of misalignment could cause distinctly different points of impact at hunting ranges.

Because a barrel's bore is seldom concentric with its outside diameter, the thickness of the barrel wall, at its thinnest point, must be determined. This may be accomplished as follows: Measure the outside barrel diameter; for example, a 12-gauge barrel may measure 0.830-inch. Then measure the inside diameter of the barrel; for example 0.700-inch. Subtracting the inside diameter from the outside diameter, and dividing the results by two, will give you the average barrel wall thickness; in this case, 0.830-inch - 0.700-inch = 0.130-inch/2 = 0.065-inch. Now measure the actual barrel thickness at the 12, 3, 6 and 9 o'clock positions. Measurements might typically be 0.061-inch, 0.064-inch, 0.067-inch and 0.065-inch. Using these measurements, we see that the barrel is thinnest at the 12 o'clock position (0.061-inch) and is smaller by 0.004-inch from the average wall thickness.

Next, consider the reamer diameter which, in the case of a 12-gauge, is 0.797-inch. (The 10-gauge reamer is 0.867-inch and the 20 is 0.677-inch.) The reamer diameter, when subtracted from the barrel outside diameter of 0.830-inch and divided by two, gives us an actual wall thickness of 0.0165-inch. Then subtract the 0.004-inch for the non-concentric bore and the result is the thickness of the barrel at its thinnest point *after choke installation*. In this example it would be 0.0165-inch - 0.004-inch = 0.0125-inch. The minimum wall thickness should always be 0.010-inch to ensure a safe and satisfactory installation (regardless of gauge). Thus, the example barrel is satisfactory for alteration to accept the screw-in choke tubes.

Be certain that the barrel is straight for a maximum of 15 inches from the muzzle. This can be accomplished by placing a 15-inch long straight edge against the outside of the barrel at the 12, 3, 6, and 9 o'clock position. A bent barrel is not suitable for screw-in choke alteration. Having determined that the barrel is suitable for the necessary gunsmithing, you need to gather the necessary tools which are:

1. Pilot of a diameter appropriate to the bore involved.
2. A vernier caliper to take accurate measurements.
3. A sturdy bench vise to hold the barrel.
4. Appropriate vise jaws or jaw padding.
5. A quantity of high sulpher content cutting oil.
6. A good brace.
7. The appropriate reamer for the gauge.

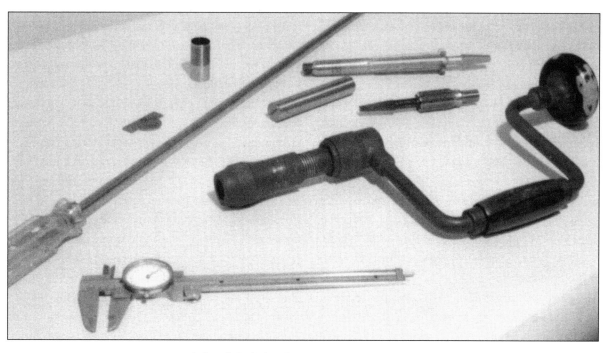

Needed tools include a brace, strong vise and verniers.

Leave a bit of play between brace chuck and reamer to allow the reamer to "float." This will help keep everything centered.

8. The appropriate tap for the gauge.

9. 35-inch long screwdriver.

Additionally, a bore caliper will prove useful for measuring actual bore diameter.

If you have purchased the choke installation kit from the manufacturer, you will have items 1, 7, 8 and 9 from the foregoing list of required tools. The pilot (item 1) is provided in five or six different sizes in 0.002-inch increments to ensure a proper fit for any barrel of normal tolerances. Again, avoid barrels that are above or below the suggested bore diameters.

Having satisfied all of the dimensional requirements we have mentioned, secure the barrel in the vise. A set of leather-faced wood jaw blocks, with an appropriate barrel channel, will ensure that the barrel is not crushed or marred. Both barrel and vise must be secured so that there is absolutely no potential of movement.

If it is not equipped with a rib, a barrel can be shortened to any desired length beforehand (ribbed barrels should be left at their original length). Slip the appropriate pilot into the barrel from the chamber end. Its slotted end should be toward the chamber. The proper size pilot is one that is less than 0.002-inch under the bore diameter. Slop of 0.002-inch or more in pilot fit will defeat the intended purpose of the pilot, to keep the bore and choke tube concentric and straight. Move the pilot forward in the barrel until it touches the internal choke taper (if applicable). Using the long screwdriver, carefully assemble

the pilot and reamer. Be absolutely certain that the mating surfaces of both the pilot and reamer are clean. These units are designed to align properly with a minimum of torque. Do not over-tighten the threads. Hand pressure on the screwdriver while holding the reamer shank is all that is required.

Be sure that the vise holds the barrel in a comfortable working position. Then close the brace over the reamer shank, but leave a bit of play. This will allow the reamer and chuck junction to float, thus enabling the reamer to follow the pilot without stress and helping to avoid misalignment.

Push the reamer gently to the front of the bore, lubricate it generously with cutting oil and, using moderate pressure, turn the reamer clockwise, starting the cut. Do not, under any circumstances, turn the reamer counterclockwise. This could ruin the reamer. Flush the chips away with cutting oil. Keep the reamer turning, slowly, as you continue cutting.

Continue reaming in this manner until the stop portion of the reamer is between 0.060-inch and 0.075-inch away from the muzzle. This will completely remove the original choking and open the barrel to the correct diameter for threading. When this position has been reached, remove the reamer and pilot from the barrel. Thoroughly clean all traces of metal chips from the bore. Remove the pilot from the reamer and assemble it to the tap. Be certain that both mating surfaces are absolutely clean.

Thoroughly lubricate the tap and slowly start it into the

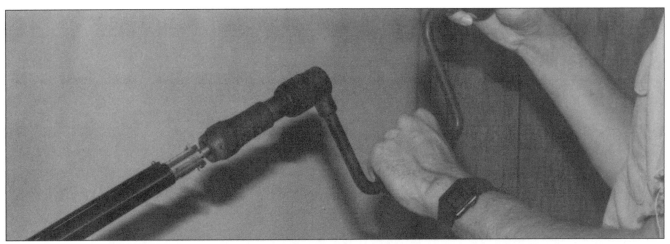

Ream carefully and never, repeat NEVER, rotate the reamer in a counterclockwise direction.

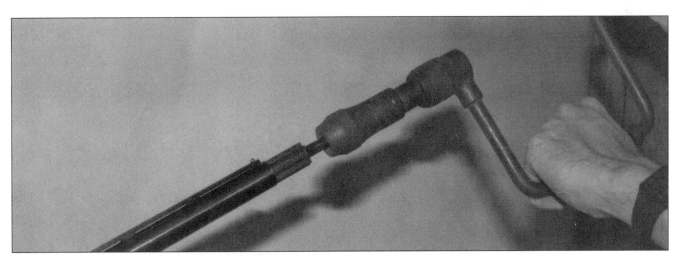

After cleaning the barrel of all chips, thread the reamed barrel very carefully.

After threading, make a final and very careful ream, bringing the internal shoulder to a shape and positive profile.

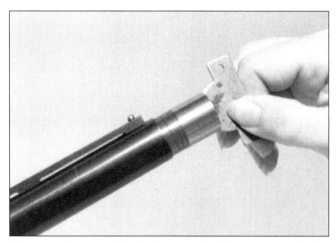

After cleaning away all chips from inside the barrel it is ready for the choke tube of the shooter's choice.

bore, rotating it no more than four revolutions. Squirt plenty of cutting oil into the bore, as far as possible, and then make another four revolutions. Continue squirting oil and turning the tap a maximum of four revolutions until the tap first meets increased resistance. This resistance is caused by the end of the tap striking the necked-down section of the bore. Reverse the tap and back it out slowly.

Clean the barrel again, removing all chips and grit. Reassemble the pilot to the reamer and very gently ream in until you feel the reamer stop its cutting action and begins to turn freely. Use care not to damage the freshly cut threads. Remove the reamer/pilot and clean the barrel, removing all traces of steel, chips, grit, and cutting oil. This operation sharpens the step which the choke tube will rest against.

Then screw in a choke tube, finger tight, followed by using the choke tube installation wrench to gently snug it up. Never overtighten the tube.

Check the bore/choke tube junction (from both ends) using a good light. There should be a slight step down from bore to the back edge of the choke tube.

In some instances, it may be necessary to chase the threads with the tap once again, before the choke tube will screw in without undue resistance. If so, be certain not to damage the final reaming operation which leaves a true ninety degree step in the barrel against which the choke tube seats.

As with all gunsmithing tasks, the quality of the job will depend upon how well it is thought out beforehand and how slowly and carefully the work proceeds.

Naturally, the reamer and tap must be kept sharp. Doing the job with dull tools may well end with a ruined barrel. While some local machine shops can properly sharpen reamers and taps, I prefer to return mine to the manufacturer for such work.

With screw-in chokes, the shooter has the advantage to fine tune his pattern to meet his specific requirements for a specific lot of ammunition. When test firing the gun, remember that a minimum of ten patterns are needed to give a fair estimate of actual average pattern density.

Also keep in mind that with very large shot sizes (i.e. 1, B, BB, BBB, T, F), a choke tube with somewhat less constriction might well provide a denser pattern than a choke tube with slightly more constriction. Steel pellets, naturally, tend to pattern very densely. Seldom is there reason to use more choke than a modified choke with steel shot. Certainly it is counterproductive to use a choke tighter than improved modified with steel pellets.

Interchangeable choke tube conversion, like any gunsmithing task, should be first attempted on an easily replaced, inexpensive barrel. A careful individual should encounter no difficulties, but best to be safe than sorry. After a few installations have been completed, you can easily pay for the tooling by doing a few choke tube conversions for friends. It's easy and, after your first try, shouldn't take more than forty minutes or so.

22

REPAIRING STOCK BREAKS AND SPLITS

Wood is fragile, at least fairly so. Sooner or later, anyone who spends sufficient time working on firearms will be faced with a broken or cracked stock. Stock breaks usually occur in the wrist/pistol-grip area. However, broken-off stock toes are not uncommon, nor are general cracks or splits.

If the broken stock has been subjected to years of abuse in the form of oil draining from the action, it will be impossible to repair the stock. Oil-soaked wood is ruined wood. It cannot be successfully glued, not even with an epoxy compound. However, if the stock is free from oil and if the broken pieces are available, it is often possible to restore the stock to a strong and useful life.

Clean breaks are the easiest to repair. But splintered breaks can be repaired if there are no more than four or five major fractures. Attempts to repair severely splintered stocks are usually excercises in futility. Fortunately, stocks seldom break apart with many splinters. You will, of course, be best able to repair a stock if all the broken wood is available. However, it is not unreasonable to repair stocks when there is a missing piece of wood.

PREPARING WOOD FOR BONDING

First, determine if the broken pieces fit reasonably well together or if it will be necessary to splice in a piece of wood. If another piece of wood is required, no special attention, other than trying to match the grain and color, is needed. This is especially true if the missing piece is a toe or a pistol-grip end. Simply find a piece of wood that closely matches in color and grain, and then cut it so that the glued-on piece will have its grain running in the same direction as the wood against which it will be glued. It's best to make a smooth, flat surface at the point of the break if replacement wood is to be added. Two flat, matching surfaces are much easier to join with a minimal visible parting line.

Breaks requiring the addition of wood between two exist-

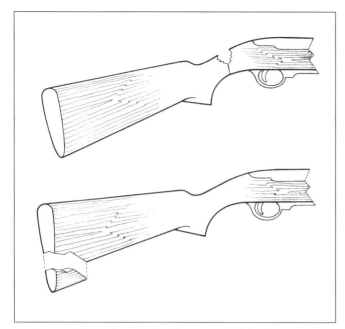

Broken or split stocks can often be repaired if the damage is not too severe. Here are two examples of typical breaks that can be repaired in your shop and extended the useful life of the stock.

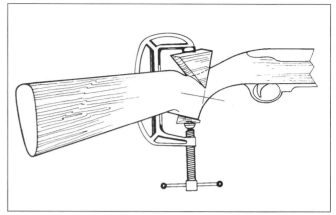

To repair a stock partially split at the pistol grip, insert a wooden wedge into the break as shown. The two parts to be joined must bear against each other for at least half their surface. Clamp the wedge in place.

ing pieces need careful consideration. It is not practical to splice in, for example, a new wrist in the pistol grip area to the remains of a fore-end and buttstock. To add in wood between two existing pieces will require that both existing pieces contact one another over at least fifty percent of the area to be repaired. Otherwise, it is unlikely that a strong and satisfactory repair can be made. Again, the sections of the original stock that will mate with the replacement wood in the repair, should be carefully worked into flats that will match similar flats on the new wood.

Do not attempt to have the replacement wood "fit" the contours and shape of the stock. The replacement piece should be left in as large a block form as possible to help it get worked into the overall profile of the stock's lines.

The replacement wood must be very carefully worked to match it to the mating surfaces of the repair. The quality of the job will be directly related to the fit on the replacement wood.

Next, make one or more grooves, depending upon the size of the working area, in both the original stock and in the matching repair block. These grooves will accept the epoxy which later on will become internal supporting ribs, solidly supporting the stock repair. The depths and widths of the grooves should be about 1/8-inch. However, if you are uncertain as to your ability to put this size groove in both the original and repair wood to have them line up at least on fifty percent of their width, make the grooves wider–up to about 1/4-inch.

If you are going to glue together two or more original stock pieces, first fit everything together. Determine what press-together or slide-together techniques will be required to have all the pieces go together as closely as possible to the original shape.

CLAMPING REQUIREMENTS

All parts must be solidly held together during the curing of the epoxy. This means one or more clamps will be required. You should determine the best clamping method for your repair before applying the epoxy. Put everything together in a dry run and clamp up the work. Use pieces of soft wood to protect the original stock from damage from clamping. You may want to rasp a flat on any replacement wood to best accept firm, even clamping pressure. It is important that you find a way to position the clamps effectively, squeezing the repair surfaces together firmly.

EPOXY BONDING PROCEDURE

When you are certain you know how to hold the broken parts together and you have the proper clamps and know exactly how they should be positioned, prepare the epoxy. Mix up an adequate amount to cover all the surfaces of the repair. Then, place some tape on your clamp jaws and cover the tape with epoxy-release compound. Do this carefully. You do not want to glue the clamps to the work. The same epoxy and release agents as used for glass-bedding a rifle are ideal for stock repairs. Match the dying of the epoxy to the color of the wood. A little too light will look better than a bit too dark.

Coat all the surfaces of the repair with the epoxy, then assemble and clamp everything securely. If there are portions of the stock that will need to be protected from the epoxy, (such as checkered areas or large finished areas), they should be covered with masking tape before mixing and applying the epoxy. Set the clamped repair aside to harden for about five hours.

After the repair begins to harden, without disturbing the clamps, remove any excess epoxy from the outside of the

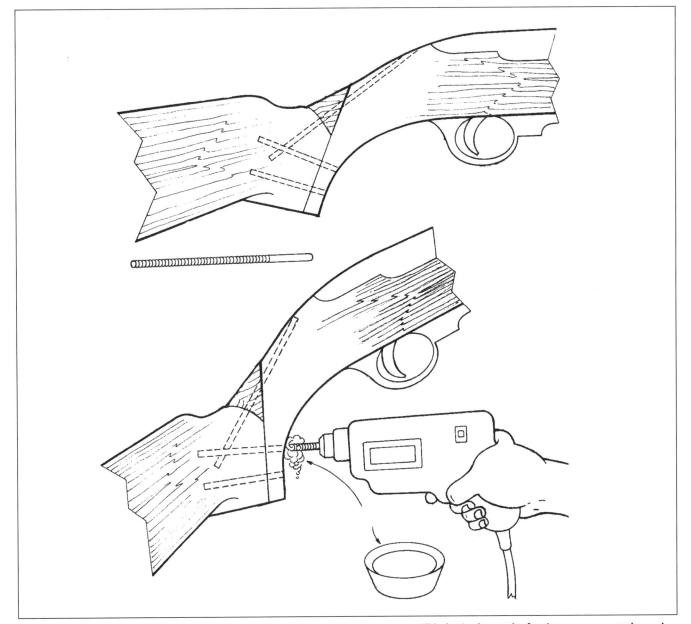

Top - When the epoxy hardens, shape the new wood to match the stock contour. Drill holes in the stock of a size to accept stock repairs. Bottom - Chuck the pin up into a cariable speed drill, cover it with epoxy and then drive it into the hole.

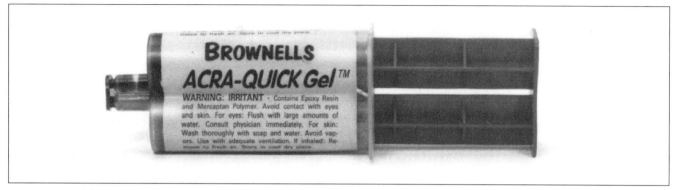

Some epoxies, like Brownells' Acra-Quick Gel, work very quickly with a working life of two to three minutes and reach full strength in twenty-four hours. (Copyright 2003 Brownells)

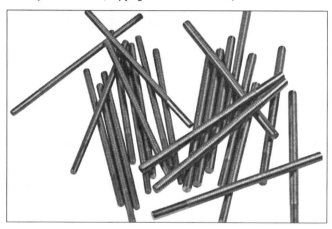

Stock-repair pins are available from gunsmithing supply houses, like Brownells. (Copyright 2003 Brownells)

Stock shellac sticks come in various shades to help match the new wood to the original stock. (Copyright 2003 Brownells)

work. Then, let the whole job harden and cure for at least seventy-two hours.

Remove the clamps and, with a medium-coarse rasp, shape any repair replacement wood into the lines of the stock. Also rasp away any excess epoxy. Do not work so fast as to rasp any of the original stock. If no replacement wood has been used, carefully remove any heavy excess of epoxy.

PINNING FOR EXTRA STRENGTH

The repair is about one-third done! Now pin the stock to give it the needed strength. Brownells' stock repair pins are strongly suggested. These are available in 3/32-inch or 1/8-inch diameters. They are about 2½-inches long and are threaded to hold some anchoring epoxy compound. Determine at what angle or angles the pin or pins will need to be installed to provide the maximum strength to the repair. Generally speaking, the pins should be placed at right angles to the original break. Do not overuse the pins. Carefully consider the extent of the repair. One pin for every 1½-inch of length in the repair area is quite adequate. If the repair involves a broken pistol grip or wrist, place two pins to form an X through the repair area.

When you have decided on how many, where, and at what angle you will place pins, drill a corresponding hole with a bit the same size as the repair pin. Then coat the repair pin with a bit of stock-bedding epoxy. Chuck the pin up into a variable speed drill and run it into the pre-drilled hole at low speed. Allow seventy-two hours for complete curing and then cut off the pins flush with the repair.

CONTOURING AND FINISHING

Now bring the repair surface into full and matching contours with the original stock. Do not remove excess amounts of original finish around the repair. However, you will need to feather the area to make it more feasible for spot finishing. The brass repair pins are easily filed to match stock contours. Put a drop of paint on each end before refinishing if you find the brass dots objectionable.

If there are small chips, small bits of missing wood, or tiny spots where epoxy did not fill in, correct these before refinishing. There are a number of ways to do so. One way is to mix up some additional epoxy to fill in voids. A bit of shellac of matching color can be worked into place with an electric hot knife. Or, if the spots are tiny enough, you can simply rub in a bit of Fil-Stik before refinishing. All the necessary items are available from most wood working outlets and gunsmith suppliers such as Brownells.

RESTORATION OF CHECKERING

If the repaired area includes portions of stock checkering, obviously the checkering will need to be recut or need to be extended across any replacement wood. Checkering, at best, is not a task for the inexperienced person. But repairing a broken stock is the ideal time to learn.

A carefully worked single-line cutter following the original checkering as a guide, will work well. You may find the task easiest with a cutter that has a smooth edge to follow existing checkering and a separate single cutting edge. By beginning in an area with checkering and recutting some of the original checking rows, you can slowly progress until you are actually cutting new checkering rows over the repaired area. Entire books have been written on checkering and it's impossible to tell all in a single chapter. But go very slowly, beginning in existing checkering and work carefully outward over the repair.

Remember to cut all the lines running in one direction before cutting diagonal lines. Work new cuts carefully from existing lines and realize that these cuts must meet properly with existing cuts on the other side of the repair. Work from both sides of the repair gradually to ensure the cuts are aligned. Simply scribe original cuts very, very shallow until you are sure everything lines up, then go back and carefully cut your scribed lines deeper.

GAINING EXPERIENCE

Stock repairs necessarily demand an innovative approach. No two repairs will be exactly alike. Patience in fitting everything together, in selecting matching color and grain for replacement wood, in dying the epoxy, and in careful use of repair pins and touch-up material are essential. Every step is equally important to a satisfactory repair. Mixing the epoxy must be exact to afford the needed strength; and, many epoxies are sold in containers that dispense pre-measured amounts to eliminate the need to measure and mix epoxies on your own. And the placement of repair pins requires a certain insight into the need for strength.

I've found that the best stock repairs are made by those who have had the experience of a number of repair jobs. So if there's an old discarded stock lying about, you may just want to deliberately break it in half through the wrist and attempt to repair it, before you begin a similar effort on a favorite gun.

If the repair involves a split, but not completely separated, stock give some thought to get the epoxy down into every area of the split. You may have to pry the split apart to do this. In some instances, it may be best to completely separate the stock at the split. It will require careful judgment to decide what is required for a satisfactory repair.

I cannot overemphasize the need to work the repair through on a dry run. Aligning the pieces and then clamping them, should not be first undertaken after applying the epoxy.

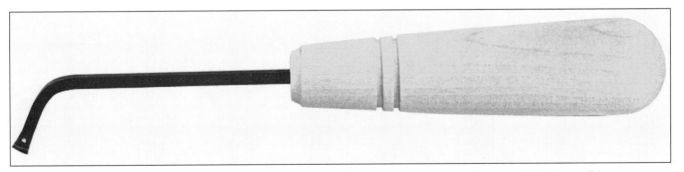

This checkering tool gets into tight corners, curves, and out-of-the-way places. (Copyright 2003 Brownells)

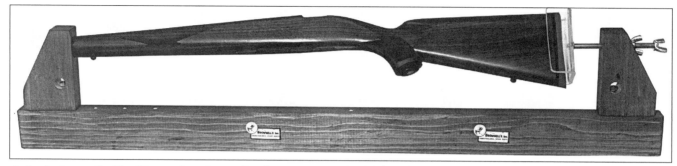

A checkering cradle, like this one from Brownells, allows you to work with both hands and rotate the stock as you checker across the pattern. It also prevents the back-and-forth wobble that stops the cutting action of the checkering tools. (Copyright 2003 Brownells)

It's essential that this be done before the epoxy is mixed.

It is possible to use glue on some stock breaks. Where strength is not important, one of any of the good waterproof glues may prove satisfactory. Glues are generally a bit easier and more convenient to use than a stock-bedding epoxy. But, overall, an epoxy will prove to be the best and strongest substance.

23

DRILLING AND TAPPING FOR SIGHT INSTALLATION

There is no surer way to destroy any rifle, shotgun, or handgun than to drill and tap it for sight installation without an adequate drill jig, sharp drill bits and taps, and knowing how to proceed. It is virtually impossible to achieve a one hundred percent perfect job without using a drill jig. .

Thus, this chapter is meant only for those who have (or will acquire) the necessary equipment. That includes, at a minimum, the B-Square Pro-Scope Mount Jig, which comes complete with a base block, a bore align arbor, two V-bushings, a #31 drill bushing, jig bars for both Mauser and Springfield receivers, cap screws, and a wrench. With this tool you can drill Springfield, Enfield, and Japanese receivers with one jig bar and Mausers with the other. This unit, however, does not

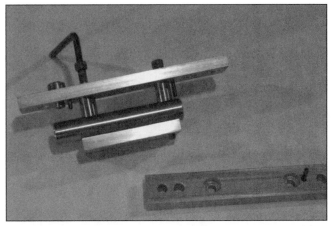

The B-Square Pro-Scope Mount Jig is the minimum essential for proper scope mount drilling and tapping of undrilled military style receivers.

include the necessary tap guide. A B-Square Tru-Tapper is strongly suggested.

The B-Square Pro-Scope Jig uses a flat base plate to provide a suitable flat work surface for the drill press table. To use the jig, the bore align arbor is inserted into the rifle's receiver (after removing the stock, trigger, bolt stop, or other encumbrances). Next, place both V-bushings, with the "V" contacting the arbor, over the holes in the arbor. Then place the appropriate jig bar over the V-bushings so that the two recesses in the jig bar go over the V-bushings. Drop the Allen screws down through the jig bar V-bushings and bore align the arbor to hold everything in place. Finally, position the base block against the bottom of the receiver and turn the Allen screws loosely into it.

Note: The two holes in the jig bar with the narrowest spacing should be positioned at the rear of the receiver. These holes have a 1/2-inch spacing.

Before tightening the Allen screws, slide the whole assembly forward until the jig-bar stop pin contacts the rear of the front receiver ring. This is an important step and will properly locate the screw holes. Then, tighten the Allen screws securely. The rifle's receiver is squared with the jig as a result of the receiver's bottom flat being securely held by the flat base block. It is important to note that this type of jig cannot assure correct alignment of the screw holes in relationship to the bore. In most cases, all holes will properly align. But if the barrel is not central and square with the receiver, there can be difficulty in proper mount alignment with the bore.

Place the correct drill bushing in the appropriate hole in the top of the jig bar, place the entire unit on the drill press table, clamp it in alignment with the drill bit, and you are ready to drill holes. Be sure to set the drill-stop to *not* drill into the barrel with the forward hole on the front receiver ring. The three remaining holes can be drilled through the receiver. Blind holes (the front hole on the front receiver ring) present some special tapping problems, so drilling through the receiver whenever possible is best. If you can drill the front receiver hole without a barrel in place, all the better.

Always be certain that the holes in the scope base (bases), that you wish to use, properly align with those in the jig bar. When installing Weaver blocks on a Springfield 03-A3, use the rear stop pin in the jig bar to properly locate the single rear receiver hole. To do so, simply slide the entire jig rearward (after drilling the forward holes) until the stop pin contacts the edge of the old rear sight's dovetail.

Always check mounts equipped with a recoil shoulder to

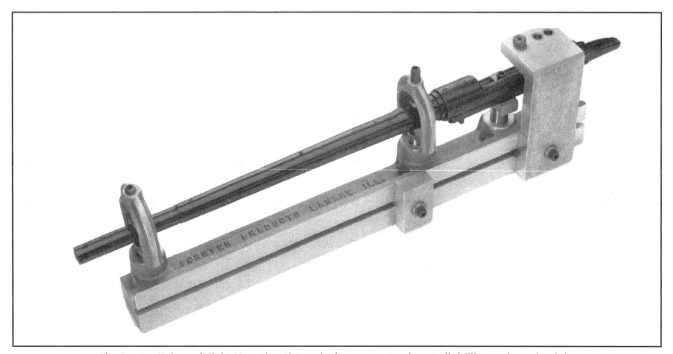

The Forster Universal Sight Mounting Fixture is the answer to almost all drilling and tapping jobs.

The raceway of the drilling jig must be kept meticulously clean to insure positive alignment of the over arm and locator block.

ensure they properly fit the receiver. The forward jig stop pin must contact the receiver at the same spot where the mount's recoil shoulder makes contact. Also, be certain that the V-bushings do not contact the left hand side of the receiver (especially on small ring models) as this will misalignment the jig.

If necessary, file or grind the V-blocks to get proper clearance.

DRILLING RECOMMENDATIONS

When drilling, use as short a drill bit as possible (screw machine drill bits are ideal) to prevent the drill from wandering. It is a good idea also to use a new high-speed drill for each job. Do not use carbide drills. If the receiver is too hard to drill with a standard high speed drill, it is too hard to be tapped. If you can drill successfully only with a carbide drill, you are sure to break off the tap when attempting to thread the hole. Avoid this and drill only those holes you can make with standard drills. If the receiver is too hard, have it spot annealed by someone experienced in this procedure, to soften the area to be drilled.

TAPPING RECOMMENDATIONS

After the holes are drilled, carefully tap them. Use a new tap for each job. This is cheap insurance against breaking a tap. Broken taps can sometimes be removed successfully. However, the risk of a ruined receiver (or barrel) is a real possibility whenever a tap breaks in a hole. So play it safe and use a new tap for every job. Fluteless taps work best on very thin receiver sections. Fluted taps are used for all holes of normal

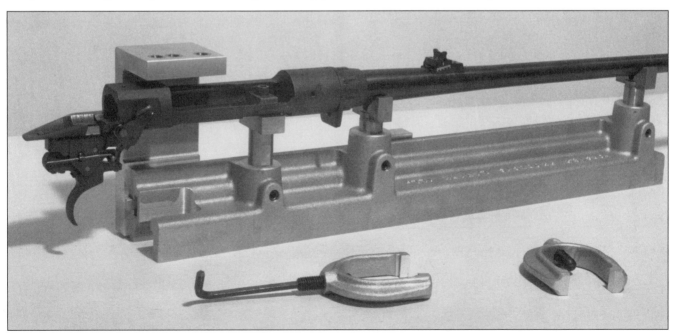

A properly installed barrelled action will see the V-blocks carefully adjusted for the correct height, the action properly leveled on the action support post, with V-block and support post clamps tightened securely.

The aluminum pads supplied with the Forster jig will prevent the clamps from damaging the barrel finish.

or greater depth. Be sure to run the tap through all drilled through holes. Tapping should be done progressively. If the tap binds even just a tad, back it out, clear away any chips in the hole and on the tap, relubricate the tap, and proceed. It is sometimes necessary to back out the tap several times before the hole is fully threaded. Always use tapping compound–not cutting oils–when tapping.

With blind holes, be careful not to run the standard tap too deeply–resulting in a broken tap. You will have to form the last three or four threads in a blind hole using a bottoming tap. Again, be careful not to solidly bottom the tap.

JIG RECOMMENDATIONS FOR DEMANDING JOBS

The B-Square jig is adequate for occasional jobs. But if you are going to be drilling and tapping receivers frequently, or if you need to drill and tap barrels for front and rear sights, you will need to purchase a unit like the Forster Universal Sight Mounting Fixture. This unit allows you to drill holes on the side of a receiver (for side mounts and peep sights) with perfect bore alignment. And when needed, this fixture can be used to drill holes that, when necessary, do not align with the bore.

The Forster jig has remained virtually unchanged for many years simply because has not needed to be changed; and, it is durable. Beginning in the mid-1950s I used one extensively for twelve years. Since then it has continued to see occasional use. Today, the jig is as reliable as it was in the 1950s. It

Drilling and tapping for a front ramp is an easy task with the Forster jig.

has proven near foolproof for getting scope mount bases, or sights of any type, installed right–the first time. Like any other specialized tool it does, however, require some knowledge to use it properly.

For example, the Forster jig uses a raceway along its rear edge to position the over-arm in proper alignment. If drilling chips get into the raceway, or if an accumulation of any crud is allowed to build up in it, the over-arm will not properly align and the drilled holes will not be where they are supposed to be. Ditto for the spacer bar. Always carefully clean the raceway before each use and clean out any chips that accumulate during use before moving the over-arm or space bar.

The stock will need to be removed from the gun before placing it in the jig. Only the fore-end must be removed on firearms that have separate fore-ends and buttstocks. However, a buttstock left attached may make it awkward to properly position the drill fixture on the drill press table. More than one gunsmith has had a drill fixture and gun fall to the floor because a buttstock was hanging out in the air. The best procedure is to remove the buttstock.

Inaddition, remove any magazine tube or appendages that hang below the barrel to properly clamp of the barrel in the fixture's V-blocks. It is, however, seldom necessary to remove

When the drilling or tapping bushings touch the receiver (or barrel) the chance for breaking the drill bit or tap is greatly reduced.

triggers, as the jig is appropriately positioned for these. Bolt stops and safeties can usually be left in place. Just be certain that triggers, bolt stops and the like do not come in contact with any portion of the jig, as this can cause misalignment of the barrelled action.

When using the jig the action locking screw and bar should be removed from the action supporting post. Then lay the barrel in the V-blocks with the action on the left end of the fixture (cut out for the trigger). The action should rest on the flat, action support post so that the top of the action just contacts the under surface of the drill bushings in the overarm.

The rear V-block (one closest to the action) should contact the barrel on a cylindrical section. This, however, is not always possible. Nonetheless, move the entire barrelled action forward or rearward, as necessary, to accomplish this.

The front V-block must be elevated precisely to keep everything level. Measure the barrel diameter at both the rear and front V-blocks. Also measure the height of the rear V-block from its bottom flat edge to the machined-top of the fixture. To arrive at the exact height needed for the front block, proceed as follows: Subtract the barrel diameter at the front V-block from the barrel diameter at the rear block. Then multiply the difference by 0.707. This number should be added to the height of the rear V-block for a total measurement for the front V-block height.

When tightening the V-blocks, be certain to temporarily move the action-support block to prevent any tipping of the barrelled action. Then lightly lock the barrel into the V-blocks using the supplied clamps. Be sure to use the supplied aluminum pads between the barrel and the clamp screws. Do not tighten the screws as the barrelled action must now be levelled with respect to left and right orientation. Do this by carefully bringing the action support bar against the receiver bottom (assuming it is flat). Rotate the receiver so that it lies perfectly flat on the support post. Do not tighten the support post screw.

Install the action-locking block and screw and securely tighten. Now tighten the action-bar support post screw and then snug up the V-block clamps. It is important that all the support post screws are tightened against the flat milled on each post. If this is not done, serious misalignment can occur.

If the action does not have a flat bottom, it will be necessary to use a level on a flat surface. Make sure the action is lev-elled within the jig. Use the machined surface on the back edge of the jig or the machined top surface of the over-arm (be sure it has been snugged up first) to use as a comparison.

Sometimes the rear V-clamp will interfere with the appro-priate positioning of the over-arm. If so, remove it, but only after the action and barrel have been secured with the action-support bar clamp and the front clamp screw.

Next, carefully position the base or mount (with the over-arm moved out of the way) on the receiver. Then carefully scribe the front receiver hole using a pencil or steel scribe. If two-piece bases are used, locate the holes so that if, at a later date, you want to use a one-piece base, the holes will be cor-rectly positioned. In doing so, keep a one-piece base on hand and align the holes with it. Then the rear base of a two-piece unit can be positioned to drill the fourth hole (not used with a one-piece base).

After scribing the front hole position, situate the over-arm with the locating pin in its front hole, and the pin's center in exactly the middle of the scribed area. Then lock the over-arm into position, install the correct size drill guide and you are ready to drill the first hole.

Set the drill press stop to drill almost through the receiver but not into the barrel. It is always a good idea to position the locator block firmly against the over-arm and lock it in place. Then if the over-arm must be moved for any reason, it can be returned precisely to the same position by sliding it against the locator block.

Drill the first hole and then remove the drill guide, replac-ing it with the tap guide. Tap the hole. If the drill bushing just touches the receiver (when properly bottomed on the top of the over-arm) there will be almost no chance of the drill "walking" and mislocating the hole or breaking from being flexed. Always use a new drill and tap for each new job. The grief that can come from dull cutting tools is easily avoided by using a new drill or tap on every job. With experience, you may decide that a drill or tap can be used for two or three jobs, but go slow-ly here. The amount saved in drills and taps over many decades will not pay for one ruined receiver or barrel.

Often the second front receiver ring hole can be drilled simpy by placing the drill bushing in the middle hole of the over-arm. However, do not assume this. It's best to move the

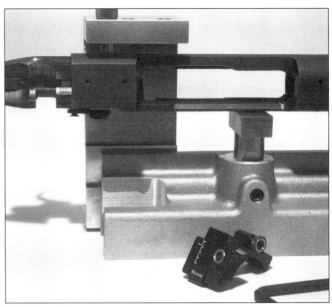

Drilling for peep sight installation is easily accomplished with the Forster jig.

over-arm out of the way and screw the mount to the receiver using the one hole you have drilled and tapped. Then careful-ly scribe the second hole. Remove the base and move the over-arm back into position, situating the locating pin in the middle of the scribe. Remove the locating pin, install the drill-guide bushing and drill the second hole. Replace the drill-guide bushing with the tap-guide bushing and tap the hole.

Always use a bit of cutting oil when drilling and a bit of tap lubricant when threading the holes. Clean away all chips and lubricants between each operation. Progress slowly with tapping. It may be necessary to back out the tap and clear away chips several times during the threading of a hole.

Drilling and tapping rear holes is best accomplished if you drill through the receiver. Before doing so, make sure that the drill will break through on a level area. If there is a step or sharp change in profile where the drill will come through, do not drill through as almost invariably a drill or tap will break when part of its diameter is free while the remainder bears against the work. There is no need to drill through the rear hole on the front receiver ring if the receiver is quite thick. On thin receivers, drill this hole through if it will not go into the barrel and if it will come through on a level area.

Be certain to position the first rear receiver ring hole to accommodate a one-piece mount. Always use an actual base (now screwed to the front receiver holes) to locate this hole. Use the locating pin in the middle hole to do this. Lock the over-arm in place and drill and tap as you did the front holes. Often, the second hole for a two-piece base can be made by simply using the rear hole in the over-arm. But always double check this as described earlier. An erroneous assumption can lead to a bad mistake.

Caution: Never drill or tap holes with the mount base(s) in place as this may negate the positive alignment of each hole with the bore's axis.

Drilling for peep sights is done in a manner similar to drilling for scope bases, except the rifle is oriented with the appropriate side of the receiver in the up position. A level then must be used to ensure that fixture and firearm are square. The action-support bar should be brought up against the action to support it during drilling. The support-bar clamp is not used. All this holds equally true for the installation of side mount scope bases.

On those rare occasions when the holes to be drilled for a peep sight or side mount scope base are not to be on the bore's axis, the over-arm is not used. In this case, great care must be taken to prevent drill bit "walk" and broken drill bits or taps.

When drilling for a front sight ramp or base, reverse the direction in which the gun is placed in the jig, if possible, to place the action-support bar under the barrel at the point of drilling. Be sure the drill bushing contacts the barrel and also be certain that everything is level. Don't forget to allow for the variation in V-block heights as previously explained.

If a barrel is to be drilled and tapped for any combination of scope bases (receiver mounted) and open rear and front

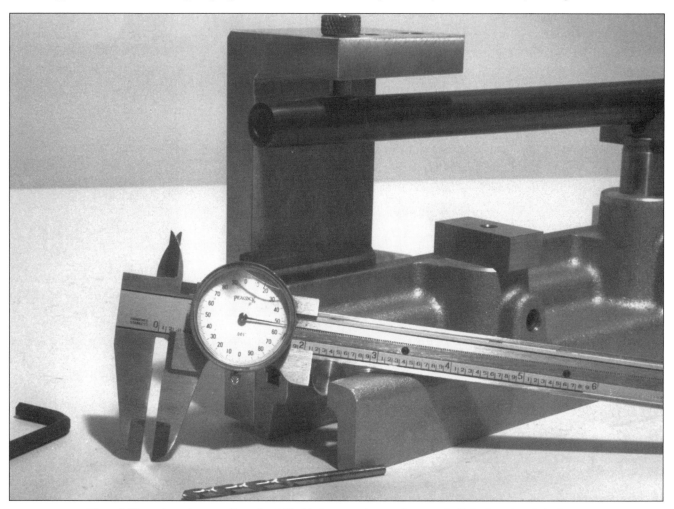

When drilling a barrel never allow the drilled hole to go deeper than one-half the barrel wall thickness.

sights (or barrel mounted scope base(s), I have sometimes found it best to do the entire job without re-orienting the gun in the jig. But if the front sight ramp holes are more than one or two inches beyond the front V-block (barrel longer than twenty inches), then it's best to re-orient the barrelled action. Drilling a barrel that is not properly supported can cause the barrel to flex away from the drill bit. This can result in a broken drill, a less than perpendicular to bore hole, or a broken tap. Obviously, a thin barrel requires closer support than a heavier one.

Drill and tap bushing sets for 3-56, 7-48, 8-40, or 10-32 thread sizes are available for the Forster jig, covering almost every possible firearm requirement.

Double check every single step. No attempt should be made to tap aluminum receivers as the steel screw will tear out the threads when properly tightened. Never drill and tap a hole that will not provide at least four full threads. With fewer turns, the screw may pull out the threads when tightened.

Don't drill too deeply into any barrel. A very thin barrel wall beneath the drilled hole is a potnetially serious problem. In general, there is no set rule for barrel thickness as the strength required depends upon the internal pressure generated at the point of the drilled hole when the gun is fired. This varies with cartridge, propellant speed, bullet weight and distance from the bolt face. A good rule of thumb is to never drill more than half the barrel wall thickness. There is little need ever to go more than six threads deep, regardless of barrel wall thickness. It is always advisable to have at least 0.020-inch barrel thickness.

Some exceptions do exist, such as a front shotgun bead hole that can be drilled through the barrel (because of the low muzzle pressure). However, do not drill through on barrels shorter than twenty inches. But even then, a minimum of four screw turns will be necessary to keep the front bead from being blown out. The bead must be fitted exactly flush on the inside barrel surface.

Always use a relatively small handled tap holder when threading. This will prevent over-torquing the tap and breaking it off in the hole. Not enough can be said about the grief of trying to remove a broken tap. The best procedure is to make sure it doesn't happen. Using a small-handled tap will also help with the "feel" of the tap and help keep everything in one piece.

Drilling and tapping a firearm for sights is perhaps one of the most common gunsmithing tasks. It can also be one of the most rewarding.

With experience, a firearm can be disassembled, set up in the jig, drilled, tapped, and bore-sighted in about forty-five minutes. And such a job can bring sufficient monetary reward to make it all worthwhile, including the quick amortization of a jig and drill press.

24

FITTING A RECOIL PAD

A well-fitted recoil pad is something almost every shooter can use. Reduced recoil means reduced shooting fatigue and this can mean improved accuracy. For a shooter who finds recoil unpleasant, or for the shooter who finds that recoil induces flinching and thus causes poor accuracy, a well-installed recoil pad can become essential. A properly installed recoil pad can also lengthen a short stock. And a recoil pad or a rubber buttplate is an excellent replacement for a cheap and fragile factory-installed plastic buttplate.

On the other hand, few things can destroy the overall appearance and value of a good gun like a poorly fitted recoil pad. Stock heel and toe lines must flow uninterruptedly across the recoil pad. Changing angles at the stock pad juncture have the same appearance as ink blots on a fine sketch. And unless wood and pad meet in a smooth edge all the way around, the job will be best left undone.

None of which is to say pad installation is terribly difficult. But it does require a great deal of time, patience, care, and a power sanding table.

There are two approaches to proper pad installation. The first is to shape the pad, away from the gun stock. This prevents marring of the stock finish. This method is the best one

A properly installed recoil pad can add accuracy to shooting by eliminating fatigue and perceived recoil levels.

for those with less than extensive experience.

The second method is to fit the recoil pad to the stock while it is attached. This method brings about the most perfect fit but it should not be attempted on a valuable firearm without previous experience. If the pad is being fitted to a stock

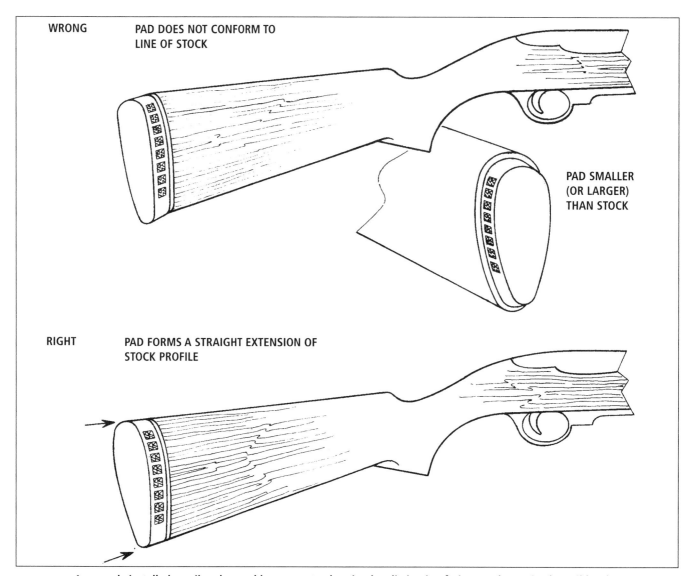

WRONG   PAD DOES NOT CONFORM TO
        LINE OF STOCK

PAD SMALLER
(OR LARGER)
THAN STOCK

RIGHT   PAD FORMS A STRAIGHT EXTENSION OF
        STOCK PROFILE

A properly installed recoil pad can add accuracy to shooting by eliminating fatigue and perceived recoil levels.

that is to be completely refinished, or to a semi-finished stock yet to see its final shaping, then this second method can be undertaken even by an amateur.

METHOD 1 - SEPARATE SHAPING

The first method requires a unit like the B-Square Recoil Pad Jig, a sanding table, a suitable screwdriver with a round shank, lubricant, and an appropriate-sized recoil pad. The pad must be large enough to continue the lines of the stock heel and toe but not too large to require excessive trimming. Cutting too deeply into a pad can ruin it.

Begin by determining how much, if any, of the buttstock is to be removed to obtain the desired length of pull. Even if the stock is not to be shortened, any curvature of the butt must be removed. This is best done with a saw cut. However, use a very fine-toothed and sharp saw in order to avoid the splintering effect that normally occurs at the bottom of the cut. Wrapping the stock with masking tape at the point of the cut will help prevent splintering. If you splinter the stock as you saw through the bottom of the cut, the stock could well be ruined.

Always use a miter box to make the cut. Be absolutely cer-

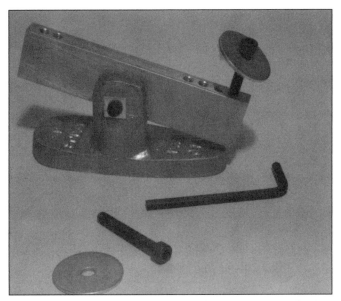

The B-Square recoil pad jig is needed for the separate shaping method of installation,

The stock should be firmly masked at the point of the cut. This will prevent splintering of the wood when the stock is cut to size.

Sand the butt perfectly flat and be certain to keep the work area clean to prevent the butt from taking on an unwanted angle.

Sand the recoil pad until it is perfectly flat. A belt sander makes this a much easier task.

tain that the stock is positioned square and level before beginning the cut. With your first attempt at cutting a stock, it is strongly advised that you make several practice cuts on a discarded stock. Cut slowly and carefully. Do not force the saw downward. Let the sharpness of the saw and its own weight supply the cutting action.

Most miter boxes will allow the cut only to be made by progressing from one side of the stock to the other. This, however, maximizes the chance of splintering on the bottom side due to the great surface area. Some gunsmiths prefer to construct miter boxes that allow for cutting from the top (heel) of the stock to the bottom (toe). This keeps any splintering con-

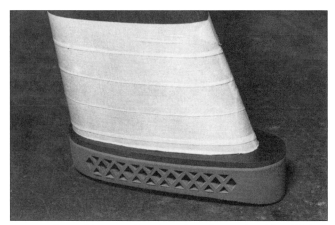

Be sure the pad is correctly oriented on the stock, with sufficient overhang at the heel and toe.

fined to the relatively small toe area of the stock. However, elaborate systems of proper stock alignment and support must be developed for cuts of this type. The beginner is probably best served with cutting in a standard miter box, proceeding from one side of the stock to the other. A sharp saw, properly used on a well-taped stock, will prevent problems.

After the cut, the flat must be sanded perfectly smooth. This will also eliminate any minor splinters. This is best done on a belt sander. Carefully bring the butt squarely onto the belt and sand until all traces of the saw cut and any minor edge splintering are removed. It requires a great deal of care and visual alignment to keep the sanding flat and perpendicular to the stock. If you sand at an angle, the job will look poor indeed. Again, practice on a discarded stock is urged.

Next, to ensure a perfect mating of the recoil pad and stock, the back surface of the pad must also be sanded flat. Do this on a belt sander and keep the pad square. Sand until all high spots disappear and the pad has a smooth, even surface.

Now you are ready to mount the pad to the stock. Begin by pushing a Phillips screwdriver, which has been properly lubricated (soap will work fine), into the back side of the pad and out of the face side so as to mark the screw hole locations. Then, using well lubricated screws (again, soap works well), push the screws into the pad from the outside surface and screw the pad to the buttstock.

It is important to locate the pad centrally on the stock. Be sure there is sufficient overhang to allow the heel and toe line to be maintained, or the job won't look right. Try to avoid excessive hangover on either end, especially with pads that have exposed vents or grooves. You don't want to wind up with a 1/2-inch overhang of solid rubber on the stock heel while pad grooves come within 1/8-inch of the toe, or you actually have no solid toe at all.

Some suggest using the same holes for the recoil pad screws as were used for the original buttplate screws. This is usually impossible if the pad is to be correctly aligned. Drill the butt with the appropriate size drill bit. Take care to ensure that the drilled holes are square and perpendicular to the buttstock. If they enter at an angle it will be difficult to screw the buttplate down flush all around with the stock.

After securing the pad to the stock, carefully trace the stock's outline on the pad using a sharp-pointed scribe. Get the outline as close to the stock as possible. If you do not, the pad will protrude around the stock when the job is finished. Then remove the pad from the stock. The pad must now be mounted on the B-Square jig.

Lubricate the machine screws supplied with the jig. Then place the face of the pad against the jig's mount bar. Place a washer over the pad's top hole and insert the mounting screw, only loosely tightening it. Then put in the bottom screw (don't forget the washer). Tighten both screws but do not tighten so much as to distort the pad's shape.

Caution: Make certain that the top (heel) end of the pad is located at the top end of the jig (double hole). If the bottom screw does not easily enter one of the jig bar's four bottom holes, relocate the top screw in the unused top hole.

Now loosen the screw holding the jig bar to the jig base. Position the jig base against the buttstock (heel to heel and toe to toe). Place one edge of a square along the bottom (toe) edge of the stock. Adjust the jig bar so that the recoil pad face aligns correcty with the other edge of the square. Tighten the jig bar/base screw to lock the pad in proper alignment.

Place the jig base on the sander so as to position the pad's toe against the sander and sand only the toe area to perfectly coincide with the line previously scribed. Be sure that the screw holding the jig bar does not loosen as this controls the proper angle of the stock toe and pad.

After only the toe area has been exactingly sanded, loosen the bar/base screw on the jig and again place the jig base against the stock. This time use the square to properly align the heel of the stock and the face of the pad. When it is correctly positioned, lock the screw. Now sand the heel area of the pad. Once again be sure the screw holding the jig in alignment does not loosen. If it does, use the square and stock to once again align the jig correctly.

After the heel has been sanded to coincide with the scribe lines, level the pad in the jig and sand the sides of the pad, blending it carefully into both heel and toe sanded areas. When the sanding is done, install the pad on the stock. If you have been careful with the scribing of the stock outline on the pad and with the blending and sanding to the scribe line, you will have a near perfect fit.

METHOD 2 - SHAPING AN ATTACHED PAD

The second method of pad installation will provide an even better fit. You will need a solid sanding belt (or disc), a steady hand, sharp eye, and a bit of masking tape. However, this procedure can easily result in a disfigured stock if the workman is inexperienced. Therefore, before attempting the following method on a good gun, practice several installations on a discarded stock.

Begin by making the previously described stock cut to bring the pad and stock combination to the correct overall length. It's good to leave an extra 1/8-inch to allow for sanding the stock and pad surfaces to a flat state. Remove the tape used

The experienced workman can install a pad and then sand it on a belt or disc sander bringing it down to the level of a layer of stock protecting masking tape.

for a cutting guide. Then pierce the recoil pad screw holes, as described earlier, and mount the pad firmly to the stock. Now carefully wrap the buttstock immediately in front of the recoil pad with two thicknesses of three inch-wide masking tape.

From this point on, the installation becomes one of art, not mechanics. Rough sand the pad on a hard disc or belt sander until you have brought it to within 1/16-inch of the taped stock. This can be done with a rough grit sanding paper. Great care must be taken to ensure that the heel and toe lines of the stock are continued into the pad. When the pad is about 1/16-inch from the tape, all the way around, switch to a finer grit paper. A large diameter sanding disc with a flexible wheel (hard rubber) back is best. Sand the pad until it is almost down to the masking tape. Now switch to a very fine grade paper and sand, very carefully, to reduce the pad dimension to the same as the top layer of masking tape. This is done by sanding through the top layer of tape without cutting into the bottom layer of tape. Sounds hard? Well, I'm not sure hard is the right description. But it does take skill, art, and patience. However, the finished job will give as perfect a fit as possible without actually refinishing the stock.

After a pad installation has been completed, some shooters remove the pad and place a thin coating of glue on it and the stock and then screw the pad back on. This helps keep the pad positioned, but if it ever needs to be removed, it could be difficult. If glue is not used, a coating of waterproof finish is a good idea to reduce moisture absorption.

Installing recoil pads is not for the faint of heart. You will need to proceed carefully. A face mask and ample ventilation are always required. The mounds of rubber dust that pile up in the work area must be seen to be appreciated. The workman will also be covered from head to toe with this same dust. But a properly installed pad is a gunsmithing effort that justifiably carries a lot of pride.

PART 5

THE FINAL STEPS

25

AMMUNITION AND THE GUNSMITH

Functioning and accuracy problems are often gun related. For example, misfires can be caused by a short firing pin, weak firing pin spring, light hammer blow, or excessive chamber headspace. Poor accuracy may be caused by improper barrel and receiver bedding, worn rifling, bore erosion and/or corrosion, a bad crown, loose sights, and so on.

However, function and accuracy problems are directly related to the quality of the ammunition being used. It is, therefore, important to be familiar with ammunition induced difficulties. And it is essential to know that not every box of centerfire ammunition purchased is capable of anything even closely resembling good accuracy.

Ammo-induced misfires can be caused by any of the following: primers seated too deeply, primers not seated deep enough to properly stress the priming pellet, using the wrong type of primer, cartridge cases with insufficient headspace, cushioned firing pin blows caused by frost or ice on the shoulder of a case which affords minimal shoulder support (such as the .35 Remington), missing primer anvils, missing primer pellets. Feeding problems in some semiautomatics may be caused by an incompatible bullet nose shape or overall cartridge length.

This kind of accuracy is not easy to come by.

Difficult bolt closing on a reload could be caused by a case that exceeds the maximum case length (needs trimming), incorrect sizing (faulty die adjustment or die dimensions), a rim that was bent when extracting a case from a sizing die (insufficient or poor sizing lubricant, or wrong shell holder) or a too-long overall cartridge length for the bullet ogive. Poor extraction may be caused by ammunition generating excessive chamber pressure. Poor ejection of a semiautomatic could be caused by ammo generating insufficient chamber pressure.

With a semiauto, or a pump, shotgun shells may not feed from the magazine due to a too large rim diameter (reloaded cases that have enlarged). In semiauto rifles or handguns, bullets must be securely held by neck tension. A firm crimp is also required except on straight, rimless cases. Sufficient neck tension and a good crimp prevent bullets from being driven deep into the case during feeding, which can cause excessive chamber pressure.

Indeed, the list of potential ammo-induced difficulties is quite long, but the most common problem caused by ammo is poor accuracy.

SHOOTING GROUPS TO EVALUATE ACCURACY

Not every shooter knows how to evaluate accuracy. It is not possible to judge accuracy on the basis of a single group or even several three-shot groups. It takes a minimum of five five-shot groups to gain even a basic appreciation of the potential of a firearm. Five ten-shot groups will really begin to let the shooter know the capability of his gun.

The very best way to test for accuracy is to hang up two targets perfectly superimposed over one another, at one hundred yards (shorter ranges will prove very little). Then fire the first five-shot group. If the gun will be used for prairie dog shooting or matches, a ten-shot group should be used to better reflect the intended use, which will see many shots fired with a warm or hot barrel. After the first group has been fired, remove the top target and replace it with a new one, for the next group. Be sure the new target is placed exactly over the one left in place. After each group has been fired, allow the barrel to cool down and repeat the

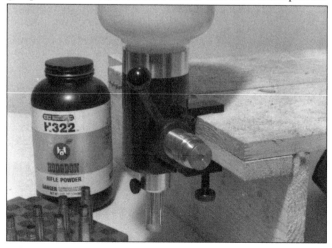

A bench rest grade powder measure (this one by Sinclair) is an essential part of loading accurate ammunition. Ordinary powder measures simply are not up to the task.

test, shooting the new group on a fresh target, while leaving the bottom original target in place. After five groups have been fired, there will be five targets each with one group on it. And there will be a sixth target with all twenty-five (or fifty) shots on it.

Examining each individual group will usually show at least a few targets with one or two so-called fliers on it. Examining the target containing all the shots fired will quickly reveal that those "fliers" really are part of the overall grouping capability of the firearm. It will be evident that most often five groups ranging between perhaps one-inch and 1¾-inch (with good reloads) actually make for a single group of perhaps 1¾-inch to two-inch. The target with all the shots on it is, of course, the better indicator of the gun and ammo combination's actual capability.

This type of testing, using a backer target, will quickly reveal that there really is no such thing as a flier shot. Those individual "fliers" in the five-shot groups disappear in the combined group target. Each shot is indeed part of the firearm and ammunition overall capability. Of course, the shooter must be up to the task. A poor shooter has no hope of realizing the potential of any firearm.

A still better way to evaluate the accuracy of any gun and ammo combination is to shoot groups as described, but to fire each group on separate days. This then will show the effects that lighting can have on accuracy, as well as the daily effects of the shooter's capability, the weather, and so on. One three-shot group may be OK for the once-a-year deer hunter. But for those with good equipment and a true desire to know actual accuracy potential, a good number of five- or ten-shot groups are necessary and these should always be supported by an aggregate target that reflects the total size of all groups fired (with a single sight adjustment, of course)

WHAT TO EXPECT FROM FACTORY LOADS

To the enthusiast, accuracy with factory ammunition is seldom impressive. Indeed, with the majority of factory centerfire rifle ammo, aggregate group sizes of under three inches are seldom seen and individual groups of two inches are good ones, while one of 1¾-inch is outstanding. It's true that some individual lots of factory ammo perform admirably in certain firearms. But the very next lot of the same type of ammo may prove disappointing.

Some factory ammo, however, does seem to do very well, lot after lot–most times, anyway. Such ammo includes Remington varmint style loads which use the Power Lokt hollow point bullets. These are available in .17 Remington, .222 Remington, .223 Remington, .222 Remington Magnum, .22-250 Remington, .243 Winchester, 6mm Remington, and .25-06 Remington. Another consistent performer is the Federal Premium 150-grain (Nosler Partition bullet) .270 Winchester load. And individual lots of Winchester 150-grain Power Point .30-06 have proven to be quite good. With .22 rimfire ammo, the premium priced CCI Green Tag and RWS R50 brand long rifle ammo are both outstanding.

When you do encounter a particularly good shooting lot of ammunition, take note of the lot number (printed on the inside flap, on the outside back of the box, or, in the case if plastic ammo boxes, a heat-embossed lot number may be used) and purchase all of it that you can. Such ammo is not always easy to come by.

As factory ammo goes, there are only two cartridges and loads that I have encountered that will consistently shoot 3/4-inch or less groups and do it with ten-shot groups. This is the Sako brand .22 PPC (52-grain hollow point boattail bullet) and the 6mm PPC (70-grain hollow point boattail bullet). But any factory ammo that produces one-inch to 1¼-inch groups with five shots is considered by myself to be outstanding. And any ammunition that will consistently produce one-inch to 1¼-inch five-shot, one hundred-yard groups is entirely adequate for most firearm accuracy testing.

But because such ammunition is comparatively rare, shooters who wish to test for accuracy often must reload for ammo requirements. Much has been written about the need to develop, through extensive testing, a load that performs well in each individual rifle or handgun. In truth, extensive testing is seldom needed. If it were, it would not be possible for factories or arsenals to manufacture large lots of match grade ammunition that produce fine results in a great many firearms. And such match grade ammo has been, and will be, produced many times.

INGREDIENTS OF ACCURATE HANDLOADS

The secret, if there really is one, to assembling top accuracy ammo is, first, to be a proficient handloader, and second, to use proven components. This chapter cannot possibly undertake to explain the myriad of details required of a handloader.

Such information is contained in other volumes devoted solely to handloading. But what is listed are the specific load details that have proven successful for a great many others. It's not hard to do so, since for each cartridge and bullet weight combination there are usually but one or two truly outstanding propellant powders. If you do not find a listing for a particular cartridge in the tables, try one of the various reloading handbooks that single out the better-performing loads.

Also included is a list of factory ammunition which has proven to be consistent in performance with sufficient accuracy to be used for serious firearm accuracy evaluation. Keep in mind that ammunition can vary notably from one lot to another. Therefore, it is possible that someday one of the listed factory loads may fail to perform as expected. It is also possible to find an unlisted factory load that performs outstandingly. There is always the proven performance of good reloads to rely on when good factory ammo is not available or affordable.

Keep in mind that the conditions of reloading, the operator's methods, and the dimensions of the assembled ammo, as well as variations in components from lot to lot, can bring about substantial ballistic changes. Therefore, the listed loads may not be safe when assembled by your methods, or with tolerances or component lots that differ from the test conditions.

Always begin reloading efforts with a powder charge a full ten percent below the listed charge. Then, as pressure indications (which must be learned from worthwhile reloading manuals) permit, increase the load in half-grain increments. Never exceed the listed load and completely discontinue the use of any component combination that shows any outward indications of excessive pressure before or at the maximum charge. No reload that results in difficult extraction after firing, enlarged case head diameters, cratered primers or any other problem indications should even be used. Fire at least ten rounds at each load increment before proceeding to the next.

MAINTAINING AMMO UNIFORMITY FOR TESTING

Reloading match-grade ammo to be used for accuracy testing does demand special attention. Every single powder charge should be weighed exactly or thrown using a bench rest powder measure. Only match-grade primers should be used. I strongly favor the Federal 210M match-grade large rifle

SOME FACTORY LOADS THAT HAVE PRODUCED HIGH ACCURACY LEVEL

Caliber	Brand	Bullet Weight in grs.	Bullet Type	Actual Velocity in fps	Velocity in fps	Test Bbl. Length (inches)	Test Rifle	Test Scope	Accuracy Average
.22 LR	CCI	40	Green Tag	1138	1080	22	Kimber 82	6x Leupold	1" [2]
.22 LR	RWS	39	R50 Match	1070	1080	22	Ruger 77/22	8x Leupold	3/4" [2]
.22 PPC	Sako	52	H.P.B.T.	3400	3400	24	Sako Varmint	12x Leupold	7/10"
.222 Rem.	Rem.	50	Power Lokt H.P.	3140	2960	18½	Rem. Model 7	10x Zeiss	1⅛"
.223 Rem.	Federal	55	Amer. Eagle FMC	3240	3110	18½	Ruger Mini-14	4x Leupold	2"
6mm PPC	Sako	70	H.P.B.T.	3200	3140	24	Sako Varmint	12x Leupold	5/8"
.270 Win.	Norma	130	Soft Point	3060	3000	22	Rem. 700	3-9x Redfield	1¼"
.270 Win.	Federal	150	Nosler Part.	2850	2810	22	Win.70 Feath.	4x Leupold	1"
7mm-08 Rem.	Rem.	140	Soft Point	2860	2675	18½	Rem. Model 7	1.5-5x Leupold	1¾"
.308 Win.	Rem.	150	Ptd. Core Lokt	2820	2770	22	Win. 70 Feath.	4x Leupold	1¾"
.30-06 Spfd.	Federal	125	Soft Point	3140	3100	22	Rem. 700	4x Redfield	1¾"
.380 Auto	Win.	85	Silvertip	1000	915	3¼	Walther PPK		2" [3]
.38 Special	Win.	148	H.B.Wadcutter	710	740	6	S&W Model 19		2" [4]
.357 Magnum	Win.	145	Silvertip	1290	1220	2½	S&W Model 19		3" [4]

(1) Average accuracy for five five-shot groups at one hundred yards except (2) which was five ten-shot groups at fifty yards and (3) which was five five-shot groups at twenty-five yards and (4) which was five five-shot groups at fifty yards.

RELOADS FOR MATCH-GRADE ACCURACY

Caliber	Weight (grs.)	Bullet Brand	Type	Powder Charge wgt. in grains	Test bbl Velocity in fps	Length (inches)	Test Rifle	Test Scope	Accuracy Average[1]
222 Rem.	50	Nosler	Match	23.0/Hodgdon H335	2920	18½	Rem. Model 7	6x Zeiss	3/4"
223 Rem.	55	Hornady	Cannelure	27.0/Hodgdon H335	3110	18½	Rem. Model 7	10x Zeiss	1"
224 Wea. Mag.	50	Nosler	Match	30.0/Hodgdon H335	3450	24	Weatherby MKV	12x Leupold	1"
22 PPC	52	Nosler	Match	24.5/Hodgdon H322	3120	24	Sako Varmint	12x Leupold	1/2"
22-250 Rem.	55	Speer	Soft Pt.	38.0/Hodgdon H380	3500	24	Rem. 700	12x Leupold	3/4"
6mm PPC	68	Berger or Watson	Custom	26.5/Hodgdon H322	3010	24	Sako Varmint	12x Leupold	1/4"
243 Win.	100	Nosler	Partition	40.0/IMR 4350	2820	18½	Rem. Model 7	6x Leupold	1¼"
257 Roberts	100	Speer	H.P.	45.0/IMR 4350	3000	22	Ruger 77R	6x Leupold	1"
270 Win.	90	Sierra	H.P.	55.0/IMR 4350	3000	22	Rem. 700	4x Leupold	1⅛"
270 Win.	130	Speer	Spitzer	55.0/IMR 4350	3000	22	Win.70 Feath.	4x Leupold	7/8"
270 Win.	150	Speer	Spitzer	52.0/IMR 4350	2800	22	Win.70 Feath.	3-9x Redfield	1"
7mm-08 Rem.	145	Speer	Spitzer	47.0/IMR 4350	2600	18½	Rem. Model 7	1.5-5x Leupold	1⅛"
30-06 Spring.	125	Sierra	Spitzer	55.0/IMR 4064	3085	22	Rem. 700	4x Redfield	7/8"
30-06 Spring.	150	Speer	Spitzer	52.0/IMR 4064	2900	22	Rem. 700	4x Redfield	7/8"
300 H&H	180	Nosler	Partition	68.0/IMR 4350	2950	24	Rem. 700	4x Leupold	1⅛"
9mm Luger	100	Speer	H.P.	5.0/Herc.Bullseye	1265	4	S&W Model 59		2" [2]
.38 Special	148	Speer	H.B.W.C.	3.0/Win.231	750	6	S&W Model 29		2" [2]

(1) Average accuracy of five five-shot groups at one hundred yards except (2) which is an average accuracy of five five-shot groups at fifty yards.

Reaming the primer pockets of cartridges is essential to achieve maximum accuracy.

primer and the Federal 205M match grade small rifle primer. CCI also sells match grade primers, in large and small rifle sizes, which perform admirably. When possible, use Federal match grade cases. Unfortunately, these are available in only a limited caliber selection.

Primer seating should be done with meticulous care, each primer being seated from 0.003-inch to 0.008-inch below flush with the case head. Primer pockets should be carefully cleaned and inside case necks should be brushed to remove any accumulated crud. On the first loading, primer pockets should be carefully reamed, to a uniform depth, with special tools available for the purpose.

Cases should be exactly trimmed to identical lengths and bullet seating must also be controlled to very small tolerances. When testing, always use full-length resize cases to ensure that there will be no difficulty in feeding, chambering, and extraction. But for accuracy testing, neck size just the first 1/16-inch of the case. Naturally, neck-sizing only is not practical if the fired cases are used in any gun other than that in which they were originally fired. For safety, never use a case beyond the point where it requires a fifth trimming. Most importantly, keep all ammo carefully segregated by lots.

Ammunition for accuracy testing should be properly stored. A cool, dry place is needed, not a damp cellar or hot attic or the -10°F garage. A temperature range of 45°F to 75°F, with a humidity of twenty to fifty percent, is appropriate. Properly stored ammunition should have a rather long shelf life. Do not load more ammunition than can be used over a span of two to three years.

When you change a lot of powder, primer, bullet, or case–begin a new ammo lot. Lot numbers are on all worthwhile component packaging. Lot variations can occur and, by loading and segregating by lot number, you will ensure the maximum uniformity. The best criteria to apply to match grade reloads is to ask yourself of each round: "Is it the same as, truly identical to, the last round loaded?"

SETTING UP A STABLE SHOOTING BENCH AND GUN REST

Good ammo alone will not make for an effective accuracy test. It will be necessary to get a very solid rest from a bench shooting position. Sand bags and leather or plastic sand-filled front and rear contoured bags are a minimum requirement. With two twenty-five pound shot bags (filled with sand) and a suitable set of front and rear contoured bench rest bags, one has the making of a rock steady shooting rest.

The sand bag approach, however, while inexpensive and effective, is not the most convenient way of solving the need for a stable shooting platform. The sand bags seldom are of the correct height to allow for proper alignment on a distant target. Thus, a lot of jury-rigging takes place at the range to bring everything into proper alignment. An easier solution is to use one of the adjustable benchrests offered by several manufacturers.

Whatever shooting stand you select be sure it has at least half-inch felt padding at all the contact points to prevent damage and to ensure maximum accuracy. When shooting from sand bags, or a shooting stand, special techniques should be used to ensure the best accuracy. It is important to adjust the rest and the firearm so that the sight alignment can be properly maintained on the target without influence by the shooter.

Sand bags are inexpensive and will give satisfactory shooting results. (Courtesy: Battenfeld)

The Sinclair rest is a good rest for accuracy testing. (Courtesy: Sinclair)

Place your shoulder as lightly against the butt as practical for the caliber being used. With .22s and most 6mm rifles, the shoulder contact should barely exist. As caliber and recoil levels intensify, shoulder contact should be increased so as to prevent a painful impact of the butt against the shoulder. The use of a thick, highly recoil-absorbent shoulder pad is beneficial in helping to keep shoulder pressure against the gun to a minimum. Shoulder pressure can cause gun movement in the stand. Therefore, keep it as light and as uniform as you can. The gun should not be held in any other manner. Do not grasp the pistol grip with the trigger finger hand.

The trigger is released by placing the index finger on the trigger and the thumb on the back of the trigger guard. The trigger is then "pinched" between the index finger and thumb. This method is not practical on rifles with a recoil level of the .30-06 or greater. Generally, bench rest shooting techniques are required for best accuracy results.

CALIBER IDENTIFICATION

Caliber identification is often the task of any gunsmith or shooting enthusiast. Proper caliber identification for American firearms is seldom difficult, though sometimes confusing. For example, not everyone may recognize a barrel stamped .25 WCF, .32 WCF, .38 WCF, or .44 WCF as meaning .25-20 Winchester, .32-20 Winchester, .38-40 Winchester, or .44-40 Winchester. Or, the fact that a barrel marked .25-35 Marlin or

.30-30 Marlin is chambered for the .25-35 Winchester or .30-30 Winchester is not always obvious to inexperienced shooters. A table of cartridge-name variations will help identify appropriate cartridges.

The metric cartridge designation on European firearms is not always an easy task to unravel. For example the 8x57 Mauser (or 8mm Mauser) may well be marked 7.9x57 JS on the barrel. But similar markings such as 7.9x57JR or 7.9x57J could lead to serious problems if they were interpreted as being one and the same as the 7.9x57JS. Another table in this chapter provides common European metric designation and equivalent American or English nomenclature for thirty cartirdges. By referring to this table, you may be able to identify quite a few puzzling European markings.

Additionally, a custom firearm clearly marked .22-250, 22 Varminter, or perhaps .25-06 may or may not be suitable for standard .22-250 or .25-06 Remington cartridges. Many custom chambers were reamed with reamers made before the industry standardization of these cartridges–when they were still wildcats. Such chambers varied considerably from gunsmith to gunsmith, depending upon who made the reamers.

And some chamber markings may not necessarily mean it's safe to use current ammo of the same designation. For example, a Winchester lever action Model 73 or an old Colt single action clearly stamped 44 WCF (.44-40 Winchester) would not be safe with current ammo. These guns were originally designed for ammunition loaded with black powder. Today's smokeless powder ammunition produces pressure much too high to allow for its safe use in guns designed for black powder.

The same warning applies for Damascus (twist) steel shotgun barrels. They were meant only for black powder. And they may no longer be safe even with black powder loads if the laminated steel has suffered internal corrosion over the many decades.

It is not advisable to shoot certain high-velocity rounds in guns originally chambered when only standard-velocity loads were in use. For instance, a Colt .32-20 revolver should not be used with .32-20 high velocity ammo, nor should some of the old .22 Long Rifle handguns and rifles be used with modern loads.

It is hoped that the tables in this chapter will aid in proper caliber identification, but an entire book would be required to deal thoroughly with cartridge identification and proper cartirdge use. In fact, a number of such volumes have been published, and you should add one or more to your shooting library if you'll be handling old or uncommon calibers.

The wrong caliber ammo or ammo with the wrong pressure level, can burst a gun and injure the shooter and any bystanders. It is essential to ensure that the cartridges used in any firearm are appropriate. Assume nothing! When the slightest doubt exists, discuss the problem with someone well-versed in caliber identification.

Finally, remember that many guns have been rechambered without any indication of the correct cartridge. I have examined barrels clearly marked for one cartridge, such as the .300 Savage, while chambered for another, such as a .308 Winchester. Sometimes, barrels are re-bored or re-lined with no reference to the new caliber (for example, a .30-06 was re-bored to 35 Whelen or re-lined to .25-06). Always be certain, there's no other way to be safe.

Caution: Many old cartridges have sound-alike names with other cartridges but bear no resemblance to, or any interchangeability with, similar sounding cartridges. For example, the .25-20 Single Shot and the .25-21 Stevens both are unique cartridges and not at all like the .25-20 Winchester. Nor does the .30-30 Wesson round, a much older cartridge, have any connection with the .30-30 Winchester. Others, such as the .32-40 Bullard, .38-40 Remington-Hepburn and .38-56 Winchester have nothing in common with the sound-alike cartridges. Further confusion can exist as some old cartridges bear identical names, yet are considerably different in shape. These include the .40-90 Sharps (straight case) and .40-90 Sharp (bottleneck case); or the .44 Extra Long (Ballard) and the 44 Extra Long (Wesson); the .44-90 (Remington Special), the .44-90 (Sharps Necked); and the .44-90 (Remington Straight). There are others, such as the .44-100 (Remington) and the .44-100 (Ballard) or the .45-75 (Winchester) and the .45-75 (Sharps straight). How about the 303? Is it the .303 Savage round or the .303 British?

Rare cartridges such as the .45-150 (3½-inch) Hepburn might be encountered, though it is listed almost nowhere. In fact, one otherwise unimpeachable source at one time listed it as non-existent and a figment of someone's imagination. That

author purchased my near mint condition Remington Hepburn, so chambered, and undoubtedly regretted his earlier strong words, though he was obviously delighted with his new purchase.

Obviously, the fact that a given cartridge can be slipped into a chamber does not mean it's the right cartridge, and yet most problems have perhaps resulted from using the wrong cartridge simply because it would chamber.

Below is a list of cartridges that have been, or can be, dangerously misapplied. A few of these make the shooter stop and wonder how an individual could possibly close the bolt on some of the combinations. But it has happened. So be careful when attempting to determine the appropriate cartridge for any firearm. Remember that, for safety's sake, this listing should never be considered complete. Naturally, it is always dangerous to shoot any shotgun with a shell length longer than that for which it was chambered. A 3-inch shell should not be used in a 2¾-inch chamber, nor should a 2¾-inch length shell be used in a 2⁹⁄₁₆-inch chamber (beware, users of old 16-gauge guns).

Metric cartridges can bring on equal, if not greater, confusion to American shooters. As mentioned earlier, the 8x57mm Mauser, sometimes marked as 7.9x57JS, but never to be confused with 7.9x57J. Another example is the fact that early Mannlicher Schoenauer rifles clearly marked 6.5x53 M.S. should be used with current ammo carrying the headstamp 6.5x54 M.S. Also, remember that a 7x57mm Mauser cartridge should never be used when a 7x57R cartridge is required. The "R" in metric cartridge designation frequently means a rimmed cartridge. And metric designations have the same kind of confusing similarities that plague American nomenclature–for example: 6.5x57 and 6.5x57R; or 6.5x58R (Sauer) or 6.5x58R (Krag-Jorgensen) or 9x56 and 9x57, and so on. As with U.S. rounds, sometimes different names are identical. Examples are shown in the list.

AMERICAN CARTRIDGE IDENTIFICATION

Barrel Marked:	Correct Cartridge:	Barrel Marked:	Correct Cartridge:
5.56mm	.223 Remington	8x57mm, 8x57mmJS, 7.92mm, 7.92x57mm, 7.92x57JSmm	8mm Mauser (not to be used in .318" diameter barrels, which are chambered for the 8x57J cartridge)
244 Remington	6mm Remington		
25ACP, 25CAP, 6.35mm(auto), 6.35mm Browning (auto)	.25 Automatic		
		32WSL, 32 Win.SL	.32 Winchester Self Loading (obsolete)
25WCF, 25-20 Marlin, 25-20 Win., 25-20	.25-20 Winchester., .25-20 Winchester High Velocity)[1]	33WCF	.33 Winchester (obsolete)
		35WSL, 35 Win.SL	.35 Winchester Self Loading (obsolete)
25-35 Marlin	.25-35 Winchester		
250 Savage	.250-3000 (Savage)	35WCF, 35 Win.	.35 Winchester(obsolete)
7x57mm	7mm Mauser	351SL, 351 Win.SL, 351WSL	.351 Winchester Self Loading
7mm Express Remington	.280 Remington		
7.65mm Para., 7.65 Parabellum,7.65 Luger	.30 Luger	38WCF, 38 Win., 38 Winchester, 38-40 Remington, 38-40 Marlin, 38-40	.38-40 Winchester (also 38-40 Winchester High Velocity)[1]
30-30 Marlin, 30 Marlin, 30 Savage, 30 W.C.F.	.30-30 Winchester		
30 Krag,	.30-40 Krag	44WCF, 44 Win., 44 Winchester, 44-40 Remington, 44-40 Marlin, 44-40	.44-40 Winchester (also .44-40 Winchester High Velocity)[1]
30-06 Govt.	.30-06 Springfield		
7.62mm (NATO)	.308 Winchester	45 Govt., 45-70 Marlin, 45-70-405, 45-70-500	.45-70 Government
30 Carbine	.30M1 Carbine		
32WCF, 32 Win., 32 Winchester, 32 Marlin, 32-30	.32-20 Winchester (also 32-20 Winchester High Velocity)[1]		
32 Colt New Police	.32 Smith & Wesson		
32ACP, 7.65mm (auto), 32CAO, 7.65 Browning ,	.32 Automatic		

[1]Higher Velocity cartridges in this caliber are no longer loaded, though old inventories may still be present on some dealers' shelves or among household contents.

One of the methods often used to determine the correct cartridge for a firearm combines two steps to give the investigator the information needed. The first is to slug the bore, with a soft lead slug. This method employs the use of a one hundred percent pure soft lead ball, slightly oversized, which is very carefully driven into the muzzle. After it has been forced into the bore three or four inches, it is driven back out. The careful investigator will then be able to measure the lead slug and determine the bore's groove and lands diameters, a big step in caliber identification.

In combination with the foregoing, a chamber cast is made, often using a Cerro-Safe non-shrinking alloy which is melted and then poured into the chamber (with the rifling lead properly plugged). When cooled, the chamber cast is removed and measured.

Both processes require a great deal of experience to prevent firearm damage. And an in depth understanding of chamber and bore dimensions is essential. Simply comparing the chamber cast's dimension with a maximum cartridge drawing will never give identical numbers. Because of the experience and knowledge required, these methods are best attempted only by qualified persons. But knowing of such procedures, the reader may care to attempt them on an old and perhaps worthless (or nearly so) firearm in order to begin to develop the necessary skills. You will, of course, need reference cartridge drawings. These are, in many cases, available from RCBS.

Cartridge identification can indeed be tricky. However, armed with the information set forth in this chapter, even the novice can begin to make correct investigations. With increasing experience the reader can broaden his knowledge by referring to books devoted exclusively to ammunition.

DANGEROUS OR MISMATCHED CARTRIDGES

Firearm Chambered for:	Wrong Cartridge for Firearm–DANGEROUS	Firearm Chambered for:	Wrong Cartridge for Firearm–Dangerous
.17 Remington	.221 Remington Fireball, .30M1 Carbine	.264 Winchester Magnum	.300 Savage, .303 British, .350 Remington Magnum, .375 Winchester
.17-223 Remington (wildcat)	.17 Remington, .221 Remington Fireball, 30M1 Carbine	.270 Winchester	.30 Remington, .30-30 Winchester, .300 Savage, .32 Remington, .308 Winchester, 7x57 Mauser, .375 Winchester
.223 Remington	.222 Remington		
.222 Remington Magnum	.223 Remington		
.243 Winchester	.250-3000 Savage, .225 Winchester		
6mm Remington (.244 Rem.)	.250-3000 Savage, .225 Winchester		
.257 Roberts	.250-3000 Savage	7x57mm Mauser	.300 Savage
6.5 Remington Magnum	.300 Savage	7mm Remington Magnum	7mm Weatherby Magnum, .270 Winchester, .280 Remington, 7mm Remington Express,
.264 Winchester Magnum	.270 Winchester, .284 Winchester, .308 Winchester,		

Firearm Chambered for:	Wrong Cartridge for Firearm–DANGEROUS
7mm Remington Magnum	.35 Remington, .350 Remington Magnum
.280 Remington	.270 Winchester, .30 Remington, .30-30 Winchester, .300 Savage, .308 Winchester, 7x57mm Mauser, .375 Winchester
.284 Winchester	.300 Savage, 7x57mm Mauser
.30-06 Springfield	.270 Winchester, 7x57mm Mauser, .30 Remington, .300 Savage, .308 Winchester, 8x57mm Mauser, .32 Remington, .35 Remington, .375 Winchester
.300 H&H Magnum	.30-06 Springfield, 8x57mm Mauser, .30-40 Krag, .375 Winchester
.300 Weatherby Magnum	.338 Winchester Magnum
.300 Winchester Magnum	8x57mm Mauser, .303 British, .350 Remington Magnum, .38-55 Winchester
.303 British	.32 Winchester Special
.303 Savage	.32 Winchester Special, .32-40 Winchester
.308 Winchester	.300 Savage
.338 Winchester	.375 Winchester
.348 Winchester	.35 Remington
.38-55 Winchester	.375 Winchester

Firearm Chambered for:	Wrong Cartridge for Firearm–Dangerous
.375 Winchester	.38-55 Winchester, .41 Long Colt
.22 Winchester Rim Fire	.22 BB Cap, .22 CB Cap, .22 Short, .22 Long, .22 Long Rifle
.22 Winchester Magnum Rim Fire (22WMRF)	.22 BB Cap, .22 CB Cap, .22 Short, .22 Long, .22 Long Rifle
.22 Winchester Auto	.22 CC Cap, .22 CB Cap, .22 Short, .22 Long, .22 Long Rifle
5mm Remington Rim Fire Magnum	.22 CC Cap, .22 CB Cap, .22 Short, .22 Long, .22 Long Rifle, .22 Winchester Auto
.25 Stevens Long (obsolete)	5mm Remington Rim Fire Magnum (obsolete)
.410 (shotgun)	.219 Zipper, .30-30 Winchester, .303 British, .32 Winchester Special, .32-40 Winchester, .35 Winchester, .38-40 Winchester, .44 S&W Special, .44-40 Winchester, .44 Remington Magnum

CORRESPONDING METRIC AND U.S. OR ENGLISH CARTRIDGES

Metric Cartridge Designation	U.S. or English Designation	Metric Cartridge Designation	U.S. or English Designation
5.6x35Rmm (not Vierling)	.22 Hornet	7.63x72mm	.300 Holland & Holland
5.7 x 43mm	.222 Remington		Magnum
5.56mm	.223 Remington	7.65x53mm	7.65 Argentine Mauser
5.6x52R	.22 Savage	7.7x58 Arisaka	7.7 Japanese
6.2x52mm	.243 Winchester	7.9x57mm	8x57 Mauser
6.5x50mm	6.5 Japanese	8x50R	8mm Lebel
6.5x52mm Mannlicher Carcano	6.5 Italian	8.8mm	.358 Winchester
6.5x52Rmm	.25-35 Winchster	9.5x72mm	.375 Holland & Holland
6.5x55mm	6.5 Swedish		Magnum
6.9x64mm	.270 Winchester	10.4x38R Vetterli	.41 Swiss Rimfire
7.35 Carcano	7.35 Italian	10.75x73mm	.404 Rimless Nitro Express
7.5x54 MAS	7.5 French	11.15x58R	.43 Spanish
7.62x51Rmm	.30-30 Winchester	11.15x60R	.43 Mauser
7.62x51mm (NATO)	.308 Winchester	11.43x50R	.43 Egyptian
7.62x54R	7.62 Russian	12.7x70 Schuler	.500 Jeffrey
7.62x63mm (U.S.)	.30-06 Springfield	14.7mm	.577 Snider

26

TESTING THE REPAIR

I've said it before, but it must be said again: always be sure the gun is unloaded when doing repair tests except, of course, during actual test firing. Use dummy cartridges for all function testing. Every repair, regardless of simplicity or complexity, should be fully tested.

FUNCTION TESTING

If the repair was simply the replacement of a sight, re-sighting the firearm is in itself test enough. A loose sight, one of inappropriate height, or any other difficulty will become apparent during shooting. If the repair involved any of the feeding cycle parts, extensive testing of the firearm should be done. I repeatedly cycle dummy cartridges through the firearm–a full gun load of shells until one hundred rounds have been cycled. Then an actual firing test with twenty rounds is done. Such testing should be done with any magazine follower, follower spring, cartridge guide, extractor, or ejector repair. The effects of recoil on feeding parts should never be overlooked. Therefore, actual firing is always essential.

Some repairs, such as firing pin and extractor replace-

Only dummy cartridges should be used for function testing.

ments, demand that fired cartridges be carefully inspected for normal appearance–the depth of the firing pin indent, the centered location of the firing pin indent, no deformation of the cartridge rim, and so on. Any trigger or safety repair requires the utmost in careful attention and testing to ensure that the integrity of the firearm design has not been compromised.

Always test trigger repairs to ensure that the weight of pull remains constant over at least two dozen dry firings. Use a

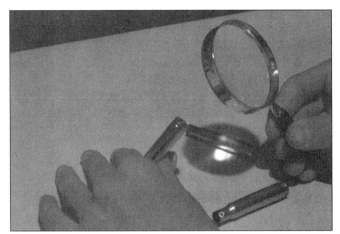

When firing pins, extractors, or ejectors have been repaired or replaced, carefully inspect fired cartridges to be sure the heads are normal.

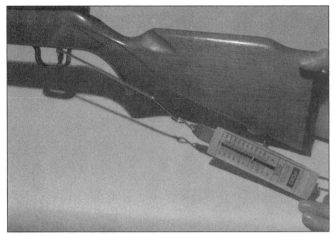

Trigger adjustments should be repeatedly tested for uniformity using a scale or weights.

scale or weights to do this testing. Do not rely on interpreted finger pressure. Check to ensure that when the gun is cocked and ready, that it will not disengage with a modest bump or blow to the firearm. Test by using a rubber mallet to strike the receiver and by bumping the butt against a padded surface. A gun that fires during these tests will, in all likelihood, fire if it is dropped when cocked. This is unsafe!

Check all safety repairs or adjustments by cocking the firearm and placing the safety switch in the safe position. Then apply pressure with the right and left index fingers, trying to pull the trigger to fire the gun. If you can, the repair is unsatisfactory! If the gun does not fire, then move the safety switch to the "fire" position. The gun should not fire as the switch is moved forward. Then, return the switch to the safe position. And repeat the entire test several times. Take no shortcuts.

Complete or partial disassembly of any firearm, whether for repair or cleaning, always should be followed by a functioning test with dummy cartridges. If the trigger or safety parts were disassembled, then a check is in order.

A stock repair always requires an actual test firing of an adequate number of rounds to ensure accuracy (bedding repairs) and/or durability (break, split, or crack repairs).

TEST FIRING

The test firing of any gun–that has had the firing pin, bolt, locking lug, bolt head, or other parts essential to the strength and integrity of the firearm replaced–should never be from the

Bumping the butt on a well-padded bench should not cause the trigger to release the sear.

shoulder. "Absence of body" is an industry phrase applied to certain ammunition testing and the proofing and test firing of any new firearm. Absence of body should also be applied to any firearm firing test that involves the mentioned repairs or similar ones, or for the verification of cartridge identification. Absence of body simply means that no person is near enough to the firearm to be hurt in the event of a catastrophic failure. Parts and pieces blown away by high pressure gases can do

Test safeties by applying maximum pressure to the trigger with two fingers.

serious bodily harm or worse. So, for the appropriate test firings, tie the firearm to an old tire or, better still, mount it in a suitable shooting jack and fire it from a remote position using a lanyard wrapped around the trigger and trigger guard. Stand at least thirty-five feet away when firing the gun.

Be certain that the recoil will not cause the gun and/or shooting jack to move and cause damage to either. It is particularly important to ensure that the recoil will not move the firearm in the shooting jack. This can cause extensive damage. The butt should bear firmly against some portion of the stand and provisions should be made to prevent muzzle jump from twisting the gun out of the stand. Furthermore, the recoil needs to be absorbed by a heavy recoil spring mechanism or the stock may bet cracked.

Do not use a shooting rest or stand designed for bench rest shooting or repair work for your test firing. Such stands do not properly support the gun and either one or both will be damaged.

ADDITIONAL CHECKS AND SAFETY PRECAUTIONS

Always use the appropriate headspace gauges after any chamber work or after repair or replacement of the barrel, bolt, or locking parts. After drilling or tapping any barrel, double

check to ensure that the drilled holes do not intrude more than half of the barrel-wall thickness. If you have tapped a shotgun barrel for screw-in chokes, be certain there is a choke tube tightly in place before testing firing.

Before firing, make sure there are no heavy deposits of oil or grease in the barrel and that no patches or brushes were left in the bore. Barrels burst easily when excessive oil, grease, or a patch is left behind.

Make sure all disassembled parts were replaced and properly assembled. When replacing stocks, always avoid excessively tightening screws to prevent stock cracks. Be sure any sight mounting screws used on the receiver do not protrude through the receiver. Be certain that the collimator spud has been removed from the gun. After a glass bedding job, double check everything to ensure that no epoxy has migrated to where it is not supposed to be.

In short, check and double check everything possible. Strange and not so strange things can happen. For example, driving a new rear open sight into a barrel just might cause a front ramp screw to loosen. Or, drilling and tapping a receiver might cause a few tiny metal particles to get into the trigger or safety mechanisms making them unsafe. Replacing or tightening a front-action screw could cause the screw to infringe deeply into the receiver's bolt-locking lug recess, making it

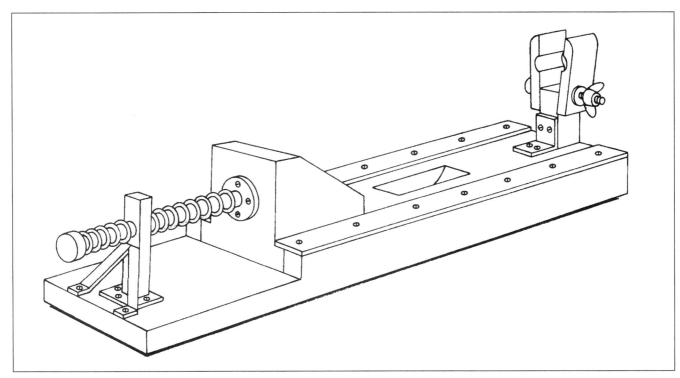

A good shooting jack for test firing. When the jack is firmly anchored, the heavy spring will absorb recoil and prevent stock cracks.

difficult or impossible to operate the bolt. A trigger job may make some safety switch work necessary. And the inverse is equally true. And so it goes.

Whatever the job, the sign of a true gunsmith is knowing what to check, besides the actual work done, after the job is completed. Take the time to think through the most important part of any repair–the completed work inspection. It will pay huge dividends.

27

SENSIBLE GUNSMITHING ALTERNATIVES

Some time long ago, a wise person said, "If it isn't broken, don't fix it." These words have been repeated countless times. Tinkering when there is no need, can soon lead to a real requirement for a bit more than tinkering. A gun often needs less fixing than at first may be supposed. A poor trigger pull can sometimes mean a need for a replacement trigger. More often than not, it simply means the trigger needs some adjusting. Most Savage 110 rifle triggers are as good as any replacement trigger I have ever used–if that 110 trigger is adjusted precisely as described earlier in this work.

A smart gunsmith figures out how much gunsmithing is required to accomplish the goal. A friend brings you his favorite scope-sighted .30-06 and says he would like to have back-up iron sights installed. The first reaction might be to drill and tap the barrel for a dovetail rear sight base and a screw-on front ramp. This means disassembling the rifle and

requires a Forster drill jig to make and thread four barrel holes. If something goes wrong, there is a risk of ruining the barrel.

A knowledgeable person would consider using a set of scope rings with sights on top of the rings. Such rings with sights are made in several configurations. For example, the Millet rings needs only a Redfield Jr. style scope mount base. If the gun already has a Redfield, Burris, or Millet base, all you need to do is change the scope rings. Ditto for Williams rings if the gun is equipped with a Williams base. And if a noncompatible scope ring base(s) is on the gun, it's a lot easier to change a scope base than it is to drill and tap four barrel holes.

The short space between scope ring open sights means they will be less accurate than barrel-mounted open sights, but open sights on a scoped rifle will probably never get used anyway. They are there simply for that one-in-five-thousand emergency–and then the ring sights will get the job done just nicely. Even the non-adjustable ones can work effectively under such circumstances if the shooter knows where his gun shoots when they are used.

As another example, why drill and tap a grooved receiver .22 for a peep sight when there are peeps that instantly slip into the receiver groove? At worst, you will have to install a higher front bead to properly align the new peep. At best, you will avoid stripping threads in an aluminum receiver or having to inlet a stock to clear that side-mounted peep.

If someone decides to have a ramp front sight instead of a plain old post, don't start drilling and tapping right away. You can purchase a Williams Shorty ramp that attaches to the barrel by means of a dovetail adapter. Any gun that has a 3/8-inch dovetail can be quickly and near effortlessly fitted with one of these ramps. Such easy gunsmithing is actually smart gunsmithing.

If there's a need for a quality scope to be mounted on a .22, there is not necessarily a need for drilling and tapping. One-inch scope rings are available to fit dovetailed .22 rifle receivers.

If the only thing wrong with a rifle's bedding is the fit of the receiver recoil shoulder in the stock mortise, try glass-bedding only the recoil shoulder in its mortise. More may look and sound great. But more may not add a bit to the rifle's performance. If simply bedding the recoil shoulder doesn't give the desired results, the remainder of the action can always be bedded later.

A smart gunsmith also tries to avoid gimmick ideas. For example, if the customer wants to inlet a compass into his rifle's stock because be always loses his compasses, suggest that he get a compass with a lanyard attached to his belt loop. The compass won't be lost and neither will the gun's full resale value. If he persists, he at least won't be able to accuse you of not keeping him informed about "gunsmithing" that detracts from firearm value.

Suppose the decision has been made to bore, ream and tap a shotgun barrel for screw-in chokes because the owner of the gun feels that he has no use for its modified choke and needs only a cylinder bore barrel. It might make a heap of sense simply to cut off 2½ inches or so of his present barrel, reinstall the front bead, and thus have a cylinder bore without spending much time and money. Naturally, this will work only on a plain barrel, as vent ribs are not designed to be cut.

If you've decided to start milling, cutting, and fitting some battery-powered sight to a revolver in order to make it useful for nighttime raccoon hunting and/or nighttime police duty, there are easier ways that don't include electrical contact switches and so on. How about using the Meprolight sights? They work on any S&W revolver (plus models for a bunch of other hand and long guns) just as long as the revolver originally has a ramp front sight with plastic insert. These work day or night, require zero maintenance, and have no switches, bells or gongs. They are self powered by a tiny quantity of radioactive tritium gas (less than thirty-one millicuries) and show up bright in the dark and as a white outline rear sight and white dot front sight when it's not. Quite simply, the total installation involves about twenty minutes.

Break out the original plastic ram inset and clean out all traces of plastic. The replacement front sight fits into the original dovetail and is glued into place using Loc-Tite 610 glue. The original rear sight blade is removed by cranking its screw clockwise until the screw bolt snaps and then the sight blade is pressed away until the bolt-retaining nut shows from the opposite side of the sight. Unscrew it and the broken bolt and you are ready to drop in the glow-in-the-dark Meprolight sight.

Why install ten recoil pads on each long gun owned if a slip-on or stick-on pad will do? Not every shooter needs a recoil pad when hunting, yet for sighting in and plinking a good pad sure is nice. For such limited applications, a stick-on pad, such as one from Smith & Wesson, will tame most recoil and save a great deal of time and money if the alternative is fitting a goodly number of recoil pads to stocks.

There are equally effective alternatives to many other actual repair efforts. Why wrestle trying to compress a coil spring, slip it onto a shaft, and then put everything into place in the gun? It doesn't make sense when someone is selling an inexpensive, easy-to-use alternative tool that gets the job done right every time. One need simply browse through a good gunsmithing supply house catalog (the Brownells catalog is a great example) to come up with dozens of ideas for doing a job easier, quicker, and right.

APPENDIX

ALPHA DRILL SIZES

Drill Letter	Dia. in inches	Drill Letter	Dia. in inches
Z	0.413	M	0.295
Y	0.404	L	0.290
X	0.397	K	0.281
W	0.386	J	0.277
V	0.377	I	0.272
U	0.368	H	0.266
T	0.358	G	0.261
S	0.348	F	0.257
R	0.339	E	0.250
Q	0.332	D	0.246
P	0.323	C	0.242
O	0.316	B	0.238
N	0.302	A	0.234

NUMERICAL DRILL SIZES

Drill Number	Dia. in inches	Drill Number	Dia. in inches
1	0.228	41	0.096
2	0.221	42	0.094
3	0.213	43	0.089
4	0.209	44	0.086
5	0.206	45	0.082
6	0.204	46	0.081
7	0.201	47	0.079
8	0.199	48	0.076
9	0.196	49	0.073
10	0.194	50	0.070
11	0.191	51	0.067

NUMERICAL DRILL SIZES (CONT.)

Drill Number	Dia. in inches	Drill Number	Dia. in inches
12	0.189	52	0.064
13	0.185	53	0.060
14	0.182	54	0.055
15	0.180	55	0.052
16	0.177	56	0.047
17	0.173	57	0.043
18	0.172	58	0.042
19	0.166	59	0.041
20	0.161	60	0.040
21	0.159	61	0.039
22	0.157	62	0.038
23	0.154	63	0.037
24	0.152	64	0.036
25	0.150	65	0.035
26	0.147	66	0.033
27	0.144	67	0.032
28	0.141	68	0.031
29	0.136	69	0.029
30	0.129	70	0.028
31	0.120	71	0.026
32	0.116	72	0.025
33	0.113	73	0.024
34	0.111	74	0.023
35	0.110	75	0.021
36	0.107	76	0.020
37	0.104	77	0.018
38	0.101	78	0.016
39	0.100	79	0.015
40	0.098	80	0.014

To convert millimeters to inches:

Multiply mm x 0.03937 = inches

To convert inches to millimeters:

Multiply inches x 25.40 = mm

To convert meters per seconds to feet per second:

Multiply mps x 3.281 = f.p.s.

To convert feet per second to meters per second

Multiply f.p.s. x 0.3048 = mps

To convert foot pounds to kilogram meters:

Multiply ft.lbs. x 0.1383 = kilogram meters

To convert kilogram-meters to foot pounds:

Multiply kilogram-meters x 7.233 = ft.lbs.

To convert pounds per square inch to kilograms per square centimeter:

Multiply p.s.i. x 0.07032 = ksc

To convert kilograms per square centimeter to pounds per square inch:

Multiply ksc x 14.23 = p.s.i.

To obtain foot-pounds (kinetic) of energy at a specific velocity:

Square the velocity, multiply by the bullet weight in grains and divide by 450,240

$$\frac{V^2W}{450,240} = \text{Foot pounds (kinetic energy)}$$

STANDARD DRILL SIZE FOR TAP SIZE

Tap	Drill
10 - 32	#21
8 - 40	#28
6 - 48	#31
3 - 56	#45

DIRECTORY OF SOURCES

CARTRIDGE DRAWINGS

RCBS Operations (Blount, Inc.)
(popular calibers)
605 Oro Dam Blvd.
Oroville, CA 95965
Toll Free (800)533-5000
Tel. (530)533-5191
Fax (530)533-1647
www.rcbs.com
rcbstech@atk.com

Sinclair International
718 Broadway
New Haven, IN 46774
Tel. (260)493-1858
www.sinclairintl.com

CLEANING CHEMICALS AND EQUIPMENT

Birchwood Laboratories, Inc.
(Birchwood Casey)
7900 Fuller Road
Eden Praire, MN 55344-2195
Toll Free (800)328-6156
Tel. (952)937-7934
Fax (952)937-7979
www.birchwoodcasey.com
mmorgan@birchwoodcasey.com

Brownells
200 South Front Street
Montezuma, IA 50171
Toll Free (800)741-0015
Fax (800)264-3068
www.brownells.com
customersupport@brownells.com
tech@brownells.com

J. Dewey Mfg. Co. Inc.
(Rods & Patches)
P.O. Box 2014
Southbury, CT 06488
Tel. (203)264-3064
Fax (203)262-6907
www.deweyrods.com
info@deweyrods.com

G96 Products Company, Inc.
P.O. Box 1684
River Street Station
Paterson, NJ 07544
Toll Free (877)332-0035
Tel. (973)684-4050
Fax (973)684-3848
www.g96.com
info@g96.com

Hoppe's Products
(Divison of Micheal's of Oregon)
P.O. Box 1690
Oregon City, OR 97045
Toll Free (800)962-5757
Tel. (503)655-7964
Fax (503)655-7546
www.hoppes.com
Sales@Hoppes.com

Kleen-Bore, Inc.
16 Industrial Parkway
Easthampton, MA 012027
Tel. (413)527-0300
Fax (413)527-2522
www.kleen-bore.com
info@kleen-bore.com

Marble's Outdoors
420 Industrial Park
P.O. Box 111
Gladstone, MI 49837
Tel. (906)428-3710
Fax (906)428-3711
www.marblesoutdoors.com
info@marblesoutdoors.com

Outers
N5549 County Road #2
Onalaska, WI 54650
Toll Free (800)635-7656
Tel. (608)781-5800
Fax (608)781-0368
www.outers-guncare.com

Shooter's Choice Guncare Products
15050 Berkshire Industrial Parkway
Middlefield, OH 44062
Tel. (440)834-8888
Fax (440)834-3388
www.shooters-choice.com
shooters@shooters-choice.com

WD-40 Company
P.O. Box 80607
San Diego, CA 92138-0607
Tel. (619)275-1400
Fax (619)275-5823
www.wd40.com

Yankee Hill Machine
(Kleen Bore #10)
20 Ladd Avenue
Northampton, MA 01060
Tel. (413)586-1400
Fax (413)586-1326
www.yhm.net/index
sales@yhm.net
service@yhm.net
info@yhm.com

COLD BLUING KITS

Birchwood Laboratories, Inc.
(Birchwood Casey)
7900 Fuller Road
Eden Praire, MN 55344-2195
Toll Free (800)328-6156
Tel. (952)937-7934
Fax (952)937-7979
www.birchwoodcasey.com
mmorgan@birchwoodcasey.com

Brownells
200 South Front Street
Montezuma, IA 50171
Toll Free (800)741-0015
Fax (800)264-3068
www.brownells.com
customersupport@brownells.com
tech@brownells.com

G96 Products Company, Inc.
P.O. Box 1684
River Street Station
Paterson, NJ 07544
Toll Free (877)332-0035
Tel. (973)684-4050
Fax (973)684-3848

Hoppe's Products
(Divison of Micheal's of Oregon)
P.O. Box 1690
Oregon City, OR 97045
Toll Free (800)962-5757
Tel. (503)655-7964
Fax (503)655-7546
www.hoppes.com
Sales@Hoppes.com

GUN-REPAIR VISES & STANDS

Decker Shooting Products
1729 Laguna Avenue
Schofield, WI 54476
tel. (715)359-5873

Hoppe's Products
(Divison of Micheal's of Oregon)
P.O. Box 1690
Oregon City, OR 97045
Toll Free (800)962-5757
Tel. (503)655-7964
Fax (503)655-7546
www.hoppes.com
Sales@Hoppes.com

GUNSMITHING ACCESSORIES, SUPPLIES, TOOLS

Brownells
200 South Front Street
Montezuma, IA 50171
Toll Free (800)741-0015
Fax (800)264-3068
www.brownells.com
customersupport@brownells.com
tech@brownells.com

B-Square Co.
P.O. Box 11281
Forth Worth, TX 76110
Toll Free (800)433-2909
Tel. (817)923-0964
Fax (817)926-7012
www.b-square.com
bsquare@b-square.com

The Chapman Mfg. Company
(screwdrivers)
P.O. Box 250
Durham, CT 06422
Tel. (860)349-9228
Fax (860)349-0084
www.chapmanmfg.com
info@ChapmanMfg.com
sales@ChapmanMfg.com

Forster Products
310 E. Lanark Avenue
Lanark, IL 61046
Tel. (815)493-6360
Fax (815)493-2371
www.forsterproducts.com
info@forsterprodcuts.com

Kimber Manufacturers
(Meprolight sight)
Toll Free (800)444-2950
Tel. (928)476-3066
www.kimberamerica.com

Lyman Products (Pachmayr, Ltd.)
475 Smith Street
Middletown, CT 06457
Toll Free (800)225-9626
Fax (860)632-1699
www.lymanproducts.com

Micheal's of Oregon
(Uncle Mike's)
P.O. Box 1690
Oregon City, OR 97045
Toll Free (800)900-4868
Tel. (503)655-7964
www.michaels-oregon.com
info@unclemikes.com

Outers
N5549 County Road #2
P.O. Box 38
Onalaska, WI 54650
Toll Free (800)635-7656
Tel. (608)781-5800
Fax (608)781-0368
www.outers-guncare.com

Six Enterprises
3200 Turtle Creek Court
San Jose, CA 95101
Tel. (408)999-0201
Fax (408)999-0216

Texas Platers Supply
2453 W. Five-Mile Pkwy.
Dallas. TX 75233
Tel. (214)330-7168

Trexler Industries
(Kwik Klip for Rem. 700)
95 Southland Drive
Bethlehem, PA 18017
Tel. (610)974-9800
Fax (610)974-9803
www.trexlerindustries.com
info@TrexlerIndustries.com

Williams Gun Sight Co.
7389 Lapeer Road
Davison, MI 48423
Toll Free (800)530-9028
Fax (810)658-2140
www.williamsgunsight.com

GUNSMITHING SCHOOLS

American Firearms School, L.L.C.
5 John Dietsch Square North
Attleboro, MA 02763
Tel. (508)695-5869
Contact: David Autrey (Gunsmith)
www.americanfirearmsschool.com
info@americanfirearmsschool.com

Lassen Community College
Highway 139, P.O. Box 3000
Susanville, CA 96130
Gunsmithing School
Coordinator - Steve Taylor
Tel. (503)251-8800
www.lassen.cc.ca.us

Montgomery Community College
1011 Page Street
Troy, NC 27371
Coordinator - Mr. Wayne Bernauer
Tel. (910)576-6222
Fax (910)576-2176
www.montgomery.cc.nc.us

Murray State College
One Murray Campus
Suite ET 117
Tishomingo, OK 73460
Coordinator - Mr. Dean Arnold
Toll Free (800)342-0698
Tel. (580)371-2371
Fax (580)371-9844
www.mscok.ed

Rochester Institute of Technology
College of Fine and Applied Arts
P.O. Box 9887
One Lomb Memorial Drive
Rochester, NY 14623-5603
Tel. (585)475-2411
www.rit.edu

Trinidad State Junior College
600 Prospect
Campus Box 319
Trinidad, CO 81082
Coordinator - Harold Thomason
Toll Free (800)937-6884
Tel. (719)846-5616
www.trinidadstate.edu

HEADSPACE GAUGES

Brownells
200 South Front Street
Montezuma, IA 50171
Toll Free (800)741-0015
Fax (800)264-3068
www.brownells.com
customersupport@brownells.com
tech@brownells.com

Forster Products
310 E. Lanark Avenue
Lanark, IL 61046
Tel. (815)493-6360
Fax (815)493-2371
www.forsterproducts.com
info@forsterprodcuts.com

PARTS

Brownells
200 South Front Street
Montezuma, IA 50171
Toll Free (800)741-0015
Fax (800)264-3068
www.brownells.com
customersupport@brownells.com
tech@brownells.com

Browning
One Browning Place
Morgan, UT 84050-9326
Toll Free (800)322-4626
Tel. (801)976-2711
www.browning.com

Colt Industries
P.O. Box 1868
Hartford, CT 06144-1868
Toll Free (800)962-COLT (2658)
Fax (860)244-1449
www.colt.com

Gun Parts Corp.
(formerly Numrich)
226 Williams Lane
West Hurley, NY 12491
Tel. (845)679-2417
Fax (845)679-4867
Orders (877)486-7278
www.gunpartscorp.com
info@gunpartscorp.com

Kimber
One Lawton Street
Yonkers, NY 10705 9701
Toll Free (888) 243-4522
Tel. (406)758-2223
Fax (406)758-2222
www.kimberamerica.com

Marlin Firearms Company
100 Kenna drive
North Haven, CT 06472
Tel. (203)239-5621
Fax (203)234-7991
www.marlinfirearms.com

O.F. Mossberg & Sons, Inc.
7 Grasso Avenue
North Haven, CT 06473
Tel. (203)230-5300
Fax (203)230-5420
www.mossberg.com

Navy Arms Co.
211 Lawn Street
Martinsburg, WV 25401
Tel. (304)262-1651
Fax (304)262-1658
www.navyarms.com

Remington Arms Co., Inc.
870 Remington Drive
Madison, NC 27025-0700
Toll Free (800)243-9700
Fax (336)548-7741
www.remington.com

Smith & Wesson
2100 Roosevelt Avenue
Springfield, MA 01104-1698
Toll Free (800)331-0852
Tel. (413)781-8300
Fax (413)747-3317
www.smith-wesson.com

Springfield Armory, Inc.
420 W. Main Street
Geneseo, IL 61254
Toll Free (800)680-6866
Tel. (309)944-5631
Fax (309)944-3676
www.smithfieldarmory.com
sales@smithfield-armory.com
customshop@smithfield-armory.com

Stoeger Industries
17603 Indian Head Hwy.
Suite 200
Accokeek, MD 20607-2501
Tel. (301)283-6300
Fax (301)283-6986
www.stoegerindustries.com

Sturm Ruger & Co., Inc.
200 Ruger Road
Prescott, AZ 86301
Tel. (520)541-8820
Fax (520)541-8850
www.ruger-firearms.com

Thompson/Center Arms Company
P.O. Box 5002
Rochester, NH 03867
Tel. (603)322-2394
Fax (603)322-5133
www.tcarms.com

Winchester Firearms
275 Winchester Avenue
Morgan, UT 84050
Tel. (801)876-3440
Fax (801)876-3737
www.winchester-guns.com

RELOADING

Forster Products
310 E. Lanark Avenue
Lanark, IL 61046
Tel. (815)493-6360
Fax (815)493-2371
www.forsterproducts.com
info@forsterprodcuts.com

RCBS Operations (Blount, Inc.)
605 Oro Dam Blvd.
Oroville, CA 95965
Toll Free (800)533-5000
Tel. (530)533-5191
Fax (530)533-1647
www.rcbs.com
rcbstech@atk.com

Sinclair International
718 Broadway
New Haven, IN 46774
Tel. (260)493-1858
www.sinclairintl.com

Savage Parts
Savage Arms, Inc.
100 Springdale Road
Westfield, MA 01085
Toll Free (800)370-0708
Tel. (413)568-7001
Fax (413)562-7764
www.savagearms.com

Small Arms Shop
Steve Simons
3262 South Eagle Point
Inverness, FL 34450
Tel. (352)637-4770
Fax (413)562-7764
www.savageparts.com
sas@savageparts.com

Scopes & Mounts
Brownells
200 South Front Street
Montezuma, IA 50171
Toll Free (800)741-0015
Fax (800)264-3068
www.brownells.com
customersupport@brownells.com
tech@brownells.com

B-Square Co.
P.O. Box 11281
Forth Worth, TX 76110
Toll Free (800)433-2909
Tel. (817)923-0964
Fax (817)926-7012
www.b-square.com
bsquare@b-square.com

Burris Optics
Box 1747 – 331 East 8th Street
Greely, CO 80631
Tel. (970)356-1670
Fax (970)356-8702
www.burrisoptics.com

Bushnell Performance Optics
9200 Cody
Overland Park, KS 66214
Toll Free (800)423-3537
Tel. (913)752-3400
Fax (913)752-3550
www.bushnell.com

Leupold & Stevens, Inc.
P.O. Box 688
Beaverton, OR 97075
Tel. (503)646-9171
www.leupold.com

Leica Camera, Inc.
156 Ludlow Avenue
Northvale, NJ 07647
Toll Free (800)222-0118
Tel. (201)767-7500
Fax (201)767-8666
www.leica-camera.com/usa

Millett Industries
(Mounts)
16131 Gothard Street
Huntington Beach, CA 92647
Toll Free (800) MILLETT
Tel. (714)842-5575
www.millettsights.com

Nikon, Inc.
1300 Walt Whitman Road
Melville, NY 11747
Tel. (631)547-4200
Fax (631)547-8518
www.nikonusa.com

Redfield, Simmons & Weaver
ATK Ammunition &
Related Products
P.O. Box 39
Onalaska, WI 54650
Toll Free (800)635-7656
Tel. (608)781-5800
Fax (608)781-0365
www.simmons-mounts.com
www.redfield-mounts.com
www.weaver-mounts.com

Williams Gun Sights
7389 Lapeer Road
P.O. Box 329
Davison, MI 48423
Toll Free (800)530-9028
Fax (810)658-2140
www.williamsgunsight.com

SHOOTING STANDS AND RESTS

Brownells
200 South Front Street
Montezuma, IA 50171
Toll Free (800)741-0015
Fax (800)264-3068
www.brownells.com
customersupport@brownells.com
tech@brownells.com

Hoppe's Products
Division of Michael's of Oregon
Airport Industrial Mall
Coatsville, PA 19320
Toll Free (610)384-6000
Fax (610)857-5980
www.hoppes.com
Sales@Hoppes.com

SIGHTS

Brownells
200 South Front Street
Montezuma, IA 50171
Toll Free (800)741-0015
Fax (800)264-3068

www.brownells.com
customersupport@brownells.com
tech@brownells.com

Lyman Products (Pachmayr, Ltd.)
475 Smith Street
Middletown, CT 06457
Toll Free (800)225-9626
Fax (860)632-1699
www.lymanproducts.com

Marble's Outdoors
420 Industrial Park
P.O. Box 111
Gladstone, MI 49837
Tel. (906)428-3710
Fax (906)428-3711
www.marblesoutdoors.com
info@marblesoutdoors.com

Micro Sight Co.
242 Harbor Blvd.
Belmont, CA 94002
Tel. (650)591-0769
Fax (650)591-7531

Millett Industries
16131 Gothard Street
Huntington Beach, CA 92647
Toll Free (800) MILLETT
Tel. (714)842-5575
www.millettsights.com

Williams Gun Sights
7389 Lapeer Road
P.O. Box 329
Davison, MI 48423
Toll Free (800)530-9028
Fax (810)658-2140
www.williamsgunsight.com

SPECIAL TOOLS, JIGS, FIXTURES

B-Square Co.
P.O. Box 11281
Forth Worth, TX 76110
Toll Free (800)433-2909
Tel. (817)923-0964
fax (817)926-7012
www.b-square.com
bsquare@b-square.com

Brownells
200 South Front Street
Montezuma, IA 50171
Toll Free (800)741-0015
Fax (800)264-3068
www.brownells.com
customersupport@brownells.com
tech@brownells.com

Forster Products
310 E. Lanark Avenue
Lanark, IL 61046
Tel. (815)493-6360
Fax (815)493-2371
www.forsterproducts.com
info@forsterprodcuts.com